MAKING SENSE OF EUROPEAN UNION LAW

This book reflects on selected issues of European law in dialogue with leading legal scholar Bruno De Witte, whose work has enlightened generations of students, scholars and practitioners of European law. The volume is designed to mark the impressive academic oeuvre of a great legal mind and true academic whose elegant and insightful writings have decisively contributed to the advancement of the study of European law.

The contributions attempt to 'make sense of European Union law', reflecting Bruno's mission as a legal scholar and commenting on some of the themes that he has worked on: constitutional Europe, differentiated Europe, social and educational Europe and minorities Europe. It culminates in reflections on the very nature of Bruno's scholarship and his academic *persona*. Not only is this book a public recognition and an expression of appreciation for all that Bruno has offered to the European legal community, but also an invitation to challenge the way many scholars think of academic careers and their ways to success.

Making Sense of European Union Law

Edited by
Monica Claes
and
Ellen Vos

•HART•
OXFORD • LONDON • NEW YORK • NEW DELHI • SYDNEY

HART PUBLISHING
Bloomsbury Publishing Plc
Kemp House, Chawley Park, Cumnor Hill, Oxford, OX2 9PH, UK
1385 Broadway, New York, NY 10018, USA
29 Earlsfort Terrace, Dublin 2, Ireland

HART PUBLISHING, the Hart/Stag logo, BLOOMSBURY and the Diana logo are trademarks of Bloomsbury Publishing Plc

First published in Great Britain 2022

A catalogue record for this book is available from the British Library.

Library of Congress Cataloging-in-Publication data

ISBN: HB: 978-1-50995-969-3
ePDF: 978-1-50995-971-6
ePub: 978-1-50995-970-9

Typeset by Compuscript Ltd, Shannon

To find out more about our authors and books visit www.hartpublishing.co.uk. Here you will find extracts, author information, details of forthcoming events and the option to sign up for our newsletters.

PREFACE

I. Making Sense of European Union Law

The contributors to this volume look at some of the many themes of EU law that Bruno De Witte has researched in his work. They engage with ideas Bruno has expressed in his impressive academic oeuvre. Our work as scholars, in Bruno's view, is to make sense of things. His own contribution to the study of European law is marked by pragmatism and an aversion to hubris, grand theory and pie-in-the-sky research. It is consistently well-informed, thoroughly researched, razor-sharp and elegantly worded. The contributions in this volume attempt to 'make sense of European Union law' by reflecting and commenting on current issues, in dialogue with Bruno. In essence they look at *Bruno's Europe*.

Bruno's work spans a period of 40 years (and counting). Educated at the Universities of Namur and Leuven, the College of Europe and the European University Institute (EUI), his first passion was cultural diversity, as shown by his PhD thesis on the protection of linguistic diversity through fundamental rights. This research was situated in international human rights law and comparative constitutional law. Yet, working at the EUI – which in Bruno's words, offered ideal research conditions despite its many temptations – it is no wonder that he would soon enter the world of European Union law. He would, however, also continue to work on minority rights and language law. This is characteristic for his entire career: a man of great academic appetite, Bruno would enter new fields and add themes to his academic menu, without however relinquishing older ones. The relations between international, European and national law; constitutional reform and Treaty revision in the European Union; the protection of fundamental rights in Europe; the internal market and non-market values; the institutional organisation of the Union, its decision-making and the legal instruments of EU law – these are all lenses through which he studied the European Union, in order to make sense of it. Through these, he would examine the developments of the European Union: the consecutive Intergovernmental Conferences (IGCs) and EU Treaties; enlargement; the rise and fall of the Constitutional Treaty; the failed accession to the European Convention on Human Rights; the euro crisis and euro-crisis law; the pandemic and the Covid-19 Recovery Plan. Underlying his work is his interest in how the law accompanies – and at times steers – developments and changes in the European integration process.

Part I, 'Constitutional Europe', looks at the European Union from a constitutional angle. Gráinne de Búrca, Claire Kilpatrick and Joanne Scott discuss the question of the legal parameters and consequences of EU accession to international agreements; a topic on which Bruno is amongst the leading authorities. They examine the practice of the Court of Justice of the European Union in relation to two important international agreements to which the EU has acceded in the field of human rights and environmental law. Marise Cremona looks at two aspects of interaction in relation to mixed agreements: the interaction between the Council's political choice to conclude a mixed agreement and the legal rules governing EU participation and the interaction between those legal rules and the political and legal management of Member State participation. She uses these examples to discuss Bruno's view that the EU suffers from an over-detailed and over-interpreted constitution. Monica Claes looks at the relation between the EU and national constitutional values. She revisits some of the ideas developed by Bruno on this topic in the early 1990s. She argues that while the issue and the lines along which solutions should be found have essentially remained the same, the context within which tensions are negotiated and the vocabulary used have changed, and so has Bruno's approach to the matter.

In Part II, 'Differentiated Europe', Ellen Vos and Deirdre Curtin discuss differentiated integration, a topic studied by Bruno in many of his writings. Ellen Vos looks at the development of differentiated integration in the EU as a steady feature of EU law, accommodating internal tensions and respecting heterogeneity, and discusses the various modes and the definition of differentiated integration. She reflects on the future of differentiation, looking in particular to the EU's response to the Covid-19 pandemic. Deirdre Curtin looks at what she terms the 3D's (ie decimation, decline and disuse) of differentiation. She observes how a renewed Europe, which potentially involves all Member States, seems to appear. She sees how the EU can go beyond turbulence as Member States continue 'flying together' and that this unity is reinforced and strengthened with every further crisis. Both authors connect with recent work by Bruno holding that differentiation is in decline.

In Part III, 'Social and Educational Europe', Diamond Ashiagbor examines what Bruno has referred to as the 'slow constitutionalisation' of social rights in the EU project and EU law. She observes that with a shift from labour law and social policy to economic policy governance the EU may be said to prioritise economic rationality over social justice. Hildegard Schneider reflects on a topic Bruno studied at the beginning of his career, namely education. She looks at the evolution towards an EU law of education, and its impact on educational policies and the recognition of diplomas.

In Part IV, 'Minorities Europe', Iyiola Solanke discusses the protection of minority rights in Europe, the legal basis for protection of minority rights and languages and the role of the European Court of Justice in providing that protection. She looks at Bruno's earlier work on linguistic equality, comparing it to her on work on racial rights. Dia Anagnostou examines minority litigation before the European Court of Human Rights and focuses in particular on the period of the 1980s and early 1990s, which was a critical turning point in the Court's engagement with the concerns and claims of ethnic and cultural minorities. Dilek Kurban examines the role of law, and specifically courts, in the protection of human rights. She asks how, why, and how effectively social movements mobilise international human rights law to contest state violence by authoritarian regimes in the context of an armed conflict.

Part V is entitled 'Scholarly Europe' and reflects on scholarly methods and approaches to academic research. Elise Muir seeks to identify some of the main characteristics of Bruno's approach to the EU legal order, in the context of the choice of framework and methods. Niamh Nic Shuibhne portrays Bruno as as a legal pragmatist and explores a concept of legal pragmatism that emerges from Bruno's extensive scholarship.

II. Making Sense of Bruno De Witte

In their contributions, the authors not only engage with the topics that Bruno has covered in his work and reflect on the various aspects of EU law addressed by Bruno, as set forth above, they also reflect on the *scholar* Bruno and the *person* Bruno. They reveal the many faces of the *scholar* Bruno: the generalist, the legal pragmatist, the pioneer, the trapeze artist, the polyglot, the fox *and* the hedgehog, the eagle – all denominations used to highlight the eminence of his scholarly work. The contributions also reveal the many faces of the *person* Bruno: generous, responsive, inclusive, warm, sharp, engaging, critical, attentive, humorous – all adjectives used to depict the personality of Bruno.

In the last contribution to this book Ruth Rubio Marín puts the many faces of Bruno together. She stresses that this *Liber Amicarum* is not only a public recognition and an expression of appreciation for everything that Bruno has offered to the academic community but also an invitation to challenge the way many scholars think of academic careers and the pathways to success. In our attempt to make sense of European Union law and the scholar and person Bruno, we may have found the need to 'rethink academia', in the words of Ruth, and hence the way we do academia and deal with the frantic demands imposed today on the academic community in relation to research grants, publications and specialisation.

III. *Liber Amicarum*

How does one celebrate the work and career of Bruno De Witte, who has published so widely on so many topics of EU law, who has contributed to the field of European law in so many ways, who has written over 250 publications, and who has worked and co-authored with over 20 scholars, supervised over 50 PhD researchers – yet who is also not a big fan of the genre *Festschrift*? How does one avoid the need to publish a multi-issue volume to do justice to his immense legacy and pay tribute to such a great scholar? How does one limit the number of contributions? The answer came from his wife Veerle: by making it a collection of contributions by Bruno's closest female academic friends, a *Liber Amicarum*. Initially baffled by the idea, we were easily convinced that this would indeed be an appropriate way to honour Bruno, who has so often professed his preference for working with women. Why does Bruno actually prefer to work with women? In her contribution Ruth Rubio Marín recalls that Veerle, when asked this question, indicated that this is 'just the way it is' and pointed to Bruno's family situation, having been raised with four sisters. Ruth herself thinks that it has to do with the type of academic person Bruno embodies: 'Bruno, unlike many other male academics of similar great prestige, is, in essence, a team player. He is a "we", rather than an academic "I".'

We were left with one final hesitation: women professors celebrating the male professor – would that not look awkward and confirm the old pattern of women serving the man? We decided that this would not be the case here, because the male professor in question is Bruno. Only for Bruno would a *Liber Amicarum* be appropriate and make sense. Ruth Rubio Marín depicts it strikingly: 'Only for Bruno because, male as he is (as far as I know he has never changed views on this), Bruno is, academically speaking, one of us. Nothing but complete "horizontality" in his approach and no secrets.'

Monica Claes and Ellen Vos

ACKNOWLEDGEMENTS

We would like to express our sincere gratitude to Sinead Moloney of Hart Publishing who embraced our proposal for a *Liber Amicarum* for Bruno De Witte with great enthusiasm. We would like to thank Sinead and her colleagues Sasha Jawed, Tom Adams and Ceri Warner for their friendly and co-operative attitude and their patience in the process of delivering the manuscript. It has been wonderful to work with them.

We would also like to thank Joana Brito Frago Nunes who has diligently formatted the text and footnotes.

Last, but not least, we would like to thank our dear friend Veerle Deckmyn who gave us the idea of this *Liber Amicarum* and helped us to select the authors for this collective volume.

CONTENTS

PART IV
MINORITIES EUROPE

PART V
SCHOLARLY EUROPE

PART VI
RETHINKING ACADEMIA: BRUNO DE WITTE

NOTES ON CONTRIBUTORS

Dia Anagnostou is Assistant Professor of Comparative Politics in the Department of Public Administration at Panteion University of Social Sciences, and Senior Research Fellow at the Hellenic Foundation of European and Foreign Policy (ELIAMEP) in Athens. She has held research positions at Princeton University, and the European University Institute.

Diamond Ashiagbor is Professor of Law at the University of Kent, UK. She is an interdisciplinary legal scholar who teaches and researches on labour law, equality, regions (European Union and African Union), trade and development, and economic sociology of law.

Monica Claes is Professor of European and Comparative Constitutional Law at Maastricht University. Her work focuses mainly on the relationship between the European and the national constitutional law, common constitutional traditions and national constitutional identities, and European fundamental rights law. Monica is co-editor-in-chief of the *European Constitutional Law Review*.

Marise Cremona is Professor Emeritus at the European University Institute, Florence. She was Professor of European Law and a co-Director of the Academy of European Law at the European University Institute (2006–2017). She was Head of the Department of Law at the European University Institute (2009–2012) and President *ad interim* of the European University Institute (2012–2013). She is a member of the Editorial Board of the Common Market Law Review. Her research interests are in the external relations law of the European Union, in particular the constitutional basis for EU external relations law and the legal and institutional dimensions of EU foreign policy.

Deirdre Curtin is Joint Chair Professor of European Union Law at the Department of Law and Robert Schuman Centre for Advanced Studies, European University Institute, Florence. She is director of the Centre for Judicial Cooperation at the Robert Schuman Centre. She is member of the Royal Netherlands Academy of Arts and Sciences; a laureate of the Spinoza prize by the Dutch Scientific Organization for research in the field of European law and governance; a holder of Honorary Doctorates in law from University College Dublin and the University of Copenhagen; and an Honorary Bencher of the King's Inn, Dublin.

Gráinne de Búrca is Florence Ellinwood Allen Professor of Law at NYU. She is Director of the Hauser Global Law School and Co-director of the Jean Monnet Center. She is co-editor-in-chief of the *International Journal of Constitutional Law*

(I•CON) and serves on the editorial boards of the *American Journal of International Law*, *Global Constitutionalism* and *Legal Studies*. She is a Corresponding Fellow of the British Academy. She is co-author with Paul Craig of the textbook *EU Law* (Oxford University Press), currently in its 7th edition, and author of *Reframing Human Rights in a Turbulent Era* (Oxford University Press, 2021).

Claire Kilpatrick is Professor of International and European Labour and Social Law at the Department of Law, European University Institute, and Co-Director of the Academy of European Law. Before coming to the European University Institute in 2011, she worked at London School of Economics and Political Science (LSE) and before that at Cambridge University. Her interests lie mainly in the law and policy construction of Social Europe, especially the EU's roles. She is a member of the Editorial Boards of the *Industrial Law Journal*, the *International Journal of Comparative Labour Law and Industrial Relations* and the *Giornale di diritto di lavoro e di relazioni industriali*.

Dilek Kurban is a Max Weber post-doctoral fellow at the European University Institute and an Adjunct Faculty at the Hertie School of Governance, Berlin. Her PhD dissertation received the Erasmus Dissertation Prize 2019 in the Netherlands. Her research interests are regional human rights courts, state violence, legal mobilisation and judicial politics, with a thematic focus on authoritarian regimes.

Elise Muir is Professor of European Law at KU Leuven and Visiting Professor at the College of Europe. She is the Principal Investigator of the RESHUFFLE project (funded by the European Research Council). Before starting at KU Leuven, Elise was a tenured Associate Professor at the Faculty of Law of Maastricht University and Associate Director of the Maastricht Centre for European law.

Niamh Nic Shuibhne is Professor of European Union Law at the University of Edinburgh. She is one of the Joint Editors of the *Common Market Law Review*. She was Joint Editor of the *European Law Review* from 2009–2014 and remains a member of its Editorial Board. She was awarded a Leverhulme Trust Major Research Fellowship (2016–2019) to examine how protection of the foundational commitment to equal treatment in EU law came to represent an ideological challenge to the sustainability of the Union more generally.

Ruth Rubio Marín is Professor of Constitutional Law at the University of Sevilla and a holder of the UNIA Unesco Chair in Human Rights. Formerly, she held a Chair in Comparative Public Law at the European University Institute in Florence, Italy where she currently forms part of the School of Transnational Governance. Her research attempts to understand how public law creates categories of inclusion and exclusion around different axis including gender, citizenship, nationality and ethnicity. Her most recent book is *Global Gender Constitutionalism and Women's Citizenship* (Cambridge University Press, 2022).

Hildegard Schneider is emeritus professor at Maastricht University. She was professor of European Law and a former dean of the Law Faculty of Maastricht University. She is member of the Dutch UNESCO Commission, The Hague. Her research interests are in EU migration law, European citizenship and recognition of diplomas. She is holder of the Dr. J.G.H. Tans medal for her contribution to the development of Maastricht University.

Joanne Scott is Professor of European Law at the European University Institute and Co-director of the Co-Director of the Academy of European Law. Before joining the European University Institute in 2017, she was professor at the Faculty of Laws, University College London (on special leave) and the Universities of Kent, Queen Mary and Cambridge and a visiting professor at Columbia and Harvard Law Schools. She was elected as a Fellow of the British Academy in 2013 and as a Fellow of the Royal Society of Edinburgh in 2012.

Iyiola Solanke is the Jacques Delors Professor in European Union Law at the University of Oxford. She is a visiting professor at Wake Forest University School of Law and the Harvard University School of Public Health and former Fernand Braudel Fellow at the European University Institute. She is the author of *EU Law* (2022), *Making Anti-Racial Discrimination Law* (2011) and *Discrimination as Stigma: A Theory of Anti-Discrimination Law* (2017).

Ellen Vos is Professor of European Union law at Maastricht University and Visiting Professor at the College of Europe. She is director of the Maastricht Centre for European law. She is a member of the Editorial Board of the European Journal of Risk Regulation and of the Advisory Board of the Maastricht Journal of European and Comparative Law. She is coordinator of a large H2020 project *REconciling sCience, Innovation and Precaution through the Engagement of Stakeholders (RECIPES).*

PART I

Constitutional Europe

1

Questioning the EU's 'Principled Openness' to International Law

An Examination of the Court's Reception of the Aarhus Convention and the Convention on the Rights of Persons with Disabilities

GRÁINNE DE BÚRCA, CLAIRE KILPATRICK AND JOANNE SCOTT

I. Introduction

The question of whether the European Union, by comparison with other significant global powers, maintains a distinctive openness to international law – a *Völkrechtfreundlichkeit* – has animated EU law scholarship for many years.[1] Yet, while the claim of openness and fidelity to the international legal order is prominent in various provisions of the EU Treaties and in early rulings of the European Court of Justice (CJEU), observers have long pointed out the tensions between the professed commitments and the actual practice of the EU, not least the practice of the Court itself. The competing concerns of protecting the 'autonomy' of the EU legal order, shielding EU political institutions from international obligations which may not be so faithfully observed by other international actors, and preserving the authoritative and gatekeeper role of the CJEU vis-à-vis the international legal order, often run sharply counter to this declared openness to international law.

[1] There is an extensive literature on the topic. For a few pertinent contributions see J Klabbers, 'Völkerrechtsfreundlich? International Law and the Union Legal Order' in P Koutrakos (ed), *European Foreign Policy* (Elgar, 2011) 95; recently, R Dunbar, 'Article 3(5) TEU a Decade on: Revisiting "Strict Observance of International Law" in the Text and Context of Other EU Values' (2021) 28 *Maastricht Journal of European and Comparative Law* 479; and more generally the contributions in E Cannizzaro, P Palchetti and R Wessel (eds), *International Law as Law of the European Union* (Brill, 2010).

We might expect, however, that the Court's concerns with autonomy, reciprocity, authority and gatekeeping would be significantly lessened, if not abated, by a decision of the EU's political institutions to take the step of accession to a particular international agreement. Surely if the EU has indicated its clear intention to be bound by the provisions of an international Treaty, and has taken legal steps to bind itself publicly and externally, we might reasonably conclude that the Court of Justice has little reason to limit or impede the inclusion of those provisions as part of the EU legal order?[2] And yet, as this brief chapter indicates, the Court has continued to do just that – to impede and limit the inclusion within EU law of provisions of international Treaties to which the EU has acceded. In what follows below, we examine a range of the CJEU's rulings on provisions of an important environmental Treaty (the Aarhus Convention) and an important human rights Treaty (the Convention on the Rights of Persons with Disabilities) to which the EU has acceded, and we note how the Court has deliberately diluted the impact and effect of these Treaties as part of EU law, imposing an array of legal obstacles to the invocation and implementation of their provisions.

II. EU Accession to International Agreements

The question of the legal parameters and consequences of EU accession to international agreements remains one of perennial interest and importance in EU law. It is also a subject on which it seems challenging to do any more than faithfully reproduce the extensive and illuminating writings of Bruno De Witte. It is a topic on which he is amongst the foremost authorities.[3] In his recent publication on

[2] See eg B De Witte, 'Accession to International Instruments as an EU Legality Constraint' in C Kilpatrick and J Scott (eds), *Contemporary Challenges to EU Legality* (Oxford University Press, 2021).

[3] See B De Witte, 'The Past and Future Role of the European Court of Justice in the Protection of Human Rights' in P Alston (ed), *The EU and Human Rights* (Oxford University Press, 1999); B De Witte and GN Toggenburg, 'Human Rights and Membership of the European Union' in S Peers and A Ward (eds), *The EU Charter of Fundamental Rights* (Hart Publishing, 2004); B De Witte, 'The EU and the International Legal Order: The Case of Human Rights' in M Evans and P Koutrakos (eds), *Beyond the Established Legal Orders: Policy Interconnections between the EU and the Rest of the World* (Hart Publishing, 2011); B De Witte and A Thies, 'Why Choose Europe? The Place of the European Union in the Architecture of International Legal Cooperation' in B van Vooren, S Blockmans and J Wouters (eds), The EU's Role *in* Global Governance: The Legal Dimension (Oxford University Press, 2013); B De Witte, 'A Selfish Court? The Court of Justice and the Design of International Dispute Settlement Beyond the European Union' in M Cremona and A Thies (eds), *The European Court of Justice and External Relations Law: Constitutional Challenges* (Hart Publishing, 2014); B De Witte, 'Beyond the Accession Agreement: Five Items for the European Union's Human Rights Agenda' in V Kosta, N Skoutaris and VP Tzevelekos (eds), *The EU Accession to the ECHR* (Hart Publishing, 2014); B De Witte and Š Imamovic, 'Opinion 2/13 on Accession to the ECHR: Defending the EU Legal Order Against a Foreign Human Rights Court' (2015) 40(5) *European Law Review* 683; B De Witte, 'The European Union in the International System of Human Rights Protection: Solo Singer or Voice in the Choir?' in E Bribosia and I Rorive (eds), *Human Rights Tectonics: Global Perspectives on Integration and Fragmentation* (Intersentia, 2018); B De Witte, V Kosta, 'Human Rights Norms in the Court of Justice of the European Union' in M Scheinin (ed), *Human Rights Norms in 'Other' International Courts* (Cambridge University Press, 2019); B De Witte, 'Accession to International Instruments' (n 2).

the subject, he suggests that '[i]nternational agreements are likely to act as an EU legality constraint, due to the principled openness of the EU legal order to international law'.[4] However, in observing a contrast between the EU's formally open stance towards international agreements and the constraints imposed by the 'direct effect' requirement that has been strictly applied by the European Court, he argues that 'it may be more plausible to call the EU legal order a 'neo-monist' (in the sense of 'not-so-monist) one'.[5]

EU accession to international instruments can be an important first step in achieving openness to parts of international law. The EU has so far acceded to only one human rights instrument: the UN Convention on the Rights of Persons with Disabilities (CRPD). A range of legal and political obstacles have beset two other notable EU attempts to accede to human rights Treaties: namely, the European Convention on Human Rights (ECHR) and the Istanbul Convention, both of which have been the subject of Opinions by the Court of Justice.[6] By contrast, accession to the CRPD was remarkably smooth and rapid. On the EU side, the competence to sign the CRPD was based on the omnibus anti-discrimination legal basis now contained in Article 19 of the Treaty on the Functioning of the European Union (TFEU), and on the internal market legal basis now contained in Article 114 TFEU.[7] The EU rapidly proceeded to sign and to ratify the CRPD in 2010 without waiting for all EU Member States to take that step. As a party to the CRPD, the EU's compliance is monitored by the UN CRPD Committee, with the first reporting cycle having concluded in 2015.[8] By contrast with the paucity of human rights agreements to which it has become party, the EU has acceded to several dozen multilateral environmental agreements,[9] including a number that have been at issue in important cases before the Court of Justice.[10]

Yet, accession, far from being the end of the matter, is simply the beginning of a further set of inquiries about how constraining the provisions of international human and environmental Treaties will be for the EU legal order. EU law places international agreements to which it is a party just below the EU Treaties and above all secondary legislation in the hierarchy of sources.[11] From this primacy

[4] De Witte, 'Accession to International Instruments' (n 2) 100.

[5] Ibid 111.

[6] On the ECHR, see Opinion 2/94 of 28 March 1996, EU:C:1996:140, and Opinion 2/13 of 18 December 2014, EU:C:2014:2454; and on the Istanbul Convention see Opinion 1/19 of 6 October 2021, EU:C:2021:832.

[7] Council Decision 2010/48 concerning the conclusion, by the European Community, of the United Nations Convention on the Rights of Persons with Disabilities [2010] OJ L 23/35.

[8] United Nations Convention on the Rights of Persons with Disabilities, 2 October 2015, CRPD/C/EU/CO/1 GE.15-16705(E).

[9] For a complete list up to 2017 see: ec.europa.eu/environment/international_issues/agreements_en.htm.

[10] See eg Case C-308/06 *Intertanko and others* EU:C:2008:312. See also Case C-366/10 *Air Transportation of America and others* EU:C:2011:864.

[11] Art 216(2) TFEU states: 'Agreements concluded by the Union are binding upon the institutions of the Union and on its Member States.'

of international agreements over EU legislation flows the requirement that a provision of EU law should, wherever possible, be interpreted or applied in a way that is compatible with an international agreement.[12] If interpretative harmony of this kind is impossible, the conflicting provisions of secondary EU law may be set aside, but only insofar as the provision in the international agreement has direct effect. Yet in the practice of the Court of Justice, the instances in which the provision of an international agreement is found to have direct effect are significantly fewer than might be expected. Instead, what is evident is a judicial reticence or reluctance to treat the provisions of international agreements – even those to which the EU has expressly acceded – as capable of being directly enforced within EU law.

Below, we examine the way the CJEU has treated the provisions of two Conventions to which the EU has become a party, with a view to seeing whether accession makes a difference to the legal impact of those provisions within EU law.[13] The first concerns rights arising under the UN Convention on the Rights of Persons with Disabilities. The second concerns access to environmental justice pursuant to the Aarhus Convention on Access to Information, Public Participation in Decision-making and Access to Justice in Environmental Matters.

III. The Example of the UN Convention on the Rights of Persons with Disabilities

The CJEU has engaged with the CRPD in over a dozen judgments since EU accession, beginning in 2013 with the *HK Danmark Ring and Werge* case.[14] Formally, the CRPD is often given top billing in these judgments, preceding EU law in the presentation of the legal context at the beginning of each judgment and with its superior status over EU legislation noted.

[12] For a recent and extensive use of the CRPD as well as Arts 21 and 26 of the EU Charter of Fundamental Rights in deciding what 'reasonable accommodation' entails in the EU directive outlawing disability discrimination, see Case C-824/19 *TC, UB v Komisia za zashtita ot diskriminatsia, VA* EU:C:2021:862.

[13] Bruno De Witte has also examined these, most recently in his 2021 book chapter (n 2) 108–11.

[14] Case C-335/11 *HK Danmark acting on behalf of Ring and Werge* EU:C:2013:222; Case C-356/12 *Glatzel* EU:C:2014:350; Case C-363/12 *Z* EU:C:2014:159; Case C-354/13 *FAO acting on behalf of Kaltoft* EU:C:2014:2463; Case C-198/15 Invamed Group EU:C:2016:362; Case C-395/15 Daouidi EU:C:2016:917; Case C-406/15 Milkova EU:C:2017:198; Opinion 3/15 on the Marrakech Treaty EU:C:2017:114 (CRPD included in the list of relevant sources but not used in the reasoning); Case C-679/16 A EU:C:2018:601; Case C-397/18 Nobel Plastiques Ibérica EU:C:2019:703; Case C-795/19 *Tartu Vangla* EU:C:2021:606; Case C-824/19 *TC, UB v Komisia za zashtita ot diskriminatsia, VA* EU:C:2021:862; Case C-485/20 *HR Rail* EU:C:2022:85. There are also two decisions of the General Court: Case T-343/13 *CN v Parliament* EU:T:2015:926; Case T-613/19 *ENIL Brussels Office and others v Commission* EU:T:2020:382.

A. The Interpretive Obligation

In *HK Danmark Ring and Werge* the CRPD was used by the CJEU to help define the concept of disability and 'reasonable accommodation' for the purposes of disability discrimination in the EU directive prohibiting such discrimination (Directive 2000/78/EC[15]). As Advocate General Bot put it in one of the cases where the provisions of the Convention used, the CRPD has supported the adoption in EU law of 'an evolving and relatively broad definition of the concept of disability' as well as related concepts.[16] This has included drawing on the CRPD to acknowledge its provisions on the right to work; to interpret the provision of positive action for persons with a disability in the EU directive (*Milkova*); to conclude that a denial of reasonable accommodation constitutes disability discrimination in EU law (*Nobel Plastiques Ibérica; HR Rail*); and to find that failure to reasonably accommodate excludes the establishment of a Genuine Occupational Requirement (*Tartu Vangla; TC and UB*).[17]

In *Glatzel*,[18] however, the Court took the view that the interpretative obligation reached its limits. The CJEU stated, as its entire reasoning on the issue:

> point 6.4 of Annex III to Directive 2006/126 provides unequivocally that drivers of motor vehicles in categories C1 and C1E must have minimum visual acuity of 0,1 for the worse eye. In those circumstances, it does not appear possible to give that provision of secondary law an interpretation which would enable it to circumvent the clear rule laying down that minimum value.

It is worth noting that there is a considerable difference between the way the CJEU applies the interpretative obligation in this context, where it is EU law that should be re-read in light of international obligations, as compared with the way the Court requires the interpretative obligation to be applied by national courts when re-reading national law in light of EU obligations. As will be noted below, the interpretative obligation enunciated by the CJEU in the latter context seems to be in many cases considerably more demanding and far-reaching than it seems to be when applied to the interpretation of EU law in the light of international agreements. In other words, the CJEU is far more insistent on the implementation-by-interpretation of EU law within the Member States than it is on the implementation-by-interpretation of international law within the EU legal order.

[15] Council Directive 2000/78/EC of 27 November 2000 establishing a general framework for equal treatment in employment and occupation [2000] OJ L 303/16.

[16] C-395/15 *Daouidi* Opinion AG Bot, para 40.

[17] Case C-406/15 *Milkova* EU:C:2017:198; Case C-397/18 *Nobel Plastiques Ibérica* EU:C:2019:703; Case C-485/20 *HR Rail* EU:C:2022:85; Case C-795/19 *Tartu Vangla* EU:C:2021:606; Case C-824/19 *TC, UB* EU:C:2021:862.

[18] Case C-356/12 *Glatzel* EU:C:2014:350.

B. Direct Effect

According to a consistent line of case law of the Court of Justice on direct effect and the obligation of harmonious interpretation, when interpretation in line with an international agreement is not possible (eg when it would lead to a *contra legem* reading), then provided the provision in the international agreement has direct effect, it should be directly applied so that conflicting EU law could be set aside. However, what we see instead is that in all of the relevant case law on the CRPD, the direct effect requirement has been constructed by the CJEU as a very high barrier which the Convention has not surmounted. In the strangely restrictive judgment in *Z*, the Court of Justice found that the employment focus of the Employment Equality Directive meant that the general definition of disability in the CRPD could not be relied upon to broaden the scope of the Directive beyond discrimination with regard to employment and occupation – even though the case itself was directly concerned with a woman's conditions of employment in circumstances in which she had a child by surrogate.[19] As Bruno De Witte has noted,

> [t]he main reason for this restrictive view was that the CRPD requires its parties to take implementing measures to achieve the objectives of the Convention. Yet, as the EU's employment discrimination directive could very well be considered as such an implementing measure, the Court could have reviewed it in terms of whether it constituted an adequate implementation of the EU's international obligations.[20]

This puzzlingly broad refusal to countenance direct effect for any provision of the CRPD – on the peculiar basis that it is a 'programmatic' Treaty, which is something that could be said of virtually all international agreements – has been repeated in subsequent cases. Hence in *Glatzel*, where the Court concluded that, due to the limited nature of the interpretative obligation as applied by the CJEU in that case, the only option for giving effect to the provisions of the Convention would be by setting aside the conflicting EU law, the CJEU went on to rule that:

> since the provisions of the UN Convention on Disabilities are subject, in their implementation or their effects, to the adoption of subsequent acts of the contracting parties, the provisions of that convention do not constitute, from the point of view of their content, unconditional and sufficiently precise conditions which allow a review of the validity of the measure of EU law in the light of the provisions of that convention.[21]

This rejection of the possibility of direct effect of the CRPD was despite, as the CJEU itself acknowledges, the express inclusion of the Directives at issue in the annex to the EU accession instrument: 'it is clear from the appendix to Annex II

[19] Case C-363/12 *Z* EU:C:2014:159. See also AG Wahl's Opinion in *Z* (EU:C:2013:604) especially paras 81 and 114: 'the CRPD is drafted in a programmatic form and accordingly cannot be relied upon to challenge the validity of EU law'.

[20] De Witte, 'Solo Singer' (n 3).

[21] Case C-356/12 *Glatzel* EU:C:2014:350, para 69, citing Case C-363/12 *Z* EU:C:2014:159, paras 89–90.

to Decision 2010/48 that, as regards personal mobility, Directive 2006/126 is one of the legal acts of the European Union which refer to matters governed by that convention'. In other words, the refusal to view legislation expressly annexed to the EU accession instrument as an intended 'implementation' of that international agreement creates a self-denying ordinance. What then could possibly ever constitute an implementing measure for the purposes of recognising direct effect? The Court of Justice seems to have decided to exclude the provisions of the CRPD from direct application in EU law, despite the fact that the EU chose expressly to accede to this human rights Treaty, and despite the fact that the EU political institutions explicitly pointed to a range of implementing measures in the annex to the EU ratification instrument.

The consequence of these two additional sets of boundaries constituted by the CJEU's unusually restrictive approach to direct effect and to the limits to the interpretative obligation, mean that accession is very far from the magic bullet one might imagine. The outcome is that EU law is rarely significantly altered by accession to international agreements.

IV. The Example of the Aarhus Convention

The European Community (as it then was) ratified the Aarhus Convention on 17 February 2005.[22] Among the rights that this set out is Article 9(3) concerning access to environmental justice. This requires that members of the public have access to administrative or judicial procedures to challenge acts and omissions by private persons and public authorities which contravene provisions of its national law relating to the environment. The concept of a public authority excludes bodies or institutions acting in a judicial or legislative capacity.[23] Article 9(4) requires that the procedure in Article 9(3) shall provide adequate and effective remedies and be fair, equitable, timely and not prohibitively expensive.

A year after its ratification of the Aarhus Convention, the EU adopted a Regulation on the application of the provisions of the Aarhus Convention on Access to Information, Public Participation in Decision-making and Access to Justice in Environmental Matters to Community institutions and bodies (the EU Aarhus Regulation).[24] Despite this, the Aarhus Compliance Committee

[22] UNECE Convention on Access to Information, Public Participation in Decision-Making and Access to Justice in Environmental Matters (Aarhus Convention) and Council Decision 2005/370/EC of 17 February 2005 on the conclusion, on behalf of the European Community, of the Convention on access to information, public participation in decision-making and access to justice in environmental matters [2005] OJ L 124/1.

[23] Ibid Art 2(2)(d).

[24] Regulation (EC) No 1367/2006 on the application of the provisions of the Aarhus Convention on Access to Information, Public Participation in Decision-making and Access to Justice in Environmental Matters to Community institutions and bodies [2006] OJ L 264/13.

has found that the European Union 'fails to comply with article 9, paragraphs 3 and 4, of the [Aarhus] Convention with regard to access to justice by members of the public because neither the EU Aarhus Regulation, nor the jurisprudence of the CJEU implements or complies with the obligations arising under those paragraph'.[25] The Committee observed shortcomings in the CJEU's restrictive case law concerning standing under Article 263(4) and concluded that these shortcomings were not corrected or compensated for by Article 10(1) of the EU Aarhus Regulation because it applies only to non-legislative measures of individual scope.[26]

While, as noted previously, the CJEU accepts at least in theory that international agreements entered into by the EU bind the EU institutions and prevail over acts adopted by them,[27] it has strongly resisted allowing the Aarhus Convention to impact on the legality or, in practice, the interpretation of EU law, even when EU law is clearly noncompliant with Aarhus obligations. As we will see below, while some positive change is coming, this has been induced by the intervention of the EU legislature rather than the EU courts. The following sections will examine the case law of the CJEU regarding the status of the Aarhus Convention in the EU legal order, examine the limits to its interpretative effects before the European Court, and finally, discuss recent amendments to the EU's Aarhus Regulation.

A. Primacy and Direct Effect

While the CJEU recognises that the Aarhus Convention may prevail over acts adopted by the EU institutions, it does not – as explained above – consider that it has primacy over the EU Treaties.[28] This has led the CJEU to conclude that 'derogation from the fourth paragraph of Article 263 TFEU cannot be accepted on the basis of [the Aarhus] agreement'.[29] The Court's longstanding restrictive reading of the standing conditions for non-privileged applicants in that fourth paragraph therefore remains unaffected.

Equally, even though the Court accepts that the Aarhus Convention may prevail over EU secondary legislation, it has established strict conditions that must be met if the Convention is to be relied on as a basis for challenging the legality of an EU act. It insists that the Aarhus Convention can only be relied on in an action for annulment where 'first, the nature and the broad logic of that agreement do not preclude it and, secondly, those provisions appear, as regards their

[25] UNECE, 'Findings and recommendations of the Compliance Committee with regard to communication ACCC/C/2008/32 (part II) concerning compliance by the European Union' ECE/MP/PP/C.1/2017/7 (17 March 2017), para 122.

[26] Ibid.

[27] See eg Joined Cases C-401/12P and C-403/12P, *Vereniging Milieudefensie* EU:C:2015:4.

[28] Case T-600/15, *Pesticide Action Network Europe (PAN Europe) and others* EU:T:2016:601, para 56.

[29] Ibid.

content, to be unconditional and sufficiently precise'.[30] The Court does not accept that Article 9(3) of the Aarhus Convention meets this second condition, which is one of the classic conditions for direct effect in EU law, because the rights of individuals under the Aarhus Convention are rendered subject to 'criteria, if any, laid down in (…) national law'.[31] For this reason, Article 9(3) is viewed by the Court as being 'subject, in its implementation or effects, to the adoption of a subsequent measure'.[32]

A chink in the armour deployed by the CJEU to resist the application of provisions of the Aarhus Convention within EU law appeared fleetingly as a result of the judgment of the General Court in *Stichting Natuur en Milieu*.[33] Here, the General Court upheld a plea of illegality pertaining to Article 10(1) of the EU Aarhus Regulation on the basis that it was incompatible with Article 9(3) of the Aarhus Convention. In so doing, it found the scope of Article 10(1) to be excessively narrow, confined as it was to 'acts of individual scope'.[34] The Aarhus Regulation thereby excludes non-legislative acts of general application which do, by contrast, fall within the ambit of Article 9(3) of the Aarhus Convention.

The willingness of the General Court to entertain a plea based on the Aarhus Convention in this case flowed from its conviction that the usual restrictive conditions which prevent an international agreement from being invoked to challenge EU law do not apply where the measure that is being challenged was intended to implement an obligation imposed on the EU by an international Treaty ('the *Nakajima* exception') or where the measure makes express reference to that agreement ('the *Fediol* exception').[35] The General Court concluded that the EU Aarhus Regulation was adopted to meet the EU's international obligations under Article 9(3) of the Aarhus Convention and it noted that there was an express reference to Article 9(3) of the Aarhus Convention in recital 18 of the EU Regulation.[36]

On appeal, however, the European Court of Justice did not agree.[37] It rejected the application of the *Nakajima* exception on the basis that Article 10(1) of the EU Aarhus Regulation could not be considered to be implementing specific obligations under the Aarhus Convention because the Contracting Parties enjoy a broad margin of discretion under Article 9(3) of the Convention.[38] It likewise rejected the *Fediol* exception on the basis that Article 10(1) of the EU Aarhus Regulation did not make direct reference to specific provisions of the Aarhus Regulation or

[30] Case C-240/09 *Lesoochranárske zoskupenie VLK v Ministerstvo životného prostredia Slovenskej republiky* EU:C:2011:125, para 44.

[31] Ibid para 45.

[32] Ibid para 44.

[33] Case T-338/08 *Stichting Natuur en Milieu and Pesticide Action Network Europe v European Commission* EU:T:2012:300.

[34] Ibid para 83.

[35] Ibid paras 53–56.

[36] Ibid paras 57–58.

[37] Joined Cases C-404/12 P and C-405/12 P *Stichting Natuur en Milieu* EU:C:2015:5.

[38] Ibid para 51.

confer a right on individuals.[39] As a result, the European Court largely eviscerated the *Nakajima* and *Fediol* exceptions by incorporating within them criteria – such as an absence of precision and the conferral of individual rights – that are reminiscent of the criteria that it uses more generally to assess direct effect even outside the scope of these exceptions. As an aside, it is interesting to observe that a recent amendment to the EU's Aarhus Regulation confirms the view that the 2006 Aarhus Regulation was indeed 'adopted in order to contribute to the implementation of the obligations arising under the Aarhus Convention by laying down rules on its application to Union institutions and bodies'.[40] The Court of Justice, it seems, is so vigilant to prevent the provisions of international law from being invoked as part of EU law that it is determined to exclude them even in the face of clear evidence of political intent to include them.

B. The Interpretative Obligation

While the CJEU has denied direct effect to Article 9(3) of the Aarhus Convention, it has insisted nonetheless that *national* courts have an obligation to interpret their national rules in accordance with the objectives of Article 9(3) and the objective of effective judicial protection and, indeed, to do so 'to the fullest extent possible'.[41] Equally, Article 9(3) must not 'be interpreted in such a way to make it in practice impossible or excessively difficult to exercise rights conferred by EU law'.[42]

While the CJEU has paid lip service to the proposition that EU law should be interpreted in light of the Aarhus Convention,[43] it has, at the same time, drained this interpretative obligation of impact in its application to the EU, as opposed in its application to the Member States and to their courts. Two aspects of its reasoning come to the fore in this respect.

First, the CJEU has chosen to characterise a softening of the standing requirement in Article 263(4) TFEU as constituting a 'derogation' from the Treaty as opposed to an Aarhus-friendly interpretation of the Treaty.[44] For the Court, a broader reading of the individual concern requirement to confer standing on persons whose rights are affected and to environmental interest groups which have

[39] Ibid para 50.

[40] Regulation (EU) 2021/1767 of the European Parliament and of the Council of 6 October 2021 amending Regulation (EC) No 1367/2006 on the application of the provisions of the Aarhus Convention on Access to Information, Public Participation in Decision-making and Access to Justice in Environmental Matters to Community institutions and bodies [2021] OJ L 356/1 recital 2.

[41] Case C-240/09 *Lesoochranárske zoskupenie VLK* EU:C:2011:125, para 50.

[42] Ibid para 49.

[43] Case C-784/18 P *Mellifera eV, Vereinigung für wesensgemäße Bienenhaltung* EU:C:2020:630. For a full discussion, including of the influence of Aarhus Compliance Committee findings and the Aarhus Implementation Guide, see I Hadjiyianni, 'The CJEU as Gatekeeper of International Law: The Cases of WTO Law and the Aarhus Convention' (2021) 70 *International and Comparative Law Quarterly* 895.

[44] Case T-600/15 *Pesticide Action Network Europe* EU:T:2016:601.

a demonstrable interest in the question arising would have the effect of 'setting aside' the condition of individual concern.[45] As Advocate General Jacobs convincingly showed in his opinion in *UPA* many years ago, this claim clearly flies in the face of the open-textured nature of the concept of 'individual concern'.[46] But while the CJEU accepts that it is possible to envisage a different system of judicial review, it declared that it considers it to be for the Member States rather than the Court to reform the system that is laid down in the Treaty.[47] Yet, as many have pointed out, it is the Court of Justice whose highly restrictive interpretation of the open-textured notion of 'individual concern' that has led to a very narrow system of standing for individuals, rather than a deliberately narrow system chosen by the Member States.

Second, even when looking to the Aarhus Convention in the course of interpreting EU secondary legislation, the CJEU has emphasised the limits that attach to this obligation. Thus, the Court has refused to construe the process of internal review created by Article 10(1) of the EU's Aarhus Regulation as extending to non-legislative acts of general application on the basis that such an interpretation would be *contra legem*.[48] This is despite the recognition by both the General Court and the Aarhus Compliance Committee that Article 10(1) EU Regulation as it is currently interpreted is not compatible with Article 9(3) of the Aarhus Convention, and despite the more demanding nature of the interpretative obligation that the Court of Justice has insisted on when applying it to the obligation of national courts to construe their legislation in the light of EU law.

C. Legislative Effect

At each turn, the CJEU has resisted allowing the Aarhus Convention to shape the contours of EU law, despite an express finding by the Aarhus Compliance Committee that the EU is breaching its obligations under this convention, and despite the evident intent of the EU political institutions to comply with the Aarhus Convention by acceding to it and implementing it in an EU Regulation. And indeed, under intense pressure from environmental non-governmental organisations (NGOs),[49] the EU legislature has recently stepped in to amend aspects of the EU Aarhus Regulation.[50]

[45] Case C-297/20 P *Peter Sabo* EU:C:2021:24, paras 34–35.

[46] Case C-50/00 P *Unión de Pequeños Agricultores (UPA)* EU:C:2002:462; AG Jacobs' Opinion EU:C:2002:197.

[47] Case C-297/20 P *Peter Sabo* EU:C:2021:24, para 33.

[48] Case C-784/18 P *Mellifera eV* EU:C:2020:630, para 27. The concept of an administrative act is defined in Art 2(g) of the EU Aarhus Regulation as a measure of individual scope. Therefore, as in Art 263(4) TFEU, the interpretative question focuses on the term 'individual'; individual concern in the case of the former and individual scope in the case of the latter.

[49] See eg Client Earth, 'A 20-year journey towards access to justice – timeline' available at www.clientearth.org/latest/latest-updates/news/a-20-year-journey-towards-access-to-justice-timeline.

[50] Regulation (EU) 2021/1767 on the application of the provisions of the Aarhus Convention.

Crucially, the recent amendments to the EU Aarhus Regulation expand the scope of the kinds of acts that may be subject to a request for internal review under Article 10(1) of the Aarhus Regulation. This now includes any non-legislative act that contravenes environmental law, including those of general application, as well as administrative omissions.[51] Moreover, the right to seek internal review extends not only to NGOs but also to other members of the public who meet the criteria in Article 11 of the revised EU Aarhus Regulation.[52] Members of the public may seek internal review if they can demonstrate impairment of their rights caused by the alleged contravention of EU environmental law and they are directly affected by such impairment compared to the public at large.[53] They are also required to demonstrate a sufficient public interest and to show that the request is supported by at least 4000 members of the public residing or established in at least five Member States, with at least 250 members of the public coming from each of those Member States.[54] A body called upon to conduct internal review will be required to consider a request unless it is manifestly unfounded or clearly unsubstantiated.[55]

V. Ways Forward: How to Ensure Respect for Environmental and Human Rights Agreements Ratified by the EU in the Face of Obstacles Erected by the CJEU?

A. Leveraging the Gap between Interpretive Obligations

There is a clear and widening gap apparent between the interpretive obligations placed by the CJEU on national courts to interpret national law in accordance with binding EU law and those it places to interpret EU law in accordance with binding international law. Indeed, looking to the *Slovak Brown Bear* case, the Aarhus Compliance Committee observed that 'if the EU Courts had been bound in the same way as national courts' by the principle of effective protection of environmental law, 'the EU might have moved towards compliance' with the Aarhus Convention.[56] This growing gap, and the double-standards it implies, could be invoked by litigants and lawyers to challenge the consistency of the Court's reasoning. While the CJEU has also set limits on the interpretative obligation of national courts vis-à-vis EU law, saying it cannot require an interpretation *contra legem*, the case law suggests that these limits are considerably looser than those imposed

[51] Ibid Art 1(1).
[52] Ibid Art 1(2).
[53] Ibid Art 1(3).
[54] Ibid.
[55] Ibid Art 1(2)(2).
[56] UNECE, 'Findings and recommendations' (n 25) para 83.

by the Court when interpreting EU law vis-à-vis its international obligations, and the CJEU has regularly encouraged national courts to do everything they can to read national law in compliance with EU law. Hence, 'the principle that national law must be interpreted in conformity with EU law requires national courts to do whatever lies within their jurisdiction, taking the whole body of domestic law into consideration and applying the interpretative methods recognised by it' and further includes a judicial obligation 'to change established case-law, where necessary, if it is based on an interpretation of national law that is incompatible with the objectives of a directive'.[57] We see a far weaker and more circumscribed interpretative obligation being outlined by the Court of Justice when it comes to the interpretation of EU law in conformity with the provisions of international law, even when it concerns an international agreement to which the EU has acceded and which it has expressly chosen to implement.

B. Re-engaging with what Implementation Requires for Direct Effect

The CJEU case law discussed above highlights one key aspect of its case law on the direct effect of international agreements. Both in relation to the CRPD and the Aarhus Convention, the Court did not accept that the provisions relied upon were sufficiently clear and precise to allow them to be directly invoked, ostensibly due to the need for further implementation of the Treaties. As noted already, this is a highly unconvincing argument in relation to the CRPD, which is a human rights Treaty imposing fairly clear obligations on its signatories, but in so far as the CJEU's argument has some plausibility, it could be argued that because the CRPD is later in time than the relevant EU Directives, the Court did not treat those directives as sufficient to constitute implementation of the international agreement.[58] The EU legislature, which is also bound by the CRPD, could accordingly make clear in future legislation (or older legislation, by amendment) that this legislation is to be considered as an implementation of the CRPD.

Similarly, in relation to the Aarhus Convention, the CJEU's approach to implementation is flawed. On the one hand, it is not clear why Article 9(3) is viewed as being subject to the adoption of implementing measures given that it does not require Member States to lay down criteria for access to judicial or administrative procedures. It merely makes access subject to such criteria where

[57] See Cases C-569/16 and C-570/16 *Bauer* EU:C:2018:871, paras 67 and 68.

[58] Needless to say, this attempt to explain the CJEU's reasoning is not particularly convincing either, since the Court has made quite clear, in relation to the obligation of harmonious interpretation imposed on national courts, that this obligation should apply to national law adopted prior to as well as subsequent to the EU law in question. In other words, an implementing act, for the purposes of the obligation of harmonious interpretation, can be an act adopted prior to as well as subsequent to the Treaty or EU law in question.

they happen to exist. On the other hand, the Court's reading of the *Nakajima* and *Fediol* exceptions is ludicrously constrained, effectively nullifying the purpose and effect of these two exceptions which the Court itself had created and articulated in earlier case-law. Building on the General Court's judgment in *Stichting Natuur*,[59] we would also encourage the CJEU to relax the conditions for invocation of these crucial exceptions, and to return to its earlier and more commendable treatment of the international obligations of the EU in line with the evident decision of the EU's political institutions to ratify, implement and comply with them.

C. Leveraging Other Opinions at the Court of Justice

One way of finding opportunities for legal change is to look for authoritative differences of opinion within the jurisprudence of the Court of Justice and indeed between the CJEU and other international courts or tribunals. The role of the Aarhus Compliance Committee in building pressure on the EU to expand opportunities for access to environmental justice is telling in this respect. Equally, within the EU legal order, the General Court's judgment in *Stichting Natuur* offers important insights into how the *Nakajima* and *Fediol* exceptions could and should be used to extend the scope of direct effect to international agreements which the EU legislative and political institutions clearly intended to comply with.[60] By contrast, the Opinions of the Advocates General concerning the CRPD provide slim pickings. Indeed, in many cases, the Court itself is considerably more diligent in considering the CRPD's potential in relation to EU law. Nonetheless, this remains an important avenue for promoting alternative ways of increasing the effectiveness of these important human rights and environmental obligations. The recent Opinion by Advocate General Rantos in *HR Rail*[61] is the first time any member of the Court of Justice has cited and examined in detail a Communication of the CRPD Committee under the Optional Protocol to that agreement. This is a significant step beyond simply looking at the words of the Convention, which has been the practice of the Court to date, and considering the interpretation of that provision amongst the relevant communities of interpretation. Another avenue is for national courts, and the lawyers appearing before them, to include and sharpen their questions on the CRPD, when invoking EU law and particularly when contemplating preliminary references to the CJEU.[62]

[59] Case T-338/08 *Stichting Natuur en Milieu* EU:T:2012:300.

[60] Ibid.

[61] Case C-485/20 *HR Rail* EU:C:2022:85.

[62] Although most preliminary references refer to the Charter of Fundamental Rights of the European Union rather than the CRPD, exceptions include Case C-406/15 *Milkova* where Milkova's lawyers developed arguments based on the CRPD, referenced and rejected in AG Saugmandsgaard Øe's Opinion.

D. Recognise the Potential for Legislative as Opposed to Judicial Intervention

While Bruno De Witte has rightly observed that there is a trend in favour of 'political exclusion' of direct effect of international agreements entered into by the EU,[63] the Aarhus example shows how legal mobilisation efforts directed at the EU legislature can sometimes bear fruit. The findings of the Aarhus Compliance Committee against the EU, together with the EU's refusal to endorse these findings at the Meeting of the Parties in 2017, 'led to strong opposition from certain non-EU states, NGOs and other institutional actors'.[64] This in turn led the Council to request the Commission to carry out a study examining the EU's options for addressing the findings of the Aarhus Compliance Committee.[65] Observing the very real constraints facing NGOs in gaining access to justice, this study honed in on the Aarhus Regulation 'as a means of redress'.[66] When it comes to securing access to environmental justice, the EU legislature has taken a step forward, while the CJEU unfortunately remains at the back of the queue.

VI. Conclusion

Inspired by Bruno De Witte's remarkable scholarly oeuvre on the relationship of EU law and international law, and particularly by his recent work on the relevance of accession by the EU to international agreements, this chapter has examined the practice of the Court of Justice in relation to two important international agreements to which the EU has acceded in the field of human rights and environmental law. Far from cementing the EU's supposed openness and 'friendliness' to international law, it seems that accession by the EU to the Aarhus Convention and to the UN Convention on the Rights of Persons with Disabilities has made no difference to the Court of Justice's reluctance to permit the enforcement of the provisions of international agreements as part of EU law. Rather than encouraging the harmonious interpretation of EU law in light of the obligations imposed by these two important Treaties and allowing their provisions to have direct

[63] Kilpatrick and Scott, *Contemporary Challenges* (n 2) 111.

[64] A Friel, 'The Aarhus Regulation Amendment: Cause for cautious celebration' (6 November 2020) at www.clientearth.org/projects/access-to-justice-for-a-greener-europe/updates/the-aarhus-regulation-amendment-cause-for-cautious-celebration.

[65] Council Decision (EU) 2018/881 of 18 June 2018 requesting the Commission to submit a study on the Union's options for addressing the findings of the Aarhus Convention Compliance Committee in case ACCC/C/2008/32 and, if appropriate in view of the outcomes of the study, a proposal for a Regulation of the European Parliament and of the Council amending Regulation (EC) No 1367/2006 [2018] OJ L155/6.

[66] DG Environment, 'Report on European Union implementation of the Aarhus Convention in the area of access to justice in environmental matters' SWD (2019) 378 final, 28.

effect when they are clear obligations which the EU fully intended to implement, the CJEU has construed the interpretative obligation narrowly and has refused to grant them direct effect in a range of cases. We have suggested a number of avenues open to litigants, activists and lawyers who are concerned to ensure the effectiveness of these international agreements within EU law, to overcome the reluctance or caution of the Court of Justice in this respect, and to restore some of the 'principled openness of EU law to international law' of which Bruno has reminded us.

2

Mixed Agreements and Constitutional Gaps

MARISE CREMONA

I. Constitutional Overload and Mixed Agreements

In a characteristically elegant and challenging contribution to a collaborative endeavour soon after I joined the European University Institute, Bruno De Witte questioned whether EU foreign relations were burdened by 'Too Much Constitutional Law'[1] and argued for greater attention to the virtue of constitutional parsimony. While what amounts to 'constitutional overload' in a particular system is both variable and debatable, he argued that the EU suffers from an over-detailed and over-interpreted constitution, combined with the inertia resulting from the difficulty of constitutional amendment. And in relation to foreign policy specifically Bruno speaks of '[a] feeling of uneasiness (…) that things really get too complicated, and that we now definitely have too much confusing and unhelpful constitutional law of foreign relations in the EU'.[2] At the same time, and perhaps contributing to that uneasiness, the Court's judgments tend to focus on technical institutional issues rather than questions of substantive foreign policy, a tendency which is – I would argue – the result of the constitutional framing of EU foreign policy powers in terms of process and fields of activity (trade, development, defence, …) rather than policy outcomes.[3]

Since Bruno's paper, written in 2008, things have not got less complicated. And yet there is a degree of paradox here. Bruno rightly mentions mixed agreements as a prime example of the incomprehensibility and complexity of EU external relations, confusing to legal specialists as well as third countries. But arguably one of the sources of this confusion is precisely the absence of clear rules in the

[1] B De Witte, 'Too Much Constitutional Law in the European Union's Foreign Relations?' in M Cremona and B De Witte, *EU Foreign Relations Law: Constitutional Fundamentals* (Hart Publishing, 2008).

[2] Ibid 10.

[3] See further M Cremona (ed), *Structural Principles in EU External Relations Law* (Hart Publishing, 2018).

Treaties on the negotiation and conclusion of mixed agreements by the EU. This short reflection on some of the implications of this phenomenon emerging from recent judgments of the Court of Justice, looks at the interplay between the legal framework of Article 218 of the Treaty on the Functioning of the European Union (TFEU) and the Council's political choices in the conclusion and management of mixed agreements. 'Interplay' in this context refers to the way in which one may influence the other as well as the balance between them.

As Bruno says, the EU's constitutional rules on external relations were not always abundant. They have grown at every Treaty revision, not only in adding more explicit external powers, but also adding considerable detail to the procedure for Treaty negotiation.[4] Despite this, the Treaties make no mention of how to handle mixed agreements; in the rules which determine competence, legal basis and Treaty-making procedures, mixed agreements are invisible. It is as though, for the EU Treaties,[5] the participation of the Member States in a Treaty negotiation alongside the EU is a separate matter for the Member States to decide on and organise. In practice, of course, Member State participation impacts the EU at each stage of negotiation, conclusion and implementation, throwing up sometimes tricky questions, legal as well as political, which have had to be resolved by the Court case-by-case. And this case-by-case construction is no doubt one reason for the complexity of the rules.

If the complexity and obscurity of the EU constitutional framework for mixed agreements is compounded by the absence of provision for them in the EU Treaties, the reason for this absence may be easily conjectured. Bruno, in his 2008 paper, makes the point that the abundance of primary law on external relations stems from the increasing desire of the Member States to control the powers conferred on the Union, as those external powers were widened and strengthened.[6] By the same token, there would be little incentive for the Member States to seek to predetermine the ways in which they might wish to exercise their own Treaty-making powers alongside the EU, to circumscribe in advance their available political choices. In mixed agreements we see operating together the political choices of the Member States and of the Council and the constraining legal framework of (constitutional) procedural rules in which, as already mentioned, mixed agreements are invisible. Let us look here at two aspects of that interaction

[4] Art 218 TFEU. A Dashwood, 'EU Acts and Member State Acts in the Negotiation, Conclusion, and Implementation of International Agreements' in M Cremona and C Kilpatrick (eds), *EU Legal Acts: Challenges and Transformations* (OUP, 2018); J Heliskoski, 'The Procedural Law of International Agreements – A Thematic Journey through Article 218 TFEU' (2020) 57 *Common Market Law Review* 79.

[5] Mixed agreements are in fact explicitly envisaged in the Euratom Treaty: see Art 102 of the Treaty establishing the European Atomic Energy Community and Ruling of the Court of 14 November 1978, 1/78/Euratom, EU:C:1978:202.

[6] '[I]n the case of the EU, enactment of constitutional rules is not so much a case of self-commitment (…) but a means for the Member States' governments to bind others, namely the EU institutions': De Witte, 'Too Much Constitutional Law' (n 1) 6.

in a few recent judgments of the Court of Justice. First, the interaction between the Council's political choice to conclude a mixed agreement and the legal rules governing EU participation. And, second, the interaction between those legal rules and the political and legal management of Member State participation. We find the Court on the one hand giving wide (too wide?) space to the Council's political choice, and on the other its strict (too strict?) insistence on compliance with procedural rules and at times an uneasy attempt to negotiate between the two.

II. Mixed Agreements and the Council's Political Choice

Mixity will be 'facultative' (that is, optional) where the whole envisaged agreement is covered by shared competence, or by a combination of shared competence and exclusive EU competence: the agreement may be concluded by the EU alone, but it may be decided that the Member States will also take part.[7] It now seems clear that the decision for mixity in such a case is a political one, and – less obviously – that it is for the Council to decide, acting in the framework of Article 218 TFEU. In Opinion 2/15, commenting on the Council's argument that in cases of shared competence mixity is 'a political choice', Advocate General Sharpston said that 'the legal safeguards underpinning that political choice' lie in the procedural provisions of Article 218 TFEU.[8] In *COTIF I* Advocate General Szpunar agreed,[9] and the Court, referring to its earlier statement in Opinion 2/15 that certain provisions of the draft agreement between the EU and Singapore, which fell within shared competence 'could not be approved by the Union alone', explained that this statement should not be taken to signify that mixity was obligatory, but rather that it was the Council's decision.

> [T]he Court did no more than acknowledge the fact that, as stated by the Council in the course of the proceedings relating to that Opinion, there was no possibility of the required majority being obtained within the Council for the Union to be able to exercise alone the external competence that it shares with the Member States in this area.[10]

So, the choice is political, but is taken by the Council as an EU institution exercising its Treaty-making powers under Article 218 TFEU, not by the Member States

[7] On facultative mixity generally, see M Chamon and I Govaere (eds), *EU External Relations Post-Lisbon: The Law and Practice of Facultative Mixity* (Brill, 2020).

[8] Opinion 2/15, Opinion of AG Sharpston EU:C:2016:992, para 74.

[9] 'The question of when and how the European Union exercises that [shared] competence is essentially a political one which is covered by the procedure laid down in Article 218 TFEU.' Opinion of AG Szpunar in Case C-600/14 *Germany v Council (COTIF I)* EU:C:2017:296, para 78. See also Opinion of AG Wahl in Opinion 3/15 (Marrakesh Treaty) EU:C:2016:657, para 119: 'The choice between a mixed agreement or an EU-only agreement, when the subject matter of the agreement falls within an area of shared competence (or of parallel competence), is generally a matter for the discretion of the EU legislature.'

[10] Case C-600/14 *Germany v Council (COTIF I)* EU:C:2017:296, para 68.

acting independently or collectively; as the Court's phrasing makes clear, there would need to be a 'required majority,' normally a qualified majority,[11] in Council to agree that the Union should act alone. Once the Council has decided in favour of EU participation (mixed or not) that participation is governed procedurally by Article 218 TFEU, and substantively by the principle of conferral and the rules governing choice of legal basis. The Court's position has always been that choice of legal basis is of constitutional significance and should therefore rest on objective factors including the aims and content of the agreement,[12] and that 'the rules regarding the manner in which the EU institutions arrive at their decisions are laid down in the Treaties and are not at the disposal of the Member States or of the institutions themselves'.[13] In other words, we move from political choice to legal rules.

However, the Court's ruling in Opinion 1/19 shows that things may not be so straightforward.[14] According to the Court, the Council, having decided in favour of mixity, may then go on to exercise a further political choice to restrict EU participation in the agreement to certain of its elements: 'the decision whether or not to act on the proposal to conclude an international agreement, and, if so, to what extent (…) fall within the Council's political discretion'.[15] The Opinion concerned the Istanbul Convention on preventing and combating violence against women, and was a request by the European Parliament concerning the appropriate legal basis for the decision on conclusion; the possibility of splitting that decision into two depending on choice of legal basis; and whether, as a mixed agreement, the Council should wait for the 'common accord' of the Member States to accede to the Convention before concluding it on behalf of the EU. In this section, I will focus on aspects of the first question, and in the next on the issue of 'common accord'.

In general, where the signature or conclusion of an international agreement is concerned, the enquiry as to 'aim and content' and 'centre of gravity' of the measure is directed at the agreement itself taken as a whole.[16] The Council decision is inseparable from the agreement to which it refers (and hence the agreement becomes an 'act of an institution' which may inter alia be referred for interpretation to the Court of Justice). However, in this case the Court, following Advocate General Hogan,[17] accepted that legal basis should depend on those parts of the agreement that the Council had decided to conclude. It did this

[11] Art 218(8) TFEU states that the Council shall act unanimously when the agreement covers a field for which unanimity is required for the adoption of a Union act, for association agreements, agreements referred to in Art 212 TFEU with States which are candidates for accession, and for the agreement on accession of the Union to the European Convention for the Protection of Human Rights and Fundamental Freedoms.

[12] See recently, Case C-180/20 *Commission v Council (CEPA)* EU:C:2021:658, paras 32–34.

[13] See eg Case C-28/12 *Commission v Council (hybrid decisions)* EU:C:2015:282, para 42.

[14] Opinion 1/19 of the Court (Istanbul Convention) EU:C:2021:832.

[15] Ibid para 252.

[16] See eg Opinion 1/15 (PNR) of the Court EU:C:2017:592.

[17] Opinion 1/19, Opinion of AG Hogan EU:C:2021:198, para 85.

by relying on the concept of 'envisaged agreement' in Article 218(11) TFEU, in respect of which the Parliament was seeking its Opinion:

> It is, in the first place, for the Council and the Parliament to specify to the Court the scope of the 'agreement envisaged', within the meaning of Article 218(11) TFEU, which is the subject matter of the present proceedings and in respect of which it is necessary to identify the legal basis on which any Council act concluding that agreement on behalf of the Union must be based.[18]

And although the Commission and Parliament had apparently envisaged that the Union would accede to all aspects of the Convention falling within its competence (exclusive or shared) the Court accepted the Council's statement that the necessary majority in the Council extended only to those parts of the Convention falling within exclusive Union competence,[19] being guided in this also by the legal bases chosen for the decisions on signature, which had already been adopted. There is some logic, certainly, in holding that if it is the Council's political choice to conclude a (mixed) agreement, it may also choose the extent to which the EU will participate. However, the Court's willingness to accept this extension of political choice raises more questions than it answers, not least in terms of international law.

First, and perhaps least important, this approach creates a circularity in determining the appropriate legal basis, which would inevitably depend not on an objective assessment of the scope, aims and content of the agreement but on the Council's own determination of the reach of Union participation, as evidenced in its own statements and instruments (such as, here, the unchallenged decisions on signature[20]). The hitherto accepted rule that legal basis does not depend on the Council's (or any other institution's) own assessment of the agreement and the relative importance of its components is challenged.[21] Legal basis is, we are told, a matter of constitutional significance, and although in practice the political institutions have always been able to frame an act so as to suggest a specific legal basis (for example in the drafting of a preamble) this is, for obvious reasons, less easy in the case of an international agreement. Focusing on the terms of the Council's decision (which, as in this case, may amend the Commission's proposal) to determine the extent of EU participation will extend the role of political negotiation with a resulting increase in uncertainty. Would it be possible, for example, to alter the extent of EU participation between the decision on signature and the decision on conclusion?[22] Would partial conclusion be possible for *any* mixed agreement?

[18] Opinion 1/19, para 278.

[19] Opinion 1/19, paras 281–282.

[20] On the reliance on the decisions on signature as evidence of the Council's intention and thereby of the scope of the 'envisaged agreement', see Opinion 1/19, para 282. On the failure to challenge the decisions on signature, see Opinion 1/19, paras 216–20.

[21] See eg Case C-180/20 *Commission v Council (CEPA)* EU:C:2021:658, paras 32–33.

[22] The Court insists that decisions on signature and conclusion 'are two distinct legal acts giving rise to fundamentally distinct legal obligations for the parties concerned' (Opinion 1/19, para 201); such a practice would of course create unwelcome uncertainty for the EU's Treaty partners.

The use of the term 'envisaged agreement' in the passage quoted above, borrowing from Article 218(11) TFEU to justify limiting the scope of the Convention under consideration, though clever, is hardly faithful to its specific procedural context and will prove less helpful when the question of legal basis arises in other contexts, such as judicial review. It also moves away from the Court's approach since *Haegeman*, which is to link the agreement with the EU's concluding decision in order to bring the agreement within the scope of Union law.[23]

Second, and following from this last point, to accept political choice in determining the degree to which the EU participates in a mixed agreement creates uncertainty in drawing the line between Union and Member State exercise of competence, and consequent multiple uncertainties: over the scope of Member State obligations;[24] over the Court's interpretative jurisdiction;[25] the degree to which the provisions of the agreement are binding on the EU and thereby condition the legality of secondary legislation;[26] and the determination of international responsibility – in any case a potentially difficult question in the case of mixed agreements.[27]

Third, the Istanbul Convention is a multilateral mixed agreement. The Court in its Opinion says nothing about the difference between bilateral and multilateral mixed agreements, but the choice for or against mixity is framed differently for bilateral and multilateral (facultative) mixed agreements.[28] In the case of bilateral agreements, the conclusion of the agreement by the EU is determined first, and only then will it be decided whether the agreement is to be mixed. Put another way, while Member State participation may be facultative, EU participation is not. In the case of multilateral mixed agreements, on the other hand, EU participation is not a given; the EU may accede to a multilateral agreement before, alongside or after its Member States, or not at all. Could it really be open to the Council to decide to conclude a bilateral mixed agreement (eg an association agreement) only in part? It has been clear since *Demirel* that the conclusion of an agreement (mixed or not) by the EU does not predetermine whether its obligations will be implemented by the EU or the Member States.[29] The conclusion of the agreement by the EU creates obligations for the Member States so that their fulfilment of its obligations is not simply a matter of international law but also EU law, deriving

[23] Case 181/73 *Haegeman* EU:C:1974:41.

[24] Case C-459/03 *Commission v Ireland (Mox Plant)* EU:C:2006:345.

[25] On this, see the Opinion of AG Ćapeta in Case C-500/20 *ÖBB-Infrastruktur Aktiengesellschaft v Lokomotion Gesellschaft für Schienentraktion mbH* EU:C:2022:79, paras 36; 84–86.

[26] Case C-308/06 *Intertanko* EU:C:2008:312 para 42; Cases C-402/05 P and C-415/05 P *Kadi and Al Barakaat International Foundation v Council and Commission* EU:C:2008:461, para 307; Case C-266/16 *Western Sahara Campaign* EU:C:2018:118, para 47.

[27] See generally M Cremona, A Thies and R Wessel (eds), *The European Union and International Dispute Settlement* (Hart Publishing, 2017).

[28] I Boss-Platière and M Cremona, 'Facultative Mixity in the Light of the Principle of Subsidiarity' in M Chamon and I Govaere (eds), *EU External Relations Post-Lisbon: The Law and Practice of Facultative Mixity* (Brill, 2020).

[29] Case 12/86 *Demirel* EU:C:1987:400; Case 268/94 Portugal v Council EU:C:1996:461.

from Articles 3(5) and 216(2) TFEU.[30] But if the EU's conclusion relates to part only of the agreement, the Member States' obligations in relation to the rest of the agreement would derive no backing from EU law. Given that the objective of a bilateral agreement is to establish a relationship between the EU and its Member States on the one hand, and the third State on the other, partial conclusion by the EU would be inherently problematic. Whether or not one agrees with the Court's approach, it is unfortunate that in Opinion 1/19 it gave no indication that its broad acceptance of the Council's political choice might carry problematic implications for different types of mixed agreement.

Multilateral agreements may be less sensitive to such issues, but they are not absent. Responding to arguments that partial conclusion might not be consistent with the Union's obligations under the Convention, the Court simply stated that its Opinion was concerned with compatibility under Union law, not public international law:

> [T]he potential liability which the European Union might incur at the international level when implementing the Istanbul Convention, because it could not properly fulfil its commitments, would not, as such, be capable of calling into question the validity of the decision by which the Council concluded that convention on behalf of the European Union.[31]

Given the purpose of the Opinion procedure, which is primarily to forestall problems at the international level caused by internal constitutional difficulties,[32] the compatibility of the Council's proposed political decision with the agreement it is purporting to conclude should, one may think, be relevant.

This brings us to a further unwelcome result of accepting partial participation by the EU in cases of facultative mixity, that is, the creation of a disconnect between the position under international law and under EU law. Advocate General Hogan recognised that an internal decision that the EU should conclude the Convention only in part by a selective exercise of its competence would not alter the fact that by concluding the Convention, the Union is bound in international law.[33] If, by concluding a mixed agreement, the EU and its Member States are jointly responsible for its performance at an international level, what then does the Council's choice of partial conclusion actually mean at the internal, EU, level? It does not

[30] Case 12/86 *Demirel* EU:C:1987:400, paras 10–11.

[31] Opinion 1/19, para 272.

[32] See eg Opinion 1/19, para 193.

[33] 'From the point of view of international law, in the case of mixed agreements, the EU and the Member States are considered to accede to them jointly and not in parallel. Consequently, unless a reservation relating to the distribution of competences is made – which supposes that the agreement does not rule out such a possibility – the conclusion by the Union of an agreement entails an obligation on its part to apply it as a whole. Issues such as the legal bases chosen to conclude such an agreement or the mixed nature of the agreement are considered to be issues internal to the European Union legal order, which in themselves cannot prevent liability on an international level in the event of unjustified non-execution. However, from the point of view of EU law, when the Union accedes to an international convention, it does so to the extent of the competences exercised to adopt the decision to conclude that agreement.' (footnotes omitted) Opinion 1/19, Opinion of AG Hogan, paras 81–82.

necessarily determine which parts of the agreement will be implemented by the EU and which by its Member States, including decisions adopted under Article 218(9) TFEU.[34] As we have seen, its primary internal result is the impact on choice of legal basis for the concluding decision by the Council, and the resulting impact on its status within the EU legal order. It may affect the interpretative jurisdiction of the Court of Justice[35] – an unwelcome complication given the potential responsibility of the Union with respect to the agreement as a whole and the need for conforming interpretation of secondary EU law.

This disconnect would disappear if, once the Council has decided both that an agreement should be concluded by the EU and that it should be mixed, EU conclusion were held to cover all elements of the agreement for which the EU has competence, exclusive or shared, with the legal basis for the concluding decision being determined by reference to the agreement as a whole. In the absence of the inclusion of the possibility of reservations in the agreement itself, State parties do not have this political choice in favour of partial conclusion. The EU, of course, is not a State and its competences are limited (if extensive): a lack of Union competence with respect to part of the agreement would render mixity obligatory, not facultative, and would require a specific understanding with the other parties; but this is a legal consequence of the Union's limited powers (the principle of conferral), not a political choice.

III. Managing Member State Participation in Mixed Agreements

So far, we have focused on the EU dimension of mixed agreements. However, the procedural rules on EU participation also affect the ability of the Council to 'manage' signature and ratification by the Member States.[36] From one perspective, it might be argued that Member State ratification has got nothing to do with the Union and that for the Council to get involved might compromise not only the national Treaty-conclusion processes but also the autonomy of action of the Union institutions. On the other hand, in a bilateral context the EU and its Member States conclude the agreement together: they will normally be described as 'of the one part'. And even in a multilateral context their participation will often be mutually inter-dependent (for example in the exercise of voting rights) and will carry EU law obligations for the Member States.[37] In terms both of the smooth functioning of the agreement and the efficacy of Union external action, coordination

[34] See eg Case C-600/14, *Germany v Council (COTIF I)* EU:C:2017:296.

[35] For a detailed discussion of the relevant case law, see the Opinion of AG Ćapeta in Case C-500/20, paras 25–86.

[36] We will not touch here on the important question of the implementation of mixed agreements.

[37] Case C-246/07 *Commission v Sweden (PFOS)* EU:C:2010:203.

is normal and expected. Indeed, the duty of cooperation in this context has long been emphasised.[38] However the Court has drawn a line between cooperation and the joint adoption of the legal act of signature, holding that the bringing together of the Council decision and the decision of the representatives of the Member States in a single act on the signature and provisional application of an agreement interfered with the procedural rules laid down in the Treaties and the institutional role of the Council.[39] This was not just a matter of voting; the Court was clearly concerned that the autonomy of Union decision-making would be compromised. Close cooperation must not interfere with the respective competences of the Union and Member States: 'The contracting parties to a mixed agreement concluded with third countries are, first, the European Union and, secondly, the Member States. When such an agreement is negotiated and concluded, each of those parties must act within the framework of the competences which it has while respecting the competences of any other contracting party'.[40] Heliskoski has suggested that at least in the case of a bilateral mixed agreement, a hybrid decision of this type could be acceptable, on the ground that the Union and its Member States are treated in the agreement as 'of one part'; therefore 'the Union and the Member States would *in any event* be required to exercise their respective competences jointly'.[41] This approach recognises the legal as well as the practical reality of mixed agreements.

The struggle between the practical management of the signature and ratification of a mixed agreement, the political discretion of the Council, and the need to protect the procedural framework established by Article 218 TFEU, was also visible in Opinion 1/19. One of the questions put to the Court by the European Parliament concerned the Council's practice not to adopt the decision concluding a mixed agreement (in this case, the Istanbul Convention) until there was a 'common accord' among the Member States to ratify the Convention themselves.[42] The Court accepted the discretion of the Council to decide whether, and when, to conclude the Convention. But the Council could not, the Court said, subject the procedure laid down in Article 218 TFEU to any external condition, such as the common accord of the Member States.[43] The decision to conclude must be adopted by the 'required majority', which will generally be a qualified majority. Thus, the Court established a path between political choice and legal rules: the Council may decide to wait but could not make conclusion conditional upon

[38] Opinion 2/91 EU:C:1993:106; Opinion of the Court 1/94 EU:C:1994:384.

[39] Case 28/12 *Commission v Council* EU:C:2015:282. See also Opinion of AG Sharpston in Case C-114/12 *Commission v Council (Broadcasting Organizations)* EU:C:2014:224

[40] Case C 28/12 *Commission v Council* EU:C:2015:282, para 47.

[41] Heliskoski, 'The Procedural Law' (n 4) 93 (italics in original).

[42] 'Is the conclusion by the [European] Union of the Istanbul Convention in accordance with Article 218(6) TFEU compatible with the Treaties in the absence of a common accord of all the Member States giving their consent to being bound by the convention?', Opinion 1/19, para 1.

[43] Opinion 1/19, paras 245–49.

the Member States' common accord. The length of the wait would in practice be determined by the need to achieve a qualified majority.

This ruling may be formally in line with Article 218 TFEU but of course in practice there is no doubt that it may be difficult for the EU to conclude certain mixed agreements if not all Member States are parties. This has always been true of bilateral mixed agreements, as recent cases where Member State ratification has been problematic have proved.[44] Although the Council decision on conclusion may not legally be made subject to prior Member State ratification, a bilateral mixed agreement will not enter into force until all Member State ratifications are complete.[45] Indeed, accession to bilateral mixed agreements by new Member States is expressly provided for in the relevant Act of Accession. In the case of multilateral mixed agreements, on the other hand, EU conclusion does not necessarily await ratification by all Member States, and indeed not all Member States may ratify (so-called partial mixity).[46] Where the EU concludes the agreement as a whole, it will be binding on all Member States as a matter of EU law.[47] However, the practice of partial conclusion of a multilateral mixed agreement by the EU may make partial mixity problematic. There would be a discontinuity in the application within the EU of those parts of the agreement not concluded by the EU if not all Member States are bound. We might respond, of course, that since those parts of the agreement are not part of EU law the variation in application does not threaten the EU system. But – depending on the precise nature of the agreement – this is hardly helpful to its effective implementation and may have implications for the operation of internal Union law.[48] And it is perhaps precisely where there is a difficulty in finding a qualified majority in Council for the full participation of the EU that we are most likely to see non-ratification by some Member States. One can see, therefore, that the acceptance of partial conclusion by the EU of multilateral mixed agreements makes the question of Member State ratification both more important and more delicate. No wonder 'common accord' became an issue in the case of the Istanbul Convention.

Whether or not one agrees with the view offered here that partial conclusion of mixed agreements should be confined to cases of legal necessity, it can I think be agreed that we lack a coherent approach to the legal implications of mixity. The Court's case law is inevitably complex given that by its nature it

[44] See eg the difficulties over the ratification of the Association Agreement with Ukraine, and over the CETA. See further G Van Der Loo and R Wessel, 'The Non-Ratification of Mixed Agreements: Legal Consequences and Solutions' (2017) 54 *Common Market Law Review* 3.

[45] Art 102 Euratom Treaty makes provision for mixed agreements and specifies that they may not enter into force until all Member State parties have completed their domestic ratification processes.

[46] See eg the Canberra Convention for the Conservation of Antarctic Marine Living Resources. See further I Boss-Platière and M Cremona, 'Facultative Mixity in the Light of the Principle of Subsidiarity' in M Chamon and I Govaere (eds), *EU External Relations Post-Lisbon: The Law and Practice of Facultative Mixity* (Brill, 2020).

[47] Art 216(2) TFEU.

[48] See by analogy, Opinion 1/13 of the Court EU:C:2014:2303.

responds to specific scenarios and legal problems case by case. To some extent the non-contentious Opinion procedure allows the Court to step back and take a broader view and in some Opinions the Court will take the opportunity to summarise, almost pedagogically, the current law. However, the particular 'envisaged agreement' and questions under dispute will remain the focus. The invisibility of mixed agreements in the Treaties' provisions on treaty-making leads to an application of the procedural rules without reference to the mixity context. And in the absence of Treaty rules the Court has not been prepared to circumscribe the Council's political choice on the EU's exercise of shared competences. Bruno may well have been right that the constitutional law on EU external relations is over-long, but the Union's foreign relations law, especially as regards mixity in Treaty-making, manages to combine being over-rigid and incomplete.

3

The European Union and National Constitutional Values

MONICA CLAES

I. Introduction

One of Bruno's main fascinations in EU law is the tension between national constitutional values and European law. This can be seen as a natural continuation of his original research interest in linguistic diversity within States and the role of fundamental rights to protect such diversity, which was the subject of his remarkable PhD thesis, written and defended at the European University Institute (EUI).[1] The co-existence of the diverse Member States within the Union is, in a sense, simply another guise of the co-existence of several language groups within one State. It also chimes with his love for the continent he has travelled so much, its many languages (several of which he speaks fluently), its cultural traditions and its inhabitants.[2] In a way, the study of the law that seeks to govern integration and diversity of the continent offered Bruno a good excuse to be on the road, and to meet up with old friends and make new friends sharing his fascination for Europe.

Along with his fascination for Europe's cultural and legal diversity comes his interest in constitutions and 'the constitutional', both in the form of the emerging European constitution, and the co-existence of that 'constitution' with those of the Member States. In 1991, that is *before* the Maastricht Treaty was concluded and signed, Bruno published an article on 'Community law and national constitutional values' – one of the first products of his extensive line of research on the relationship between European and national law.[3] In the article, he discussed some of the possible conflicts between European law and national constitutional values as well

[1] See B De Witte, *The Protection of Linguistic Diversity through Fundamental Rights* (PhD Thesis, 1985, EUI, available in open access on cadmus.eui.eu/handle/1814/4825).

[2] See eg B De Witte, 'Culturele verscheidenheid en Europese Unie' in *Redes gehouden op de 20e Dies Natalis van de Rijksuniversiteit Limburg 12 januari 1996* (Maastricht, Maastricht University, 1996) cris.maastrichtuniversity.nl/ws/portalfiles/portal/47005499/5f18b723-1360-425b-ade7-a77e552a6cff.pdf.

[3] B De Witte, 'Community Law and National Constitutional Values' (1991) 2 *Legal Issues of European Integration* 1. The first is probably his magisterial paper: B De Witte, 'Retour à Costa: La primauté du droit communautaire à la lumière du droit international' (1983) 49 *EUI Working papers.* In this paper

as proposals on how tensions might be addressed. What is immediately striking is that he does not take sides on the issue: he does not over-dramatise constitutional opposition to European law, nor does he advocate a strict hierarchy of one over the other; the article seeks ways to find consensus and achieve peaceful co-existence in mutual respect.

Since 1991, the context within which the challenge of the tension between commonality and diversity is played out has changed considerably. The European Union today is a very different organisation than the European Communities pre-*Maastricht*. The period since 1991 has witnessed several major Treaty revisions, as well as four rounds of accession.[4] The Union is now involved with so much more than integrating markets, and is active in all areas of life, including fields that were in 1991 and even until very recently considered to belong to the province of the Member States.

This chapter revisits some of the ideas Bruno discussed in his 1991 article. It opens with a brief account of the article, as a reflection of his early work on the issue as well as a time capsule. It then seeks to revisit some of the ideas contained in that article in the context of the present-day European Union. It will become clear that the challenge of balancing European law and national constitutional values has essentially remained the same, and so have the lines along which solutions should be found. Yet there are also a few important differences: much more so than in 1991, the Union is involved in the business of 'values' and presents itself as a Union of Values. Moreover, the vocabulary to negotiate the tensions between European and national values has changed, with the concept of national and constitutional identity taking centre stage today. This vocabulary is not conducive to easing tensions, but rather increases the space for conflict. More recently, the Court of Justice has coined the notion of the 'identity of the Union'.[5] Time will tell whether this may help to address tensions between Union law and national constitutional values.

he famously put into perspective the argument of the special nature of the Community Treaties as a basis for the primacy of European law. It would also lay the foundations for his work on the nature of the European Union as a branch of international law, albeit with some unusual traits, see eg B De Witte, 'The European Union as an International Legal Experiment' in G de Búrca and JHH Weiler (eds), *The Worlds of European Constitutionalism* (Cambridge University Press, 2011) 19. The relationship between European and national law is also central in many of his articles, such as: B De Witte, 'Direct Effect, Supremacy and the Nature of the Legal Order' in P Craig and G de Búrca (eds), *The Evolution of EU Law* (Oxford University Press, 1991) 177; and the updates in the second (2011, 323) and third editions (2021, 187); B De Witte, 'Article I-6 – le droit de l'Union' in L Bourgorgue-Larsen, A Levade and F Picod (eds), *Traité établissant une Constitution pour l'Europe – Commentaire article par article*, Tome 1 (Bruylant, 2007) 107; B De Witte, 'Article 53 – Level of Protection' in S Peers, T Hervey, J Kenner and A Ward, *The EU Charter of Fundamental Rights – A Commentary* (Hart Publishing, 2014) 1523.

[4] On the relationship between accession and the constitutionalisation of the Union, see B De Witte, 'The Impact of Enlargement on the Constitution of the European Union' in M Cremona, *The Enlargement of the European Union* (Oxford University Press, 2003) 209.

[5] Case C-156/21 *Hungary v Parliament and Council (conditionality regulation)* EU:C:2022:97, paras 127 and 232; Case C-157/21, *Poland v Parliament and Council (conditionality regulation)* EU:C:2022:98, paras 145 and 264.

II. Community Law and National Constitutional Values Anno 1991

As always, Bruno's 1991 article elegantly systematises the problem, and seeks to formulate seemingly modest and pragmatic solutions, steering clear from grand theories and novel concepts.[6]

The article presents the issue along the following lines. The Community Treaties, while they have been developing into the Constitution of the European Communities, are still very different from national constitutions, in that they do not express shared values and principles, but set concrete objectives to be achieved by the institutions and the Member States. Yet, when doing so, the Community may come into conflict with values enshrined in national constitutions. Supremacy is not absolute, in the sense that the national constitutional courts do not generally accept the primacy of European law over fundamental principles of the Constitution. These national constitutional values belong to different categories: on the one hand, they express universal values that are part of the common constitutional heritage of Europe (democracy, fundamental rights), and on the other hand, they relate to specific national values. This specificity may be expressed by the particular turn taken by some of the universal values (representative democracy and fundamental rights have their own national characteristics and variations), but also by institutional or substantive values that are unique features of the State concerned (such as federalism and linguistic diversity).

Bruno then reflects on a number of possible solutions for actual or potential conflicts between national constitutional values and European law. One is curtly rejected: the unilateral 'saving what each constitutional court for itself considered to be the inalienable constitutional patrimony'.[7] Remedies should rather be sought at the level of European law, 'in its present and future shape'.[8] He concludes that conflicts should not be settled according to unilateral principles of hierarchy, and that both the Court of Justice and the national constitutional and supreme courts should recognise that the relationship can be seen from two different, but equally legitimate, perspectives, and that there is now a plurality of 'supreme' texts in Europe. The dialogue might be facilitated by the fact that, on substance, there has probably never before been such a community of values among European States.

[6] Several ideas in the article can be read as reflections of what would later become known as 'constitutional pluralism' (the notion that the developing 'constitution' of the European Community ranked *alongside* 12 national constitutions; that there is a variety of reasonable but divergent interpretations on the theoretical premises of the relationship between European and national law, a 'theoretical pluralism'; that the relationship between Community law and the national constitutions is not to be settled according to unilateral principles of hierarchy; that both the ECJ and national constitutional courts should recognise that the relationship can be seen from two different, but equally legitimate perspectives; and that there is now a plurality of supreme texts in Europe), but grand theories are not Bruno's way of 'making sense of it all'.

[7] De Witte, 'Community Law' (n 3) 18.

[8] Ibid.

The challenge ahead is to make out of the national constitutions building blocks of European unity rather than bulwarks of sovereignty.[9]

III. Constitutional Tensions and Genuine Constitutional Value Conflicts

An important message of Bruno's article is that not all tensions between national constitutions and European law constitute genuine constitutional value conflicts, and even then, they do not necessarily lead to legal conflicts.[10] Indeed, many national constitutions have been amended to accommodate the requirements of membership, at the occasion of accession (thus, most of the Central and Eastern European States have included so-called Europe clauses in their Constitutions before accession) or Treaty amendment (Germany amended its Basic Law at the occasion of the Maastricht Treaty; Ireland has done so for virtually all Treaty amendments); to allow for the adoption or implementation of European legislation (such as the European Arrest Warrant which led to constitutional amendment among others in Poland and France); to respond to the pressures of EU membership on the constitutional system (like the constitutional changes to protect the federated entities in Belgium and Germany); or indeed to comply with European law as interpreted by the European Court of Justice (as in the case of *Tanja Kreil*).[11] Constitutional adaptation to the requirements of membership has also been achieved by constitutional courts, which have for instance creatively (re-)interpreted their constitutions so as to allow for European law to be applied and enforced in the domestic system (for instance Article 11 and later 117 of the Italian Constitution), or to comply with the standard of protection of a fundamental right by the European Court of Justice, in one case even lowering the standard that used to be set under the national Constitution (as the Spanish *Tribunal Constitucional* did in the aftermath of the *Melloni* judgment).[12] These are all examples of voluntary compliance by the Member States with the conditions for and consequences of membership.

There has been one timid (and failed) attempt to impose a duty on the Member States to amend their constitutions. When it became clear in 2011 that the EU rules-based fiscal framework, the Stability and Growth Pact, was not sufficient to achieve budgetary discipline, the idea was launched that balanced budget rules should be enshrined in national constitutional law to act as lasting mechanisms to better achieve sound budgetary policies in all Member States. Yet the original concept of a compulsory 'golden rule' in the national constitutions was soon watered down,

[9] Ibid 22.
[10] Ibid 18.
[11] Case C-285/98 *Tanja Kreil v Germany* EU:C:2000:2.
[12] Case C-399/11 *Stefano Melloni v Ministerio Fiscal* EU:C:2013:107; see A Torres Pérez, '*Melloni* in Three Acts: From Dialogue to Monologue' (2014) 10(2) *European Constitutional Law Review* 308.

probably because it was felt that this would be too much of an intrusion in the constitutional sovereignty of the Member States and because it would be virtually impossible to achieve in those Member States where constitutional amendment is extremely cumbersome. In the end, the Treaty on Stability, Coordination and Governance in the Economic and Monetary Union required a balanced budget rule in national law 'through provisions of binding force and permanent character, *preferably* constitutional, *or otherwise* guaranteed to be fully respected and adhered to throughout the national budgetary processes'.[13] All Contracting Parties did put in place binding and permanent balanced budget rules in their domestic legal orders. For a few those changes involved constitutional amendments, while most adopted alternative forms of binding frameworks. This approach fits with the traditional Union approach towards national constitutional systems: the principles, norms and binding aims may be set at the European level, but the way in which these are achieved is largely left to the Member States.

European law too has changed to alleviate tensions and conform to the constitutional expectations of the Member States, in particular where these are shared among the Member States. Even if this has not ended the debate on the democratic credentials of the Union, consecutive Treaty changes have aimed to make the Union more democratic. The reference in the Treaties to fundamental rights as general principles of EU law, the introduction of the Charter of Fundamental Rights, and the attempts to define the competences of the Union more clearly, can be seen as responding to the concerns expressed by Member States and their (constitutional) courts that the execution of public authority by the EU, like that of national authorities, should comply with the requirements of constitutionalism: democracy, rule of law and protection of fundamental rights.

There is still much controversy about the extent to which the European Union effectively complies with these fundamental constitutional values in its institutional structure and indeed, in its policies and daily activities. However, the notion that the Union should comply with these fundamental constitutional values has culminated in Article 2 of the Treaty on European Union (TEU) expressing the idea that the Union is founded on the same constitutional principles of democracy, rule of law, the respect for fundamental rights etc as its Member States. Article 2 TEU is the European version, so to speak, of national constitutional provisions that restrict participation of their State to a Union that complies with fundamental constitutional values, such as democracy, protection of fundamental rights and the rule of law.[14]

Another way of accommodating constitutional values diversity is differentiation and flexibility, which is another of Bruno's research themes, and which is discussed

[13] Art 3(2) of the Treaty on Stability, Coordination and Governance in the Economic and Monetary Union (the so called 'Fiscal Compact') (2012).

[14] To name just the best known example, Article 23 of the German Basic Law states that 'With a view to establishing a united Europe, the Federal Republic of Germany shall participate in the development of the European Union that is committed to democratic, social and federal principles, to the rule of law and to the principle of subsidiarity and that guarantees a level of protection of basic rights essentially comparable to that afforded by this Basic Law'.

in this volume by Deirdre Curtin and Ellen Vos.[15] National constitutional values can also be acknowledged and accommodated in European legislation.[16]

Finally, the European Court of Justice may, and should seek, where possible, to take account of national constitutional values. An evident example of this is the development of general principles based mainly on the common constitutional traditions of the Member States and the ECHR.[17] In *MAS and MB*, usually referred to as as *Taricco II*, the Court of Justice, pushed by the Italian *Corte costituzionale*, 'clarified' its position on the retroactivity of limitation periods *in peius*.[18] It did so with reference to *common constitutional traditions*, and not to the national identity claim. In some cases, the Court does allow individual Member States to derogate from obligations under EU law to protect national constitutional values, based on public policy exceptions[19] or Article 4(2) TEU,[20] or it simply allows a margin of discretion to national courts.

But there are limits to these types of 'mutual accommodation': the European Union cannot comply with all the specific, sometimes conflicting, requirements individual national Constitutions pose. There are also instances where the Union and its Court do not want to comply with (alleged) national constitutional requirements, for instance because different value choices have been made at European level. Conversely, there are instances where national constitutional actors are not willing, or do not feel able, to shape the national constitution to conform to European law. This is where genuine conflicts can occur.

[15] See chapters four and five.

[16] For example, Directive (EU) 2016/343 of the European Parliament and of the Council of 9 March 2016 on the strengthening of certain aspects of the presumption of innocence and of the right to be present at the trial in criminal proceedings [2016] OJ L 65/1 reads in its preamble that '[a]s this Directive establishes minimum rules, Member States should be able to extend the rights laid down in this Directive in order to provide a higher level of protection' (at 48), while Art 13 contains a non-retrogression clause. Another example is Directive 2010/13/EU of the European Parliament and of the Council of 10 March 2010 on the coordination of certain provisions laid down by law, regulation or administrative action in Member States concerning the provision of audiovisual media services [2010] OJ L 95/1 ('Audiovisual Media Services Directive'), which states in the preamble that '[t]his Directive enhances compliance with fundamental rights and is fully in line with the principles recognised [by Art 11 of the Charter]. In this regard, this Directive should not in any way prevent Member States from applying their constitutional rules relating to freedom of the press and freedom of expression in the media'.

[17] On the development of fundamental rights as general principles of EU law, see B De Witte, 'The Past and Future Role of the European Court of Justice in the Protection of Human Rights' in Ph Alston (ed), *The EU and Human Rights* (Oxford University Press, 1999) 859.

[18] Case C-42/17 *M.A.S. and M.B.* EU:C:2017:936; see C Rauchegger, 'National Constitutional Rights and the Primacy of EU Law: M.A.S.' (2018) 55 *Common Market Law Review* 1521 and M Bonelli, 'The Taricco Saga and the Consolidation of Judicial Dialogue in the European Union' (2018) 25 *Maastricht Journal of European and Comparative Law* 357.

[19] Case C-379/87 *Groener* EU:C:1989:599; Case C-36/02 *Omega* EU:C:2004:614; Case C-112/00 *Schmidberger* EU:C:2003:333.

[20] C-208/09 *Sayn Wittgenstein* EU:C:2010:806.

IV. Constitutional Values Conflicts: Is Primacy Absolute?

Where European Union law clashes with national constitutional values, the question arises which should be given precedence. The position in EU law is clear and has remained the same until this day: all EU law takes precedence over all conflicting national law, including of a constitutional nature.[21] The principle of primacy espoused by the Court of Justice and confirmed, albeit in an indirect fashion by the Masters of the Treaties, is still absolute.[22] However, the EU and its Court cannot annul or invalidate conflicting measures of national law, and the primacy of EU law is thus a legal reality only to the extent that national authorities including national courts accept it. The absolute version of primacy is contested, and national actors, including most prominently national constitutional courts, do not share it.[23] They base the authority and effect of EU law in the domestic legal order on the national constitution, and hence, subject it to the limits that the (core of the) constitution imposes. As a consequence, next to the European version of primacy, there are many national versions of the primacy of EU law that are more restrictive and make the authority of EU law conditional on compliance with the fundamental provisions of the constitution. It is this two-dimensional nature of primacy that made Bruno decide in 1991 that the primacy is not absolute.

The rest of the story is well-known: the constitutional courts have introduced three main types of constitutional reservations to EU law, which have been developed consecutively.[24] The first relates mainly to fundamental rights and refers to the famous *Solange* saga. On a structural level, the refusal of the German and Italian constitutional courts, later followed by virtually all constitutional and highest national courts, to accept the primacy of European law in the absence of any review of compliance with fundamental rights, contributed to the development of EU fundamental rights, first in the form of general principles, later eclipsed by the Charter. Today, the reservation relates to specific interpretations of fundamental rights and the manner in which the balance is struck in concrete cases. The second type of restrictions relates to the limits of the competences of the Union: the German *Bundesverfassungsgericht*, later joined by many other constitutional

[21] See recently Case C-357/19 *Euro Box Promotion and others* EU:C:2021:1034 and Case C-430/21 *RS (Effet des arrêts d'une cour constitutionnelle)* EU:C:2022:99.

[22] Declaration (No 17) concerning primacy, attached to the Final Act of the Treaty of Lisbon [2008] OJ 115/344, referring in turn to the Opinion of the Council Legal Service of 22 June 2007, confirming the case law of the Court of Justice.

[23] This makes Bruno question the absolute nature of primacy in the 1991 article. I believe that we agree on the substance, but I find it more logical to hold that the principle remains absolute *in EU law*, even though EU law sometimes allows for derogations based on national constitutions (eg in legislation or based on Art 4(2) TEU) and even though the principle is contested. The difference is semantic. See M Claes, 'The Primacy of EU Law in European and National Law' in A Arnull and D Chalmers (eds), *The Oxford Handbook of European Law* (Oxford University Press, 2015) 178.

[24] On the role of national constitutional courts on the matter see M Claes and B De Witte, 'Rollen der nationalen Verfassungsgerichtsbarkeit im europäischen Rechtsraum' in A von Bogdandy, C Grabenwarter and P Huber (eds), *Handbuch Ius Publicum Europaeum: Verfassungsgerichtsbarkeit in Europa: Vergleich und Perspektiven*, Vol Band VII (C.F. Müller 2021) 639.

courts, announced that it would patrol the limits of the competences of the Union, and that it would declare acts that it considered *ultra vires* to be inapplicable in Germany. Finally, with the advent of the principle of national identity, and again taking their cue from the *Bundesverfassungsgericht*, many constitutional courts developed the exception of 'constitutional identity', which usually implies that if the constitutional court should find a provision of European law to conflict with the national constitutional identity, it would not be applied in the land.

V. Genuine Conflicts: Any Solutions?

As Bruno argued in 1991, the solution of such genuine conflicts between European law and national constitutional values should be found at the European level. *Unilateral* action by national constitutional courts – and other national actors, including (constitutional) legislatures and governments, one may add – 'throwing themselves into the breach for saving what each of them considers to be the inalienable constitutional patrimony' threaten the coherence of the European legal order.[25] This is, of course, not to say that legitimate concern of national constitutional courts for the values that have been enshrined in the national constitutions should be neglected in the face of European integration. These values should be acknowledged and, where possible, be accommodated *in* European law rather than *against* it. This requires that the European institutions, including the Court of Justice, acknowledge the genuine and legitimate concerns of national actors derived on their fundamental constitutional values.

Yet, what we have seen more and more often is that national constitutional values are invoked by national actors as trump cards to block European decision-making or to justify infringements of European law. This raises the question how we can distinguish between legitimate, *bona fide* concerns for national constitutional values that should be accommodated if possible, and illegitimate references to national constitutional values that should always be rejected. It is to this issue that we shall now turn. The problem has become more pertinent than ever with the increasing use of the identity argument. Still under negotiation when Bruno wrote his 1991 article, *national constitutional identity* has these days widely been promoted as a core concept to address the relations between European law and the national constitutions. More recently, the Court of Justice has labelled the foundational values of Article 2 TEU as the 'identity of the European Union', thus providing a tool to rule out a particular type of identity argument.

[25] De Witte, 'Community Law' (n 3) 18.

VI. National Identity Protected in Article 4(2) TEU

Writing in 1991, the young Bruno seemed to have mixed feelings about a draft provision on the table in the ongoing Intergovernmental Conferences imposing a duty on the Union to respect 'the national identity' of the Member States. He appeared taken by the idea of a Treaty provision containing a duty of the Union to respect, where possible, common or specifically national constitutional values.[26] But he was not particularly impressed with the specific wording of the provision that was being negotiated: 'the Union shall have due regard to the national identity of its Member States whose systems of government are founded on the principles of democracy'. He considered the link between identity and democracy 'awkward' (which it was), and ultimately felt that the notion of identity was too vague. In order to make it legally relevant, he suggested to link it to the national constitutions as the main depositories of national identity.

The suggestion was not taken up in Maastricht. Yet with the Treaty of Amsterdam the connection between national identity and the principle of democracy was cut. 'Democracy' was transferred to the provision on the foundational values of the Union in Article 6(3) TEU, while Article 6(1) imposed the duty to respect the national identities of the Member States. In the Treaty of Lisbon, both elements were separated further. What was Article 6(3) TEU became Article 2 TEU, 'principles' became 'values', and further elements were added, including a reference to the type of society the Union envisages.[27] The *national* identities of the Member States to be respected were further explained as 'inherent in their fundamental structures, political and constitutional, inclusive of regional and local self-government', thus suggesting that what the Treaty had in mind were more structural or institutional elements, and less so constitutional *substantive values*. It was placed in Article 4(2) TEU, alongside the duty of the Union to respect the equality of the Member States as well as their essential state functions.

Nevertheless, the older Bruno has become very critical of the provision, or rather of the particular interpretation it has been given in judicial practice and in academia, and one may add, in the political debate. All too often, the provision that was intended to protect the constitutional *structures* of the Member States, is now seen as 'offering a kind of generic protection for national diversity and national constitutional values' or as 'a justification for non-compliance with EU law obligations from the side of the Member States'.[28] This can indeed be seen in several recent disputes before the Court of Justice, where governments have invoked their national constitutional identity to challenge the validity of EU law (the Polish and

[26] Ibid 20.

[27] Art 2 TEU reads: 'The Union is founded on the values of respect for human dignity, freedom, democracy, equality, the rule of law and respect for human rights, including the rights of persons belonging to minorities. These values are common to the Member States in a society in which pluralism, non-discrimination, tolerance, justice, solidarity and equality between women and men prevail'.

[28] Bruno De Witte, 'Article 4(2) TEU as a Protection of the *Institutional* Diversity of the Member States' (2021) 27(3) *European Public Law* 559.

Hungarian governments in the case concerning the Conditionality Regulation; the Polish government in the case concerning relocation of migrants),[29] or to justify derogations in the internal market based on specific conceptions of equal treatment (in *Coman*).[30] National constitutional identity is also the main theme of the decision of the captured Hungarian 'constitutional court' in its decision on the relocation of refugees,[31] and it underlies the arguments of the Polish government and the Polish 'constitutional court' on the primacy of EU law in the dispute over the EU's actions to safeguard judicial independence in Poland. What is most problematic in these last instances is that they are entirely unilateral, and that no negotiation over the relationship between European law and national values takes place at the European level.

The claims to national identity in all these cases are problematic for many reasons and they prove Bruno's point that it is better not to use Article 4(2) TEU as a kind of generic protection of national diversity and national constitutional values. Recently, the Court of Justice has chosen an alternative route to block a specific category of identity arguments: such arguments will not even be considered when they infringe the values of the European Union, the very identity of the European Union as a common legal order.

VII. The Values of the Union as the Identity of the Union

In his 1991 article, Bruno compared the 'constitution' of the European Community to the national constitutions stating that while the latter express 'the primary values held within the country', 'the Treaties, rather than expressing shared values and principles, set concrete objectives to be achieved by the Community institutions and by the Member States'. Today, it can no longer be denied that the Treaties do express shared values and principles, and many accept that the Union is also a Union of values.[32]

In its recent decision on the conditionality regulation, the European Court of Justice has stated that 'the values contained in Article 2 TEU (…) define the very identity of the European Union as a common legal order'.[33] The Court has thus

[29] Case C-156/21 *Hungary v Parliament and Council (conditionality regulation)* EU:C:2022:97, paras 127 and 232; Case C-157/21 *Poland v Parliament and Council (conditionality regulation)* EU:C:2022:98, paras 145 and 264.

[30] Case C-673/16 *Coman and Hamilton* EU:C:2018:385.

[31] Hungarian Constitutional Court, Decision 22/2016 (XII. 5.) AB on the Interpretation of Article E) (2) of the Fundamental Law; see on this decision G Halmai, 'Abuse of constitutional Identity: The Hungarian Constitutional Court on Interpretation of Article E) (2) of the Fundamental Law' (2018) 43(1) *Review of Central and East European Law* 23.

[32] See on this issue M Bonelli, *A Union of Values: Safeguarding Democracy, The Rule of Law and Human Rights in the EU Member States* (PhD Thesis, 2019, Maastricht University).

[33] Case C-156/21 *Hungary v Parliament and Council (conditionality regulation)* EU:C:2022:97, para 127; Case C-157/21, *Poland v Parliament and Council (conditionality regulation)* EU:C:2022:98, para 145.

made it clear that Article 2 TEU is not to be seen as a mere statement of policy guidelines or intentions, as argued by the Hungarian and Polish Governments, but is binding and contains *obligations de résultat*. These values 'are given concrete expression in principles containing legally binding obligations for the Member States'.[34]

It is the first time that the Court has mentioned this notion of the 'very identity of the European Union as a legal order'. The choice of wording probably aims to underline the importance of these values, which are here positioned as the European counterpart to the core values of the national constitutions – the constitutional identity – which the constitutional courts use to oppose EU law.

These European core values constitute 'red lines' for the Member States: the European Union respects the constitutional diversity of the Member States, but there are certain minimum standards that must always be complied with, and that Member States can never deviate from, not even with reference to their constitutional national identity (or essential state functions).[35]

The Court of Justice thus uses the identity of Union as a shield against certain arguments based on national identities invoked before it, which are in turn aimed to block EU law. In other words, Article 2 TEU provides a limit to the constitutional diversity allowed to the Member States. The Union respects the national identities of the Member States only in so far as they respect the fundamental values of the European Union as expressed in Article 2 TEU. In doing so, the Court introduces a distinction between legitimate or loyal identity claims, which it will entertain and balance against other interests, and those which are illegitimate. Article 2 TEU can thus be used to identify 'abuses' of national identity.

At the same time, these European values as such are not opposed to national values: the Member States share these values which are 'common to their own constitutional traditions, and which they have undertaken to respect at all times' 'vis-à-vis each other and with regard to the European Union'.[36] The Court thus suggests that the relevant Member States would not simply infringe the values of the Union, they would infringe the *common* constitutional traditions they have freely subscribed to when joining the European Union.

That is not to say, of course, that elements of national identities that do comply with Article 2 TEU can always be opposed to EU law: the claim that EU law

[34] Case C-156/21 *Hungary v Parliament and Council (conditionality regulation)* EU:C:2022:97, para 232; Case C-157/21 *Poland v Parliament and Council (conditionality regulation)* EU:C:2022:98, para 264.

[35] On the latter, see Joined Cases C-715/17, C-718/17 and C-719/17 *Commission v Poland (Compliance with Relocation Decision)* EU:C:2020:257, where the Polish government changed its focus from identity to essential state functions.

[36] Case C-156/21 *Hungary v Parliament and Council (conditionality regulation)* EU:C:2022:97, paras 127, 231 and 232; Case C-157/21 *Poland v Parliament and Council (conditionality regulation)* EU:C:2022:98, paras 263 and 264.

infringes on national constitutional identity must be assessed by the EU authorities, for example when drafting legislation or in cases before the CJEU.[37] But national identities that do not comply with the common values of Article 2 TEU are not even considered. It is for the European institutions and ultimately for the CJEU, to decide whether aspects of national identities comply with the values of Article 2 TEU.

Two challenges follow from this. First, Article 2 TEU is notoriously vaguely stated, as is often the case with provisions of a constitutional nature. The values of Article 2 TEU are rather empty and need to be fleshed out. The challenge here is, that while it may be true that the values are set out in Article 2 TEU and freely entered into, the specific obligations they give rise to are not spelled out in EU law and will have to be further fleshed out, thus requiring legislative action and/or judicial imagination, which may not always be evident. The judgment on the conditionality regulation, building on the case law starting from the *Portuguese Judges* case, contains an example of this phenomenon: the *value* of the rule of law in Article 2 TEU is made explicit in *principles* – such as the principle of judicial independence inherent in Article 19 TEU – giving rise to specific *obligations* imposed on the Member States. With respect to fundamental rights, the Charter offers more substance, but much more creativity will be needed, for instance, to formulate the obligations ensuing from, say, the values of democracy or solidarity in Article 2 TEU.

Second, while it may sometimes be rather evident that a claim based on national identity deviates from the common constitutional principles – if only because the root cause in itself infringes the national constitutional traditions by captured institutions – there will be cases where it is much harder to assess what these common constitutional traditions are in order to draw the line between a legitimate claim based on national identity which complies with the identity of the Union and a claim that does not.

VIII. Conclusion

The tension between commonality and diversity is ubiquitous in EU law, as is to be expected in a system that intends to integrate markets, states and societies into one internal market and an area of freedom, security and justice, an ever-closer union among the peoples of Europe, or even a European society, but that continues to consist of States that remain independent. The more the European

[37] See Case C-430/21 *RS (Effet des arrêts d'une cour constitutionnelle)* EU:C:2022:99, paras 69 and 70.

Union enters additional areas of life, the more likely it is that conflicts may arise between European values based on common constitutional traditions and national constitutional values. The 'community of values among European States' Bruno observed in 1991 is not as close today.[38] The challenge ahead is to foster and safeguard respect for European fundamental values – values that all Member States have freely chosen to adhere to when joining the European Union.[39]

[38] De Witte, 'Community Law' (n 3) 22.
[39] See on this M Claes, 'How Common Are the Values of the European Union?' (2019) 15 *Croatian Yearbook of European Law Policy*, VII.

PART II

Differentiated Europe

4

Differentiation and Flexibility in EU Law

ELLEN VOS

I. Introduction

In a speech of 12 January 1996, on the occasion of the 20th Dies Natalis of Maastricht University,[1] Bruno De Witte[2] addressed the topic of cultural diversity in Europe. He reminded the audience of the words of Francesco Caracciolo, a Neapolitan admiral of the 18th century, who allegedly said: 'In England there are sixty different religions and only one sauce', and subsequently noted the cultural difference with Naples, which in those days only knew one religion but at least 60 sauces.[3] In that same speech, Bruno expressed the need to find ways to maintain cultural diversity within Europe, not by setting strict prohibitions or locking people up in national fortresses but by being open for cultures of other countries of Europe and all communities that live in Europe.[4]

After having moved towards an 'ever closer union' in its initial 30 years, in the subsequent 30 years the EU accepted more differentiation and progressed according to the slogan 'unity in diversity'. Whether, and how far, Member States may introduce or maintain diversity has been debated for many years. The question of whether some Member States may move ahead in the integration process became particularly debated after the Amsterdam Treaty that introduced the flexibility clauses (now Article 20 of the Treaty on European Union (TEU) and Articles 326–334 of the Treaty on the Functioning of the European

[1] Then still called the Rijksuniversiteit Limburg. In that same year, 1996, however, the University changed its name to Universiteit Maastricht, due to the international attention the city of Maastricht had obtained following the Treaty of Maastricht, signed in 1992.

[2] Then announced as Bruno *de* Witte, although the speech was signed off as Bruno *De* Witte. In recent years Bruno has become more firm in not tolerating any diversity in the spelling of his name and consistently presents his surname with a capital D in his publications.

[3] B De Witte, *Culturele verscheidenheid en Europese Unie* in 'Redes gehouden op de 20e Dies Natalis van de Rijksuniversiteit Limburg 12 januari 1996' (Maastricht University, 1996) cris.maastrichtuniversity.nl/ws/portalfiles/portal/47005499/5f18b723-1360-425b-ade7-a77e552a6cff.pdf, 1.

[4] Ibid 14.

Union (TFEU)), which explicitly authorised enhanced co-operation between the Member States. This introduction stirred up an old debate on what has been coined 'integration at different speeds', 'variable geometry', the creation of a '*Europe à la carte*' or a 'Europe of circles'.[5] The desirability of differentiation and flexibility became again topic of debate in the discussions on responses to the financial crisis of 2009 and the prospect of Brexit.[6] We can therefore say that debates on differentiated integration are 'among the rituals of European integration'.[7]

The trajectory of differentiated integration and flexibility has been studied by Bruno in several of his publications. Soon after the entry into force of the Amsterdam Treaty, Bruno, Dominik Hanf and I dedicated a workshop to differentiated integration. Thus in 2001, Bruno edited the book *The Many Faces of Differentiation in EU Law*, together Dominik Hanf and myself, discussing institutional dimensions and policy aspects of various forms of differentiation.[8] Some 15 years later, Bruno together with Andrea Ott and myself, edited another book entitled *Between Flexibility and Disintegration: The Trajectory of Differentiation in EU Law*, to examine how differentiation had developed in EU law over the past 15 years.[9]

This chapter will look at the development of differentiated integration in the EU as a steady feature of EU law, accommodating internal tensions and respecting heterogeneity, and give an overview of modes and definitional issues regarding differentiated integration. It will offer some reflections on the future of differentiation, including in view of the Covid-19 pandemic, where the EU adopted a different response than, for example, to the economic crisis.

II. Differentiated Integration from Rome to Lisbon: Accommodating Diversity

As indicated above, the debate on differentiated integration dates back to the 1970s in the context of discussions on the nature of the EU and the stagnation

[5] See eg F Tuytschaever, *Differentiation in European Union Law* (Hart Publishing, 1999); R Barents, *Het Verdrag van Amsterdam in Werking* (Kluwer, Deventer, 1999) 85–117; G de Búrca and J Scott (eds), *Constitutional Change in the EU: From Uniformity to Flexibility?* (Hart Publishing, 2000).

[6] See eg M Markakis, 'Differentiated Integration and Disintegration in the EU: Brexit, the Eurozone Crisis, and Other Troubles' (2020) 23(2) *Journal of International Economic Law* 489; C Herrmann, 'Differentiated Integration in the Field of Economic and Monetary Policy and the Use of "(Semi-) Extra" Union Legal Instruments – The Case for "*inter se*" Treaty Amendments' in B De Witte, A Ott and E Vos (eds), *Between Flexibility and Disintegration: The Trajectory of Differentiation in EU Law* (Elgar Publishing, 2017) 237.

[7] D Thym, 'Competing Models of Understanding Differentiated Integration' in B De Witte, A Ott and E Vos (eds), *Between Flexibility and Disintegration: The Trajectory of Differentiation in EU Law* (Elgar Publishing, 2017) at 28.

[8] B De Witte, D Hanf and E Vos (eds), *The Many Faces of Differentiation in EU Law* (Intersentia, 2001).

[9] B De Witte, A Ott and E Vos (eds), *Between Flexibility and Disintegration: The Trajectory of Differentiation in EU Law* (Elgar Publishing, 2017).

of the integration process.[10] Differentiated integration in the form of a *Europe à la carte*, where states are offered the possibility to cooperate where they find common interest without being forced to do so in other fields, was then considered a means forward, to overcome stagnation.[11] Yet, in the subsequent years it became clear that a *Europe à la carte*, with the Council of Europe as an example, was not the model which would be chosen for the EU. From its very beginning, the founding treaties (in particular the EEC Treaty), dictated various substantive obligations applicable to all Member States, based on the idea of a unitary legal order. These obligations were supplemented by a large number of directives and regulations that were all binding for all Member States.[12] This uniform application of the rules 'at the same time and with identical effects of the whole territory of the Community' was viewed by the Court of Justice already in 1972, as Bruno observed, as essential to attain the objectives of the then European Economic Community.[13] Nevertheless, it is true that in the original Rome Treaty some provisions were included that limited the territorial scope of the Treaty, established specific derogations for some of the founding and some of the successive Member States, and introduced safeguard clauses.[14] In addition, the Single European Act introduced differentiation for the first time into primary EU law, by constitutionalising derogations, minimum harmonisation techniques and mutual recognition.[15] Moreover, in order to overcome political stagnation in decision-making of the 1970s to mid-1980s, the same Single Act introduced the possibility of 'opting out' from harmonisation internal market measures, as the price that had to be paid for the introduction of qualified majority voting in the new Article 100a EEC (now Article 114 TFEU).[16]

Yet, the discussion on differentiated integration gained momentum in the years leading to the conclusion of the Maastricht Treaty, where recourse to

[10] D Leuffen, B Rittberger and F Schimmelfennig, *Differentiated Integration: Explaining Variation in the European Union* (Palgrave Mcmillan, 2012) 16.

[11] See the reference to the speech of Dahrendorf by B De Witte, *The Law as Tool and Constraint of Differentiated Integration* (2019) EUI Working Paper RSCAS 2019/47, 1–2, referring to F Schimmelfennig, 'Is Differentiation the Future of European Integration?' in Björn Fägersten and Göran von Sydow (eds), *Perspectives on the Future of the EU*, Swedish Institute for European Policy Studies (SIEPS), 2019, 99, at 100.

[12] Ibid 2.

[13] Case 48/71 *Commission v Italy* EU:C:1972:65, para 8, quoted by B De Witte, 'Variable Geometry and Differentiation as Structural Features of the EU Legal Order' in B De Witte, A Ott and E Vos (eds), *Between Flexibility and Disintegration: The Trajectory of Differentiation in EU Law* (Elgar Publishing, 2017) 9.

[14] D Hanf, 'Flexibility Clauses in the Founding Treaties: From Rome to Nice' in B De Witte, D Hanf and E Vos (eds), *The Many Faces of Differentiation in EU Law* (Intersentia, 2001) 3, 5.

[15] Ibid 10. For example, Article 14 of the Single European Act [1987] OJ L 169/1 introduced Article 8c into the EEC Treaty, allowing derogations from internal market measures in view of differences in development of certain economies, provided that they were of a temporary nature and caused the least possible disturbance to the functioning of the common market. See on this issue also CD Ehlermann, *Increased Differentiation or Stronger Uniformity*? (1995) EUI Working Paper RSC 95/21, 8.

[16] Ibid 8; E Vos, 'Differentiation, Harmonisation and Governance' in *The Many Faces of Differentiation in EU Law* (Intersentia, 2001) 145–79, 150.

differentiated integration in the form of formal opt-outs from the monetary union (UK; Denmark) and social policy (UK) laid down in the Treaty became crucial to obtain agreement on that Treaty. Soon after the adoption of the Maastricht Treaty a further debate on differentiated integration was instigated in view of the discussions on enlargement of the EU to include Central and East European countries. This led to the inclusion of a formal institutional flexibility clause, called closer co-operation, by the Amsterdam Treaty. Additionally, it inserted the Schengen regime into the EU legal order which led, in turn, to new opt outs for the UK, Ireland and Denmark. The rigid conditions for closer co-operation inserted by the Amsterdam Treaty were never used in practice and the provisions were renegotiated as part of the Nice Treaty which renamed them 'enhanced co-operation' rules.[17] Despite the softening of the procedural and substantive rules the enhanced cooperation rules introduced by the Nice Treaty were never used. The Lisbon Treaty amended the enhanced cooperation provisions, again aiming at facilitating enhanced cooperation.[18] Since then, several enhanced cooperation laws have been adopted. The Lisbon Treaty also added another opt-out regime in the field of police cooperation and criminal justice, from which the UK did opt out.[19] In addition to these Treaty-based differentiation modalities, the post-Lisbon practice has resorted to other forms of flexibility mechanisms, for example *inter se* agreements such as the Fiscal Compact and the Treaty establishing the European Stability Mechanism.[20]

III. Definition and Modes of Differentiated Integration and Flexibility

The brief historical development of differentiation portrayed above reveals the variety of terms and modes of differentiated integration and flexibility. Two-speed, multi-speed, concentric circles, two-tiered, multi-tiered, variable integration … practice has not been short of terms to indicate differentiation. Yet, what is differentiation? In the legal and political science scholarly debate differentiated integration has been defined and classified in various ways. We can generally speak of differentiation in contrast to uniformity. According to Schimmelfennig and Winzen, one can speak of differentiation where at least one Member State is legally exempt or excluded from a legal rule for some time.[21] Overall,

[17] S Peers, 'Enhanced Co-Operation: The Cinderella of Differentiated Integration' in B De Witte, A Ott and E Vos (eds), *Between Flexibility and Disintegration: The Trajectory of Differentiation in EU Law* (Elgar Publishing, 2017) 78.

[18] Ibid 80.

[19] De Witte, *The Law as Tool and Constraint* (n 11).

[20] De Witte, 'Variable Geometry' (n 13) 21.

[21] F Schimmelfennig and T Winzen, 'Differentiated EU Integration: Maps and Modes' (2020) EUI Working Paper, RSCAS 2020/24, 2.

differentiated integration broadly indicates that certain laws and policies are not uniformly applied across all Member States of the EU. In defining the scope of *The Many Faces of Differentiation* book that Bruno, Dominik and I edited in 2001, we adopted a broad meaning of differentiation: 'the facilitation or accommodation of a degree of difference between Member States or regions in relation to what would otherwise be common Union policies'. Differentiation thus in this view encompassed not only the 'enhanced co-operation' mechanisms, but also addressesed the need of allowing the European integration process to proceed and function adequately, despite the existence of objective and value-based differences between the Member States or parts of these states.[22] Therefore, we included also derogation and opt out possibilities and minimum harmonisation which appeared in the Treaties and secondary legislation. Others too have adopted a broad meaning of differentiation, and referred to flexibility to indicate differentiation in the rights and duties of the Member States of the Union.[23]

The discussion on the definition of differentiation is inextricably linked to the discussion on the modes of differentiation. Alexander Stubb defined in 1996 three modes of differentiated integration varying in substance according to time, space and matter: 'multi-speed' being differentiated integration in time, whereby Member States decide to pursue the same policies and actions but at different times; 'variable geometry' being differentiated integration in space whereby Member States accept unattainable differences by allowing permanent or irreversible separation between a core of countries and looser integrated countries; and *Europe à la carte* being differentiated integration in certain matters.[24] These three characteristics of differentiated integration of time, space and matter have often been followed in the literature.[25] In this context, I would like to point out that Schimmelfennig and Winzen have recently come up with an interesting relabelling of Stubb's last two categories into 'multi tier' integration and

[22] B De Witte, D Hanf and E Vos, 'Introduction' in B De Witte, D Hanf and E Vos (eds), *The Many Faces of Differentiation in EU Law* (Intersentia, 2001) xi. In the 2017 book, we adopted the same definition, allowing us to take stock of the many faces of differentiation in EU law, see B De Witte, A Ott and E Vos, *Between Flexibility and Disintegration* (n 6).

[23] D Hanf, '*Flexibility Clauses*' (n 14) 4. Hanf points to the 'Dehaene Report' on the institutional implications of the enlargement of the European Union, which stressed the need for flexibility as a means to build on and strengthen the Union's achievements, instead of loosening the ties that would bind Member States, whereby it referred in particular to the possibility of closer co-operation. See R von Weizsäcker, J Dehaene and D Simon, *The Institutional Implications of Enlargement*, Report to the Commission, 18 October 1999, https://ec.europa.eu/dorie/fileDownload.do;jsessionid=vFykRHQdJGnz8QjB3DQYTTWtQpQLygd6QsJfShsD5HGKhq2zpFpk!-687982831?docId=252967&cardId=252967.

[24] A Stubb, 'A Categorization of Differentiated Integration' (1996) 34(2) *Journal of Common Market Studies* 283, 287–88.

[25] Eg Daniel Thym identified three similar models distinguishing between: 'multiple speeds', 'federal core Europe' and 'flexibility à la carte'. D Thym, 'Competing MODELS for Understanding Differentiated Integration' in B De Witte, A Ott and E Vos (eds), *Between Flexibility and Disintegration: The Trajectory of Differentiation in EU Law* (Elgar Publishing, 2017) 29 ff.

'multi-menu' integration, as these terms would be more in line with the first category, 'multi-speed' integration.[26] This terminology would indeed create more coherency and clarity.

Over the year, more refinements have been made. First a distinction has been made into internal and external differentiation, with internal differentiation indicating that situation in which at least one Member State is exempt or excluded from EU rules or policies and external differentiation where EU rules and policies are valid in at least one non-Member-State.[27] Bruno has moreover contributed to the debate by further refining the definition of differentiation by distinguishing according to the unity of decision-making. Thus, more than 17 years after the publication of *The Many Faces of Differentiation*, Bruno has narrowed down the definition of differentiation and defines it as the process that permits some EU Member States to go further in the integration process, while allowing others to choose not do so.[28] He herewith distinguishes differentiation from the broader forms of flexibility created by secondary EU law, such as provisions allowing derogations, exemptions, or differential application for specific countries or groups of countries which are adopted by the EU institutions according to the legislative as they see to diversity in the application of common norms, rather than to differentiation in the making of those norms.[29] More recently, in the framework of the project *Integrating Diversity in the European Union* (InDivEU), he terms these latter forms 'flexible implementation'.[30]

On the basis of the current scholarly insights, we can therefore further conceptualise and understand differentiation. We consider flexibility as the overarching terminology to accommodate diversity and the heterogeneous character of the EU. Following Bruno, flexible implementation allows the possibility to introduce flexibility to reach goals that are agreed upon by all Member States in EU legislative acts.[31] These possibilities are laid down in either the EU Treaties or in the legislative acts themselves. In line with Bruno's refinement, differentiation *stricto sensu* is then reserved to indicate the process that allows some EU Member States to go further in an integration process in which other Member States do not participate. Key hereby is to ascertain whether all Member States participate in the making of common norms or not. In line with Schimmelfennig and Winzen's relabelling, we may distinguish three modes of integration: 'multi-speed' integration, 'multi-tier' integration (also known as 'variable geometry') and 'multi-menu' integration (also known as *Europe à la carte*).

[26] Schimmelfennig and Winzen, 'Differentiated EU Integration' (n 21) 3.

[27] See 'Integrating Diversity in the European Union' at http://indiveu.eui.eu.

[28] B De Witte, 'An Undivided Union? Differentiated Integration in Post-Brexit Times' (2018) 55 *Common Market Law Review*, 228; quoting T Chopin and C Lequesne, 'Differentiation as a Double-Edged Sword: Member States' Practices and Brexit' (2016) 92 *International Affairs* 531, 531.

[29] Ibid 229.

[30] De Witte, *The Law as Tool and Constraint* (n 11) 4.

[31] See the project *Integrating Diversity in the European Union* (InDivEU), http://indiveu.eui.eu/2022/01/31/flexible-integration, which, however, distinguishes between legislative and executive and administrative discretion.

IV. The Future of Differentiation

In the aftermath of the Lisbon Treaty, several schemes of differentiation *strictu senso* have been put in place. Today, we may thus observe, for example, the above mentioned opt-out regimes for Economic Monetary Union (permanent: Denmark; temporary: Bulgaria, Croatia, Czech Republic, Denmark, Hungary, Poland, Romania and Sweden)[32] and Justice and Home Affairs (Denmark, Ireland);[33] several enhanced cooperation laws[34] (transnational divorces,[35] the European patent system,[36] financial transaction tax,[37] judicial cooperation in matters of matrimonial property and registered partnership property[38] and the European Public Prosecutor's Office[39]); and various *inter se* agreements, such as the Fiscal Compact[40] and the Treaty establishing the European Stability Mechanism,[41] – with Brexit representing 'the most important current shock' to the EU's system of differentiation.[42]

[32] See S Van den Bogaert and V Borger, 'Differentiated Integration in EMU' in B De Witte, A Ott and E Vos (eds), *Between Flexibility and Disintegration: The Trajectory of Differentiation in EU Law* (Elgar Publishing, 2017).

[33] See N El-Enany, 'The Perils of Differentiated Integration in the Field of Asylum' in B De Witte, A Ott and E Vos (eds), *Between Flexibility and Disintegration: The Trajectory of Differentiation in EU Law* (Elgar Publishing, 2017).

[34] See S Peers, 'Enhanced Cooperation: The Cinderella of Differentiated Integration' in B De Witte, A Ott and E Vos (eds), *Between Flexibility and Disintegration: The Trajectory of Differentiation in EU Law* (Elgar Publishing, 2017).

[35] Council Regulation 1259/2010 implementing enhanced cooperation in the area of the law applicable to divorce and legal separation [2010] OJ L 343/10; see Council Decision 2010/405 authorising enhanced cooperation in the area of the law applicable to divorce and legal separation [2010] OJ L 189/12.

[36] Regulation (EU) No 1257/2012 of the European Parliament and of the Council of 17 December 2012 implementing enhanced cooperation in the area of the creation of unitary patent protection [2012] OJ L 361/1. See Council Decision 2011/167/EU authorising enhanced cooperation in the area of the creation of unitary patent protection [2011] OJ L 76/53. See also Joined Cases C-274/11 and C-295/11 *Spain and Italy v Council* EU:C:2013:240.

[37] Council Decision 2013/52/EU, authorising enhanced cooperation in the area of financial transaction tax [2013] OJ L 22/11; however the Council did not manage to agree on the measure implementing enhanced cooperation.

[38] Council Decision 2016/954 authorising enhanced cooperation in the area of jurisdiction, applicable law and the recognition and enforcement of decisions on the property regimes of international couples, covering both matters of matrimonial property regimes and the property consequences of registered partnerships [2016] OJ L 159/16. See Council Regulation 2016/1103 implementing enhanced cooperation in the area of jurisdiction, applicable law and the recognition and enforcement of decisions in matters of matrimonial property regimes [2016] OJ L 183/1.

[39] Council Regulation (EU) 2017/1939 implementing enhanced cooperation on the establishment of the European Public Prosecutor's Office ('the EPPO') [2017] OJ L 283/1.

[40] Treaty on Stability, Coordination and Governance in the Economic and Monetary Union ('Fiscal Compact') [2012] Document 42012A0302(01) https://eur-lex.europa.eu/legal-content/EN/TXT/?uri=celex%3A42012A0302%2801%29. See Herrmann, 'Differentiated Integration' (n 6).

[41] Treaty establishing the European Stability Mechanism [2012] Document 42012A0202(01) https://www.esm.europa.eu/legal-documents/esm-treaty. The Treaty has been amended in 2020, see https://www.esm.europa.eu/about-esm/esm-reform. See T Beukers and B De Witte, 'The Court of Justice Approves the Creation of a European Stability Mechanism outside the EU Legal Order: *Pringle*' (2013) 50 *Common Market Law Review* 805.

[42] Schimmelfennig and Winzen, 'Differentiated EU Integration' (n 21) 20.

In *The Many Faces of Differentiation* in 2001, we concluded that differentiation was not perceived as a threat to further European integration but rather as a tool to promote further integration. We observed that differentiation could actually strengthen European unity. Fifteen years later, in *Between Flexibility and Disintegration* we concluded that differentiation and flexibility seemed key components when seeking to address tensions and reconcile differences between Member States. In that way, differentiation could still strengthen unity. At the same time, we pointed to the need to decide which forms would be preferable from democratic and efficiency perspectives and to the need to define the limits of flexibility arrangements in order to protect the core principles and values of the European integration project.[43] Importantly, Bruno then warned that differentiated integration comes at the price of lack of transparency, complicated accountability mechanisms, and a neglect of inter-state solidarity, which could turn into contributory factors in the disintegration of the EU.[44]

While one could say that the many opt-out arrangements made for the UK ultimately did lead to disintegration, today we see developments that point to more uniformity. For example differentiated integration will not be of any help in the rule-of-law crisis, and the rule-of-law conditionality of EU funding applies to all Member States.[45] Moreover, various initiatives adopted in response to the Covid-19 pandemic may indicate a move towards more uniformity. Whereas the reaction of the Member States to the Covid-19 pandemic initially was one of unilateral measures – such as relaxing state aid rules and closing borders – it soon became clear that more, and EU-wide, action was needed. This has *inter alia* led to the launch of an ECB pandemic emergency purchase programme (PEPP);[46] a short-term in-work job support programme to reinforce Member States' own initiatives (SURE);[47] a new European Health Emergency preparedness and Response Authority (HERA), as a separate DG within the European Commission;[48] an extensive funding programme (EU4health);[49] and the Next

[43] B De Witte, A Ott and E Vos, 'Introduction' in B De Witte, A Ott and E Vos (eds), *Between Flexibility and Disintegration: The Trajectory of Differentiation in EU Law* (Elgar Publishing, 2017) 6.

[44] De Witte, 'Variable Geometry' (n 13) 25–26.

[45] F Schimmelfennig, 'Differentiated Integration and the Future of Europe – Potentials and Pitfalls' (2021) 62 *INDivEU Policy Brief* 4.

[46] Decision (EU) 2020/440 of the European Central Bank of 24 March 2020 on a temporary pandemic emergency purchase programme (ECB/2020/17) [2020] OJ L 91/1.

[47] Council Regulation (EU) 2020/672 of 19 May 2020 on the establishment of a European instrument for temporary support to mitigate unemployment risks in an emergency (SURE) following the COVID-19 outbreak [2020] OJ L 159/1.

[48] Communication of European Commission, Introducing HERA, the European Health Emergency preparedness and Response Authority, the next step towards completing the European Health Union COM(2021)576 final.

[49] Regulation (EU) 2021/522 of the European Parliament and of the Council of 24 March 2021 establishing a Programme for the Union's action in the field of health ('EU4Health Programme') for the period 2021–2027, and repealing Regulation (EU) No 282/2014 [2021] OJ L 107/1.

Generation EU programme (NGEU) (the EU's Covid recovery plan).[50] The adoption of this set of EU initiatives underlines the will of the Member States to act uniformly and in solidarity to deepen integration in health issues.[51] In particular, it was the introduction of the NGEU programme, which was agreed by all Member States in the classical way without any recourse to international agreements, that has made Bruno reflect about the future of differentiated integration. He observes that the development of the Eurozone into an autonomous organisation, separate from the EU, has undoubtedly ceased with the adoption of the NGEU programme as the latter is an EU-wide programme. At the same time it calls into question the role of the European Stability Mechanism, as its pandemic crisis loan programme remained largely unused, in view of the creation of the more attractive funding programmes mentioned above.[52] Hence, Bruno asks whether at the time when the NGEU programme will expire, we will find that 'there is still a need for a euro-area specific reform instrument or whether the recovery plan has marked a decline of the trend towards differentiated integration in the economic policy domain'.[53] Time and Bruno will tell …

[50] Regulation (EU) 2021/241 of the European Parliament and of the Council of 12 February 2021 establishing the Recovery and Resilience Facility [2021] OJ L 57/17. See B De Witte, 'The European Union's Covid-19 Recovery Plan: The Legal Engineering of an Economic Policy Shift' (2021) 58 *Common Market Law Review* 635.

[51] V Schmidt, 'The Future of Differentiation' (2020) 9 Op-ed, EUIDEA, 3.

[52] De Witte, 'The European Union's Covid-19 Recovery Plan' (n 50) 679.

[53] B De Witte, 'Legal Feasibility Study of the Differentiation Options' (2022) EUI Working Paper RSCAS 2022/15, 16.

5

Recomposing the EU: Flying Together Beyond Turbulence

DEIRDRE CURTIN*

I. Recomposing Bruno

I first met Bruno De Witte some 30 years ago, more or less, when he had just been appointed Professor of European Law in the still new University of Maastricht. At that time Maastricht was modern in simply appointing chairs to European law as a whole, whereas I was appointed in 1992 to the more old-world University of Utrecht which (alongside the equally ancient University of Leiden) divided European law across two different Chairs dealing separately with substantive law and with institutional law, and across national and international law as well as European law. In 1993 the Utrecht *Europa Institute* held a large conference to commemorate its own 30-year existence with an international conference dedicated to the just-signed Treaty of Maastricht. There Bruno listened to me, a young, female, cuckoo in the nest who was not Dutch nor even really at that time Dutch speaking (and also not a graduate of the European University Institute (EUI) so we did not meet that way). In what later became my 'bits and pieces' article I criticised the new EU constitutional structure and the resulting fragmentation. Newly appointed to the old, established Chair covering (also) European institutional law, this amounted to cursing in church, as the Dutch say ('vloeken in de kerk'). Irrespective of whether Bruno agreed or not on substance or on tone, we bonded. Both outsiders, neither of us really genuflected at the altar of how European law was traditionally researched and taught in the Netherlands at that time.

Before the Maastricht Treaty, Bruno could have been described as a non-institutional EC lawyer, interested in policy topics such as culture, education, equality etc rather than the broad reach and structure of European law and the emerging European Union. After the Maastricht Treaty Bruno discovered his inner institutional (and international) lawyer and honed this over the years and in so

*I would like to thank Anna Morandini for excellent research assistance and Professor Diane Fromage for generous feedback.

many detailed and careful publications that it quickly became a defining part of his academic identity and profile. Like a trapeze artist, Bruno managed and still manages to continue to engage with the substantive policy areas he started his academic career with, but from the mid 1990s he also engaged with the bigger picture of the nature of the European Union (as it then already was) and its institutions in a very fundamental manner – always going back to first principles and the basics no matter what shift was taking place in practice and in politics. Bruno fits into his own category of having become 'thoroughly socialized in a transnational professional context' which has influenced his own recomposed legal culture.[1] Within that genuinely European legal culture, he has a profound interest in the constitutional both in the sense of the Treaties as a whole (never overlooking the detail of the individual legal provisions) and on specific themes that reach from the (international, supranational) sky right down to the (national) earth.

Turbulence is something that has surrounded the European Union in many shapes and sizes. Even if one limits the discussion to the last three decades (since the Treaty of Maastricht called into being the unitary but also differentiated European Union), there is no shortage of turbulence, much of it relating to constitutional resistance and ratification problems. Over the course of these three decades Bruno's publications have followed the changing nature of the European Union closely, recognising that the history of European integration has for many decades been one of unity but at the same time of growing differentiation. *The Many Faces of Differentiation* was the title of a book he co-edited after the Treaty of Amsterdam in 1997,[2] consisting of an elaborate account of a whole panoply of existing flexible and differentiated arrangements in the EU among different Member States. Differentiation at that time took many legal forms, ranging from primary to secondary EU law and soft law instruments, and from external agreements with third states to 'internal' agreements between the Member States themselves. Twenty-five years later, one would assume that the vista is very different. But is it? Differentiation is still today a defining feature of the European Union polity, warts and all. The follow-up book published in 2017 by Bruno, together with largely the same editors, bears the title: *Between Flexibility and Disintegration: The Trajectory of Differentiation in EU Law*.[3] Among legal scholars, differentiation and flexibility were not originally perceived as a threat to European integration but rather as a tool to promote further integration by allowing a group of Member States to forge ahead with closer cooperation, while leaving the door open for the remaining Member States to join later (eg the Schengen and Prüm Conventions).

Within the entrails of European Union scholarship there is a core understanding of differentiation as an attempt to remain together and seek new relationships

[1] B De Witte, 'European Union Law: A Unified Academic Discipline?' in A Vauchez and B De Witte (eds), *Lawyering Europe: European Law as a Transnational Social Field* (Hart Publishing, 2013) 111.

[2] B De Witte, D Hanf and E Vos (eds), *The Many Faces of Differentiation* (Intersentia, 2001).

[3] B De Witte, A Ott and E Vos (eds), *Between Flexibility and Disintegration: The Trajectory of Differentiation in EU Law* (Edward Elgar Publishing, 2017) 2.

despite the centrifugal forces of disintegration that threaten the EU. In fact, counter-intuitively, the very notion of differentiation points to a unitary legal order, which is nevertheless apt to more systematically accommodate diversity.[4] In the aftermath of a turbulent time for Europe (euro crisis, refugee crisis, Brexit, pandemic), differentiation has become not only an acceptable compromise, but even at times the preferred solution to potentially disaggregating forces and to the stalling of the EU integration process. Political scientists argue that ongoing acceptance of a differentiated future for the EU implies a change in the concept of integration itself, moving towards a more composite and fluid understanding of European integration as opposed to a traditional unitary model. For instance, Frank Schimmelfennig has extensively argued that European integration can *only* be understood through the prism of differentiation. Richard Bellamy and Sandra Kroeger have investigated under which circumstances institutional designs of differentiated integration can be considered as fair and therefore acceptable.[5] In addition, concrete proposals on how to implement differentiation in policymaking have blossomed in the past five years. The most discussed is certainly the European Commission's *White Paper on the Future of Europe*, featuring, as arguably one of the preferred scenarios for moving forward, a 'model of differentiation allowing willing Member States to do more together in specific areas' (*Scenario 3: Those who want more do more*).[6] Even more radical proposals have also come from think-tanks and academia with ideas on not flying together, or at least not all the time, or in different non-parallel modes of transport with different speeds.[7] Although the feasibility of these projects is controversial, they show that the scientific and political debate on European integration has by now accepted differentiation as an unavoidable – and sometimes welcomed – destiny.

But what is accepted even in many quarters is not written in stone and this also applies to Bruno, who is not afraid to point out his own changing evaluations. In a publication only four years ago Bruno spoke of the '*permanence* of many-faced differentiation'.[8] In 2022, however, he claims that differentiation is in *decline*.[9] Has the eagle spotted a topographical shift that others have not yet seen, and that points to more togetherness rather than separation? This is new, controversial, and

[4] See D Curtin, 'From a Europe of Bits and Pieces to a Union of Variegated Differentiation' in P Craig and G de Búrca (eds), *The Evolution of EU Law* (Oxford University Press, 2021) 375.

[5] D Leuffen, B Rittberger and F Schimmelfennig, *Differentiated Integration: Explaining Variation in the European Union* (Palgrave, 2012); R Bellamy and S Kröger, 'Differentiated Integration as a Fair Scheme of Cooperation' (2021) *Review of Social Economy* 1.

[6] White Paper on the Future of Europe, COM(2017) 2025.

[7] See notably M Demertzis et al, *One Size Does Not Fit All: European Integration by Differentiation* (Bruegel, 2018).

[8] See B De Witte, 'Structure and Evolution of Union Law' in PJ Kuijper et al (eds), *The Law of the European Union*, 5th edn (Kluwer, 2018) 57.

[9] This was first mentioned by him in B De Witte, 'The European Union's COVID-19 Recovery Plan: The Legal Engineering of an Economic Policy Shift' (2021) 58 *Common Market Law Review* 653, 679. He argues that whether NGEU will mark a decline in differentiated integration in EU economic policy or whether there is still a need for a euro-area-specific reform instrument will be questioned towards the end of the programme.

certainly not the consensus of political scientists or others looking at the details of specific policy areas. Existing literature, even the most recent, continues to investigate differentiated integration under the premise of its unwavering importance.[10]

Lifting our more pedestrian eyes from the ground (hedgehogs *and* foxes) to the bigger picture: what does, and what could, this mean for the future of Europe? Has Bruno spotted something that is emerging in one field (economic) but when put together with other equally turbulent developments indicate indeed (the beginning of) a movement away from differentiation in whole or in part for the future of the European Union? In this short contribution in Bruno's honour, I venture to stray beyond the normal debates on differentiation and unity to explore what can be observed when developments in one field (the economic and the financial) are put together with the trauma and legacy of Brexit (with the departure from the EU of its long-term 'awkward member', the UK), as well as EU institutional responses in the context of the still ongoing Covid pandemic.

What happens when what I term 'the 3 D's' – decimation, decline and disuse – are read in parallel? Emerging through the turbulence and the casting aside of old disagreements, a renewed Europe (potentially involving all Member States – 'back to the future in a sense) seems to appear, at least in outline, pushed along by positive gusts that operate as tailwinds, notwithstanding turbulence. Each of these tailwinds result from one of the 3D's and will be separately explored (sections II, III and IV) before reaching some conclusions (section V) on likely futures for Europe, with Member States potentially flying together rather than apart. Let's start at the beginning, where Bruno also started: the core legacy of the Treaty of Maastricht – structural differentiation brought about by the United Kingdom, and its intensification over time, as part of the EU legal order,[11] until the recent premature and permanent elimination of these differences following Brexit.

II. Decimation of Opt-Outs

Various forms of differentiation have become a stable feature of the EU legal system and have resulted in what Bruno terms a 'regime of legally constrained differentiation' enshrined in the Treaties.[12] The very notion that European integration may

[10] See eg S Telle, C Badulescu, and D Fernandes, 'Differentiated integration in the EU – What do the member states "think" about it?' EUI Working Paper, RSC 2021/50; M Markakis, 'Differentiated Integration and Disintegration in the EU: Brexit, the Eurozone Crisis, and Other Troubles' (2020) 23 *Journal of International Economic Law* 489; and F Schimmelfennig and T Winzen, *Ever Looser Union? Differentiated European Integration* (Oxford Scholarship Online, 2020).

[11] See B De Witte, 'Variable Geometry and Differentiation as Structural Features of the EU Legal Order' in B De Witte, A Ott and E Vos (eds), *Between Flexibility and Disintegration – The Trajectory of Differentiation in EU Law* (Elgar Publishing, 2017) 11 ff.

[12] B De Witte, 'The Law as Tool and Constraint of Differentiated Integration' EUI Working Papers, RSCAS 2019/47.

progress at varying speeds is based on the assumption that a group of Member States advances towards a common policy objective, and is later joined by those States which are unwilling or unable to do so from the start. The non-participation of some Member States in the integration of a given policy area is regarded as inherently temporary, with catch-up built in. This is visible not only in the use of transitional periods and safeguard clauses granted to those States in order to prepare for the full implementation of the instruments for the integration of that sector[13] but also in the field of EMU which is considered separately below as part of a different speed Europe (section III).

'Variable geometry', by contrast, suggests that the differing degrees of integration of the Member States may be formalised in permanent terms by using the instrument of the opt-out. Modest, more *ad hoc* or bespoke, differentiation has been facilitated almost from the very beginning of the Community as a way of taking account of immediate stresses and strains. The Treaty of Maastricht in the early 1990s made opt-outs more structural and embedded. They became in Bruno's words 'a major feature of the EU legal order'.[14] This was built on further in later revision Treaties. In the Amsterdam Treaty the Schengen regime was 'repatriated' within the legal order of the European Union, but the price that had to be paid for this move was 'reform at the price of fragmentation'.[15] Given the lack of unanimous support among all Member States it led to a new opt-out Treaty regime for the UK and Ireland, and another one for Denmark.[16] In Bruno's own words, 'a system of differentiation between EU Member States that had existed *outside* the EU legal framework was thus brought *inside* that framework, but without modifying the degree and content of the differentiation and creating, indeed, a number of frictions in the institutional functioning of the EU's immigration and border control policies'.[17]

This 'gradual spread' of opt outs seemed unstoppable for many years. Some of the more structural cases have been the UK's opt-out from the Charter of Fundamental Rights, or Denmark's opt-out from the Area of Freedom, Security and Justice (AFSJ).[18] The UK was, moreover, never in fact a full participant in the

[13] One example is the transitional arrangements for free movement of workers from Bulgaria and Romania – a seven-year period was established in the Act of Accession whereby full free movement of workers would be established gradually: Commission report on transitional arrangements regarding free movement of workers from Bulgaria and Romania, MEMO/11/773, (Brussels, 11 November 2011), available at europa.eu/rapid/press-release_MEMO-11-773_en.htm.

[14] De Witte, 'Variable Geometry' (n 11) 13.

[15] J Monar, 'Justice and Home Affairs in the Treaty of Amsterdam: Reform at the Price of Fragmentation' (1998) 23 *European Law Review* 320.

[16] See G Papagianni, 'Flexibility in Justice and Home Affairs: An Old Phenomenon Taking New Forms' in B De Witte, D Hanf and E Vos (eds), *The Many Faces of Differentiation in EU Law* (Intersentia, 2001) 101. On the ultra-complex legal position of the opt-out countries in relation to the Schengen acquis, see J Schutte, 'UK v EU: A Continuous Test Match' (2011) 34 *Fordham International Law Journal* 1346.

[17] See De Witte, 'Variable Geometry' (n 11) 13.

[18] See further, D Curtin, 'Brexit and the EU Area of Freedom, Security, and Justice. Bespoke Bits and Pieces' in F Fabbrini (ed), *The Law & Politics of Brexit* (Oxford Scholarship Online, 2017) 183 ff.

policy areas of the AFSJ. During the Treaty of Amsterdam negotiations in 1996, the UK acquired the right to 'opt out' of various EU initiatives in the field of police and judicial cooperation.[19] It never joined the Schengen Convention and maintained the right to 'opt out' from the Schengen border control system, which enabled the UK to continue exercising controls at its borders. The Treaty of Lisbon in 2009 merged police and judicial cooperation in criminal matters into the main structure of the EU, making initiatives in this policy domain subject to qualified majority voting and the supranational institutions of the EU. The UK negotiated a block opt-out at that time,[20] giving it the option to 'opt out' of pre-Lisbon police and criminal justice measures (around 100 measures) or to remain bound by them.[21] The UK exercised this block opt-out in 2014 but rejoined 35 measures, including participation in EU agencies such as Europol and Eurojust, later that year. It was quite distinctive the way the UK selectively opted back in again into specific areas, such as Europol.[22] The measures opted back into were 'the subject of a positive decision and assessment' as to necessity and national interest, and the fact is in the years leading up to Brexit there was no evidence that those assessments 'changed in the few intervening years'.[23]

Brexit put paid to all of that – national interest or otherwise; UK desire to remain part of the opt-ins or not. The defection of the UK 'may act as an incentive for other countries to advance the integration project more vigorously' predicted Bruno in 2017.[24] 2017 was the year that a veritable surge of interest in differentiation and its place in the future of European integration was seen.[25] The paradox of post-Brexit differentiation, in Bruno's own words, is that rather than the end of UK-crafted opt-outs marking the end of differentiation as we knew it, paradoxically 'at least some of the remaining 27 Member States shocked by the United

[19] J Monar, 'The "Area of Freedom, Security and Justice": "Schengen" Europe, Opt-Outs, Opt-Ins and Associates' in K Dyson and A Sepos (eds), *Which Europe? The Politics of Differentiated Integration* (Palgrave Macmillan, 2010); I Bond et al, 'Europe after Brexit: Unleashed or Undone?' (2016) www.cer.org.uk/sites/default/files/pb_euafterBrexit_15april16.pdf.

[20] Protocol No 21 on the position of the United Kingdom and Ireland in respect of the Area of Freedom, Security and Justice [2010] OJ C 83/201; House of Lords, 'Brexit: Future UK-EU Security and Police Cooperation' (2016) paras 17–19, https://publications.parliament.uk/pa/ld201617/ldselect/ldeucom/77/77.pdf.

[21] Protocol No 36 on Transitional Provisions concerning acts adopted on the Basis of Titles V and VI of the Treaty on European Union prior to the entry into force of the Treaty of Lisbon [2008] OJ C 115/322, Art 10; Research Section for European Affairs (German Bundestag), 'Consequences of Brexit for the Realm of Justice and Home Affairs: Scope for Future EU Cooperation with the United Kingdom' (2016) 11, www.statewatch.org/news/2016/oct/uk-brexit-german-bundstag-report.pdf.

[22] Curtin, 'Brexit and the EU Area of Freedom, Security, and Justice' (n 18) 185. See further, DJ Dickson, 'The UK and the Article 36 Protocol' (2015) 16 ERA Forum 305; V Miller, 'The UK block opt-out in police and judicial cooperation in criminal matters: recent developments' (2014) House of Commons Library.

[23] House of Lords, 'Brexit' (n 20) paras 17–19.

[24] De Witte, 'Variable Geometry' (n 11) 13 at 63. In a slightly different phrasing at B De Witte, 'An Undivided Union? Differentiated Integration in Post-Brexit Times' (2018) 55 *Common Market Law Review* 227, 235 ('the UK's defection acts as an incentive for some other countries to advance the integration project more vigorously').

[25] B De Witte speaks of the surge of the differentiation theme in De Witte, 'An Undivided Union?' (n 24) 229.

Kingdom's defection, envisage a further turn of the flexibility wheel to keep the European Union up and running in the post-Brexit era'.[26] Yet in 2018 Bruno deliberately held out the possible vista of an 'undivided Union' as opposed to more differentiation, acknowledging nonetheless that 'differentiated integration, in its various forms of variable geometry, will continue to exist and will thrive maybe more than ever; but a division into two or three institutionally separate blocks of Member States is not likely to happen'.[27] A post-Brexit world, for one author, 'foresees a continuation of the status quo, in which differentiation exists in various forms but as exceptions to the rule, rather than the rule itself'.[28]

It is after all not only regarding opt-outs that differentiation occurs where the assumption may (wrongly) be that the opter-outer will join in later (opt-in and not exit), but also where the exact opposite occurs. This would be where all the Member States do not advance together to integrate a new policy but where only a number choose to do so from the beginning. Schengen was an early example of a form of integration that initially took place outside the EC/EU that was later fully integrated ('repatriated') back within the framework of the EU Treaty itself. The more contemporary example relates to Economic and Monetary Union (EMU) taking place within the EU, with clear distinctions between eurozone and non-eurozone countries but with supranational integration advancing quickly within. This will now be explored in more depth as this is where Bruno discerns differentiation in 2022 to be in 'decline'.[29]

III. Decline of Multi-Speed Europe

If there is one lesson arguably to be learnt from the economic and financial crisis it is that eurozone members share a common destiny to further strengthen European integration and extend it to economic and financial policy coordination. According to Rittberger, Leuffen and Schimmelfenning, deeper integration in such areas of sensitive core state powers is particularly likely to develop forms of differentiation.[30] EMU represents only one of the two special regimes of enhanced

[26] Ibid 235.

[27] See ibid 249.

[28] See PJ Cardwell, 'The End of Exceptionalism and a Strengthening of Coherence? Law and Legal Integration in the EU Post-Brexit' (2019) 57 *Journal of Common Market Studies* 1407.

[29] Other scholars seem to be more nuanced. They argue that this change may not be long-lasting depending on whether the implementation of Next Generation EU is successful or not and they underline that in any event the divide between euro area and non-euro area Member States is bound to endure over time, considering that not all States are bound to adopt the common currency. See eg D Fromage, 'Post-COVID-19 E(M)U Interinstitutional Balance: Assessment and Outlook' in European Central Bank, 'Continuity and change – how the challenges of today prepare the ground for tomorrow', ECB Legal Conference 2021, 421–35, https://www.ecb.europa.eu/pub/pdf/other/ecb.ecblegalconferenceproceedings202204~c2e573975б.en.pdf?326d24503e8896af91efce04141760e5.,

[30] B Rittberger, D Leuffen and F Schimmelfennig, 'Differentiated Integration of Core State Powers' in P Genschel and M Jachtenfuchs (eds), *Beyond the Regulatory Polity? The European Integration of Core State Powers* (Oxford University Press, 2013) 189.

cooperation which are enshrined in the Treaties (alongside defence). Enhanced cooperation is based primarily on objective criteria (the convergence criteria in the case of EMU) while it also factors in the will of the Member States to participate, openly in the case of defence, but de-facto also in EMU, where several Member States have opted out or have deliberately decided not to respect the euro criteria. EMU blends different forms of internal differentiation (multi-speed, variable geometries) with forms of external cooperation, and makes innovative use of the EU institutional framework. The transition to the third stage of the EMU is an example of multiple speed integration primarily in terms of membership. It does not impair the functioning of the internal market as such, rather it enables a peloton group of Member States to proceed with further integration according to objectively defined criteria. The intention is that the other Member States will, with the ripeness of time, join the leading Member States on the path ahead they forged. The possibility of this leading group was explicitly accepted in the Treaty on European Union (TEU) by all the Member States, including the UK and Denmark, even if those countries obtained an opt-out for themselves. For this reason, a single institutional framework was maintained. Another explanation is that non-euro area States are de facto affected by the decisions taken by euro area Member States and should therefore have a say in such decisions (see the attitude of the UK over time, but also the extension/de facto normalisation of the Eurogroup in inclusive format).[31]

The classic reading is that there seems to be a mismatch between the idea of multi-speed differentiation enshrined in the Treaties, whereby adopting the euro is described as a common objective that must be shared and achieved by all Union's members – only at different paces – and the *de facto* development of EMU in practice. It was felt that indeed the EU may instead move towards a form of semi-permanent multi-speed or even 'core' eurozone Europe.[32] A new conceptualisation of multi-speed might indeed rest in its 'semi-permanent' character, which is understood as a dynamic relationship. Some Member States would move to, say level 4, others would move to level 3, meanwhile some of the former group would move to level 5, etc.

This trend towards the creation of a stable eurozone avant garde was strengthened by the EU response to the euro-crisis, which took an array of different forms, further complicating the relationship between eurozone and non-eurozone members. Indeed, the economic and financial crisis urgently demanded solutions and extension of powers, targeted towards only certain Member States.[33] This is

[31] See D Fromage, 'Towards Increasing Unity and Continuing Executive Predominance within the E(M)U Post-COVID?' (2020) *Legal Issues of Economic Integration* 385.

[32] See eg JC Piris, *The Future of Europe: Towards a Two-Speed EU?* (Cambridge University Press, 2012) 106 ff.

[33] T Beukers, 'The Eurozone Crisis and the Legitimacy of Differentiated Integration' EUI Working Paper, MWP 2013/36, 1: 'The Eurozone crisis confronts the Union with an interesting legal and political puzzle: that of how to operate when new powers are necessary for some – in this case for the Eurozone – but when not all member states – notably some outside the Eurozone – are willing to make this possible?'

not the place to re-elaborate how this was done in any detail.[34] The movement outside the Treaties to negotiate international agreements external to the EU is part of a broader point dealt with in section IV below.

The idea of a more semi-permanent multi-speed EU with at its very core the eurozone members seemed to take further shape in the Brexit withdrawal phase. Macron's declared policy for the EMU calls for a 'multi-speed Europe' and an 'executive' for the eurozone in the form of a prime minister or finance minister, who would be answerable to a eurozone European Parliament. A short-term idea was that the eurogroup would get a full-time chairperson, who would present the strategy and evaluate the situation in the Euro area before the national parliaments. Regular practice of the euro area summits at the level of Heads of State and Government would be restored, instead of the current tendency to bring them together only in the event of a crisis.[35]

These changes did not require modifying the Treaties and indeed in practice they are already largely in place. The Juncker Commission launched further reflection by proposing the creation of a European Minister of Economy and Finance in the framework of its reform package on EMU.[36] In the Commission's proposal the Minister would combine the positions of EMU Commissioner and permanent Chair of the Eurogroup. Interestingly, a new central executive power for the eurozone would be created at the core of the EU institutional architecture. The Finance Minister would indeed be the Minister for the Union, while at the same time effectively acting as the main executive of the eurozone. How this would play out in terms of relationship and balance between eurozone and non-eurozone members is only one of the several questions left open by the proposal.[37] In the meantime, however, the new von der Leyen Commission did not follow up this initiative.

The central involvement of the European Central Bank and the Eurogroup in the 2015 Report on 'Completing Europe's Economic and Monetary Union' showcased their growing importance within the EU. In presenting a pathway towards completing the economic and monetary union, it included several steps – most notably a European treasury, a fiscal union, and a joined representation of the Eurogroup on the international level – without shying away from possible Treaty changes. The explicit targeting of certain reform proposals towards the Eurogroup alone implied a move towards the idea of a core Europe. This could be viewed as an attempt to promote a core Europe of a potentially more homogenous group of

[34] But see T Beukers, B De Witte and C Kilpatrick (eds), *Constitutional Change Through Euro-Crisis Law* (Cambridge University Press, 2017).
F Schimmelfennig and T Winzen, 'Path Dependence: Differentiated Integration in the Euro Crisis' in *Ever Looser Union? Differentiated European Integration* (Oxford Scholarship Online, 2020).

[35] E Macron, 'Initiative pour l'Europe – Discours pour une Europe souveraine, unie, démocratique', 26 September 2017.

[36] A European Minister of Economy and Finance, COM(2017) 823 final.

[37] For more details on the legal issues raised by the Commission's proposal see M Patrin and P Schlosser, 'The European Finance Minister and the EMU Reform Conundrum' (2019) 14 *Capital Markets Law Journal* 274.

Member States, which might then simplify further enlargements within the outer circle of the Union.[38]

The debate on how to strengthen executive power in the field of economic governance and in a differentiated Union remains on the table as Europe grapples with the consequences of the Covid-19 public health and economic emergency. Yet by 2020 there had been a shift and a return to an undivided Union. The development of the eurozone into an autonomous organisation, separate from the European Union, was halted by the legal and political evolution during 2020. The EU Covid-19 recovery plan (known as Next Generation EU or NGEU), adopted in December 2020, was implemented fully within the EU legal order as such and without recourse to international agreements *inter se*.[39] The plan is being implemented by the Member States in cooperation with the EU's main institutions, and all the 27 States participate in it on the same legal terms. Both deeper integration and a certain amount of differentiated integration can be seen in different sectors of the EU's pandemic response. Yet there is a down-side in terms of democratic accountability: we have EU27 solutions prepared by the Eurogroup in inclusive format upon instruction by the European Council.[40]

Economically, the EU-level debt realised through NGEU constitutes a 'paradigmatic shift'.[41] It also highlights a retreat from extra-EU institutional experiments such as the ESM. In Bruno's own words:

> the decline of differentiated integration, can be seen as backing away from institutional experimentalism, from the creation of euro area or hybrid institutional mechanisms, in favour of more straightforward EU-law based solutions. The second trend, the rediscovery of the EU's neglected macroeconomic competences is a new form of experimentalism, which corresponds to … a fresh interpretation of the existing Treaty norms in the light of changing circumstances.[42]

IV. Disuse of International Agreements *Inter Se*

The institutional topic of the category of acts of the EU or its equivalent of 'international Treaties between Member States' was first written about extensively by

[38] F Schorkopf, 'Zukunftsorientierung oder Realitätsleugnung? Der Präsidentenbericht zur Reform derEuropäischen Union' (2015) 13 *Journal for Comparative Government and European Policy* 356. See also J Juncker et al, 'Completing Europe's Economic and Monetary Union', 22 June 2015.

[39] See further, De Witte, 'The EU's COVID-19 Recovery Plan' (n 9).

[40] See further B Dias Pinheiro and D Fromage, 'Parliamentary Oversight of the EU Economic Recovery Plan – Lessons Learned, and Which Way Forward?' in *EU Law in Times of Pandemic. The EU's Legal Response to COVID-19* (Spain, Editorial Comares, 2021); D Utrilla and A Shabbir (eds), *EU Law Live Press*, 102–16. See also B Dias Pinheiro and D Fromage, Special issue: 'National and European Parliamentary Involvement in the EU's Economic Response to the COVID Crisis' (2020) *EU Law Live* Weekend Edition no 36.

[41] V Schmidt, 'Theorizing Institutional Change and Governance in European Responses to the Covid 19 Pandemic' (2020) 42 *Journal of European Integration*, 1177.

[42] Fromage, 'Post-COVID-19 E(M)U Interinstitutional Balance' (n 29).

Bruno in 2000 and referred to as 'old flexibility'.[43] The implication was that it was in decline and the contrast at that time was the new flexibility found in the Treaty of Maastricht and described in the previous paragraph. It was vintage Bruno: a largely overlooked legal instrument of the European integration process and concerning subjects connected with the substance of the EC Treaty or the EU Treaty but which until then had not had that much political or salience from a broader European integration perspective. In this context 'chameleonic Member States' refers to the roles of Member States in (older) initiatives such as BENELUX cooperation and Schengen cooperation as well as Europol originally and many more[44] policy-specific agreements.[45] This discussion was later updated in the fourth revised edition of *The Law of the European Union and the European Communities* in the chapter on 'Legal Instruments, Decision-making and EU Finances'. By then, their newer role and even revival came about with their incremental and increasing use within EMU, and also with their use to bring about differentiation internally.

In 2012 the Fiscal Compact (Treaty on Stability, Coordination and Governance in the Economic and Monetary Union – TSCG) and the ESM Treaty were adopted under international law. The Fiscal Compact aimed at increasing budgetary discipline, inter alia by requiring Member States to enshrine into national law the 'golden rule' of a structural deficit not exceeding 0.5 per cent of GDP.[46] The ESM Treaty created a permanent emergency fund to support eurozone members in distress.[47] Whereas the Fiscal Compact was signed by 25 Member States (with the exclusion of the UK and the Czech Republic), the ESM only applied to euro-area Member States. In this way, differentiation brought about in terms of membership internally through this medium and the post-Lisbon practice led to a 'revival' of the use of these international agreements *inter se*.[48] It was followed by agreement on the signature of the Single Resolution Fund, the inter-governmental part of the Banking package.[49] The intensive use of such agreements within the scope

[43] De Witte, 'Old-fashioned Flexibility: International Agreements between Member States of the European Union' in G De Búrca and J Scott (eds), *Constitutional Change in the EU* (Hart Publishing, 2000) 31.

[44] See De Witte, 'Variable Geometry' (n 11) 21f.

[45] B De Witte, 'Chameleonic Member States: Differentiation by Means of Partial and Parallel International Agreements' in B De Witte, D Hanf and E Vos (eds), *The Many Faces of Differentiation in EU Law* (Intersentia, 2001) 231ff.

[46] B De Witte, 'Treaty Games – Law as Instrument and as Constraint in the Euro Crisis Policy' in F Allen, E Carletti and S Simonelli (eds), *Governance for the Eurozone: Integration or Disintegration?* (FIC Press, 2012) 152.

[47] A special article was introduced in the Treaties through the simplified revision procedure (Art 136(3) of the Treaty on the Functioning of the European Union (TFEU)) allowing the eurozone Member States to establish a 'stability mechanism to be activated if indispensable to safeguard the stability of the euro area as a whole'. This also meant that the financial support did not equal a bail-out which was explicitly forbidden by Art 125 TFEU. See the conditions applying according to the CJEU in the *Pringle* judgment: Case C-370/12 *Pringle v Ireland* EU:C:2012:756, para 62.

[48] De Witte, 'Variable Geometry' (n 11) 20.

[49] Agreement on the Transfer and Mutualisation of Contributions to the Single Resolution Fund, [2014] Council doc 8457/14.

of the EU Treaties has been extensively discussed elsewhere. Bruno himself has qualified them in general terms as 'quasi-instruments of EU law' as opposed to an integral part of EU law.[50] The international 'side agreements' in the context of the Euro-Area crisis is seen not as a generalised return to inter-governmentalism but rather as representing quite specific and urgent reasons, including path dependency.[51] But at the end of the day, it is their inherent flexibility at the time of their conclusion that 'make them an attractive tool'.[52]

During the response to the Covid crisis and the adoption of NGEU discussed above in section III it is noteworthy that the path agreed was different to that which applied in the EU's response to the economic crisis. It was implemented fully within the EU legal order as such, and without recourse to either new international agreements *inter se* or older ones such as the ESM.[53] No new bodies or agencies were created either within the EU or ESM type international bodies outside it. This is in real contrast to the response to the economic crisis. There was perhaps less need given the exogenous nature of the Covid crisis and the fact that some stabilisation instruments were in place already.

V. New Recompositions: Observing Shifting Outer and Inner Cores

Flying together *through* turbulence was the sub-title to this piece, which was written in its entirety before the war in Ukraine. The word 'turbulence' may cover previous periods in time such as national constitutional resistance, referendum struggles and Brexit, but it is not strong enough in the current constellation and changes we are now living through in Europe. That is why the sub-title has in this final version amended to flying together *beyond* turbulence. It implies that the EU has flown through the turbulence into a full scale and serious storm. More important than words, what matters in the context of this contribution and the book as a whole is that the EU continues 'flying together' – indeed, all the evidence is that this closeness, even unity, is reinforced and strengthened with every further crisis. My brief concluding remarks are in the spirit of Bruno's own trajectory – from more and more differentiation to, in fact and somewhat counter-intuitively, now more and more unity. This is a trajectory that has been there arguably all along according to some analyses (including mine) but it is

[50] B De Witte and T Martinelli, 'Treaties between EU Member States as Quasi-instruments of EU Law' in M Cremona and C Kilpatrick (eds), *EU Legal Acts: Challenges and Transformations* (Oxford University Press, 2018) 157.

[51] Ibid 171–76.

[52] Ibid 175. See too D Fromage, 'The Future of EMU Architecture Post-COVID' (2020) *Legal Issues of Economic Integration* 295.

[53] See further, De Witte, 'The EU's COVID-19 Recovery Plan' (n 9).

now much closer to the surface, and recent extraneous triggers – in particular Brexit and the pandemic – have delineated it more sharply. It now seems that the war in Ukraine may even reverse ('decimate') previously existing long-held national convictions and resulting opt-outs or inability to participate with the other Member States (eg Denmark and Germany).

Beyond turbulence may well lie the *volte face*. In this perspective, the recomposition of what has been termed the outer core to also include strong elements of an inner core (eg EMU) is still nascent but some signs are there already, even if the future remains as ever profoundly unknowable.

Recomposing Bruno is another matter. Bruno is one of those very rare European law academics, even in his own terms,[54] who is both vertical and horizontal; both institutional and substantive; both curious about the law, its norms and its practice, as well as the politics behind and around it. Despite his own qualification of himself as an academic fox rather than the proverbial (single-minded) hedgehog,[55] this in no way does him justice. For me there is no hint of Bruno prowling low over varied terrain, scavenging for multiple sources. I see him more as an eagle soaring high and swooping down to the ground on occasion to protect, to investigate and perhaps to disagree. Eagles are majestic and can see the big blue-sky picture, but their optics are also unusually attuned to vision in less clear, more turbulent, environments. As the environment changes, eagles are perceptive to differences and novelties even if they are in still in shadow and only partially emerging. Eagles are highflyers with acute and adapted vision despite and beyond turbulence of whatever kind. There is in fact no one who did and does see European law in all its changing facets, all its nuances, like Bruno. In seeing and placing chameleonic legal and institutional realities as they emerge, he engages in helping us to be more optimistic that the EU will continue flying together through and even beyond acute turbulence.

[54] De Witte, 'EU Law' (n 1) 101.
[55] His own qualification: see R Rubio Marín, chapter thirteen in this volume.

PART III

Social and Educational Europe

6

On the 'Slow Constitutionalisation' of Social Europe

DIAMOND ASHIAGBOR

I. Introduction

In this contribution to the 'Liber Amicarum' for Bruno De Witte, I want to reflect on two inter-related aspects of Bruno's qualities and commitments as an academic. First, his recognition of the importance of the 'social' in the European Union and what it means for EU law scholarship to take seriously the 'human face' of the EU. Second, perhaps equally importantly, Bruno's consistent modelling of good academic practice – through being intellectually curious, engaged with and supportive of the work of others, and interested in building a non-hierarchical academic community. As Ruth Rubio Marín has noted in her contribution,[1] Bruno De Witte is, at heart, a *collegial* scholar: not only in collaborating and co-writing with other researchers, in particular early career scholars; but also, in being open to research from across the spectrum of EU law scholarship, as evidenced by the range of contributions in this collection.

I share with Bruno an interest in exploring the role of 'social' and labour law in the historic, and ongoing, construction of the European Union integration project. In particular, in this contribution, I will examine what Bruno has referred to as the 'slow constitutionalisation' of social rights in the EU project and EU law.[2] My contention is that the resilience of the integration project is threatened by neoliberal responses to the present crises, which erode the EU's ability to institutionalise a labour or social constitution to counter the dominance of an economic constitution. EU labour law has long been a site for contestation between the market and the social, and for attempts to resolve the tensions inherent in the Union's aspiration to give a 'human face' to the market integration project or to create 'a highly competitive *social* market economy'. Labour law has

[1] R Rubio Marín, chapter thirteen in this volume.

[2] B De Witte, 'Two Charters and a Pillar: The Slow Constitutionalization of Social Rights in European Law' in U Belavusau and A Gliszczyńska-Grabias (eds), *Constitutionalism under Stress: Essays in Honour of Wojciech Sadurski* (Oxford University Press, 2020).

also served as a bridge between the national and the transnational, responding to tensions which arise when market integration and economic governance take place at supranational level in the absence of a supranational polity. Historically, the liberal market economies of the EU were able to establish social cohesion and solidarity domestically, and to govern or 'embed' capitalism at national level, for example, through labour standards. This has been a traditional focus of labour law scholarship: on the role of the state and its capacity, or otherwise, to regulate a territorially bounded market and to socialise economic risk. However, capital and the sphere of economic interaction have become increasingly de-territorialised, undermining the scope for market governance through labour law. On the one hand, EU trade liberalisation means national capacity to regulate markets is severely reduced due to removal of barriers to trade, mobility of capital and fear of capital flight. On the other, this state capacity was considerably shored up by being part of a *regional* integration project which shielded states from *globalisation* and carved out policy space in which Member States could maintain national systems of labour and social welfare law.

However, the historic imbalance in the EU's economic constitution between market and non-market objectives has come to the fore in recent years – as has the latent potential for a clash between labour law and social policy at national level and the principles of the internal market as seen in the jurisprudence of the Court of Justice, in particular in the *Viking* and *Laval* line of case law.[3] Such judicial incursions against labour law and labour market institutions are exacerbated by broader EU economic policy governance, now contained in the European Semester which, with its focus on strict fiscal discipline, subsumes and dilutes attempts to re-establish 'social Europe', as contained in the European Pillar of Social Rights.[4]

II. EU Social Policy as an Autonomous Field?

The initial thinness of social policy provisions within the EU integration project was premised on a consensus that the creation of a common market would not require harmonisation of labour standards or national systems of labour law.[5]

[3] Case C-438/05 *The International Transport Workers' Federation and The Finnish Seamen's Union v Viking Line ABP* EU:C:2007:772; Case C-341/05 *Laval un Partneri Ltd v Svenska Byggnadsarbetareförbundet and Others* EU:C:2007:809. See D Ashiagbor, 'Collective Labour Rights and the European Social Model' (2009) 3(2) *Journal of Law and Ethics of Human Rights* 222.

[4] European Commission Press Release IP/21/6105, 'European Semester Autumn Package: rebounding stronger from the crisis and making Europe greener and more digital', 24 November 2021. The European Semester Autumn Package includes the Annual Sustainable Growth Survey, Opinions on euro area Draft Budgetary Plans (DBPs) for 2022, policy recommendations for the euro area and the Commission's proposal for a Joint Employment Report; European Commission, Recommendation on the European Pillar of Social Rights, C (2017) 2600 final, and Communication of 26 April 2017 establishing a European Pillar of Social Rights, COM(2017) 250 final.

[5] D Ashiagbor, 'Unravelling the Embedded Liberal Bargain: Labour and Social Welfare Law in the Context of EU Market Integration' (2013) 19(3) *European Law Journal* 303.

The goal of economic liberalisation at the centre of the European integration project was founded on the understanding that competition did not necessarily require a complete harmonisation of costs; that differences, such as those in labour costs or interest rates, would tend to level up in a common market, through the free circulation of the factors of production (goods, services, capital and workers). Thus, the orthodox view at the foundation of the EU – exemplified by the inter-governmental Spaak Report on which the original EEC Treaty was based[6] – was that equalisation of labour standards would be the *result* rather than the *condition precedent* of the operation of the common market. This view was reinforced rather than undermined by the insertion of a Title on 'social policy' into the EEC Treaty (Articles 117–22 EEC).[7] With the exception of Article 119 EEC on equal pay between men and women,[8] the original social policy provisions were principally exhortatory and failed to provide legally enforceable social rights.[9] Indeed, Article 117 EEC makes clear Member States' belief that improved working conditions would ensue principally from the functioning of the common market,[10] with Article 119 one of the few exceptions to the rejection of a wider role for transnational harmonisation of social policy. Other provisions stressed the supportive role of the Community institutions whilst conferring no real power on them – the role of the Commission being to 'promot[e] close co-operation between Member States in the social field' (Article 118 EEC). Thus, whilst 'textually broad'

[6] Comité Intergouvernemental Créé par la Conférence de Messine, Rapport des Chefs de Délégation aux Minstres des Affaires Etrangères (1956) (the Spaak Report), summarised in English in (1956) 405 *Political and Economic Planning* 233: '[C]ompetition does not necessarily require a complete harmonisation of the different elements in costs; Indeed, it is only on the basis of certain differences – such as wage differences due to differences in productivity – that trade and competition can develop. (…) In addition, wage and interest rates tend to level up in a common market – a process which is hastened by the free circulation of the factors of production. This is a consequence rather than a condition of the common market's operation.' The Spaak Report had, in turn, drawn heavily on the 1956 Ohlin Report of the International Labour Organization's Committee of Experts, underpinned by the theory of comparative advantage that differences in levels of social protection, labour law or wage costs between states engaged in international trade broadly reflected differences in productivity and would level up as a result of trade: International Labour Organization, 'Social Aspects of Economic Co-operation: Report of a Group of Experts' (The Ohlin Report) (1956) 46 Studies and Reports, New Series.

[7] The social policy title has undergone radical revision since 1957. Following the coming into force of the Treaty of Lisbon on 1 December 2009, the EU's social policy provisions are now to be found in Title X, Arts 151–161 of the Consolidated version of the Treaty of the Functioning of the European Union [2012] OJ C 326.

[8] Art 119 EEC is now Art 157 TFEU. See C Barnard, 'The Economic Objectives of Article 119' in T Hervey and D O'Keeffe (eds), *Sex Equality Law in the European Union* (Wiley, 1996).

[9] For instance, Art 120 EEC (now Art 158 TFEU) exhorts Member States to 'endeavour to maintain the existing equivalence between paid holiday schemes'.

[10] Art 117 EEC: 'Member States agree upon the need to promote improved working conditions and an improved standard of living for workers, so as to make possible their harmonisation while the improvement is being maintained. They believe that such a development will ensue not only from the functioning of the common market, which will favour the harmonisation of social systems, but also from the procedures provided for in this Treaty and from the approximation of provisions laid down by law, regulation or administrative action.'

it is arguable these original social policy provisions were 'legally shallow'.[11] It thus seems apposite to claim, as Stefano Giubboni does, that the 'apparent flimsiness' of the social provisions of the Treaty of Rome was deliberate.[12]

With hindsight, it became clear that the very process of economic liberalisation was placing demands on the ability of States to maintain living and working standards: in the creation of a common market, there is arguably pressure on national economies to deregulate to remain competitive, since national capacity to regulate markets is severely reduced due to removal of barriers to trade, mobility of capital and fear of capital flight. There has been an incremental development of a framework of basic minimum standards at EU level, in response to and justified by a complex set of rationales – only one of which was the need to protect against destructive downwards competition. The key observation here is that there has been a significant development of the EU social dimension, admittedly from a very low base. Nevertheless, the social harmonisation which has emerged has never been intended as a replacement for the more substantial social provision assumed to exist at national level. As the then president of the European Commission declared in 1986, 'the creation of a vast economic area, based on the market and business cooperation, is inconceivable – I would say unattainable – without *some* harmonisation of social legislation. Our ultimate aim must be the creation of a European social area'.[13]

The approach, emerging over several decades and accelerating following the Treaty on European Union (TEU) in 1992, has been to build on the thin social policy provisions of the Treaty of Rome. Although the 1986 Single European Act (SEA) extended the use of 'qualified majority voting' (QMV) to measures relating to the health and safety of workers (eg denying the possibility for a single Member State to veto a proposal by voting against it in the Council of Ministers), measures relating to 'the rights and interests of employed persons' still required the unanimous agreement of the Council. The SEA thus enabled the enactment of directives ostensibly concerned with health and safety, such as the Working Time Directive and the Pregnant Workers Directive,[14] but failed to provide a legal basis

[11] C Barnard, 'Social Policy Revisited in the Light of the Constitutional Debate' in C Barnard (ed), *The Fundamentals of EU Law Revisited: Assessing the Impact of the Constitutional Debate* (Oxford University Press, 2007). See also P Watson, *EU Social and Employment Law: Policy and Practice in an Enlarged Europe* (Oxford University Press, 2009) especially at 47: 'Articles 117–122 were vague and repetitious, conferring no real powers upon the Community institutions, and little by way of direct rights on Community citizens'.

[12] S Giubboni, *Social Rights and Market Freedom in the European Constitution: A Labour Law Perspective* (Cambridge University Press, 2006) 16.

[13] Programme of the Commission for 1986, Statement by Jacques Delors, President of the Commission, to the European Parliament and his reply to the ensuing debate, Strasbourg, 19 February 1986, Bulletin of the European Communities, Supplement 1/86 at 9 (Emphasis added).

[14] Council Directive 93/104/EC of 23 November 1993 (Working Time Directive) [1993] OJ L 307/18; Council Directive 92/85/EEC of 19 October 1992 (Pregnant Workers Directive) [1992] OJ L 348/1.

for broader social policy interventions. It was only with the Treaty of Maastricht that the EC acquired the requisite Treaty base: a 'Protocol and Agreement on Social Policy' annexed to the TEU broadened the substantive scope for social policy at European level and, also, made the process of enacting harmonising legislation more straightforward, through the extension of QMV. However, the United Kingdom's 'opt out' from this social policy chapter cast doubt on its legal status, until the Amsterdam Treaty finally brought together the various sources of EC/EU social law into a single chapter on social policy, to which all Member States are now subject.[15] What changed over this period was a greater political willingness among the Member States to accept that social law and policy were not solely national functions, alongside a newly emerging economic consensus that there could be an *economic* justification for labour standards to smooth the process of integration – hence the willingness to change voting procedures to facilitate the enactment of social law at European level.

The EU in time evolved a supranational social dimension to protect vulnerable regions, sectors and workers from the effects of intra-EU trade liberalisation, and also to offer protection against global trade. Further, the EU also developed major redistributive policies: adjustment assistance and financial instruments to address economic and social imbalances at EU level, in the form of the European structural and investment funds. However, whilst social policy has become deeply institutionalised, it has not become constitutionalised within the EU legal order – or at least, not to the same extent as EU economic governance and coordination.

III. 'New Governance', Economic Coordination and the Constitutionalisation of the European Semester

It is relevant here to compare the 'hardness' of economic policy coordination and its unequivocal entrenchment of the economic constitution, with the relative 'softness' of EU social law and social policy. As Claire Kilpatrick reminds us, traditionally within the EU, worker protection was associated primarily with hard law,[16] with the use of the 'classic' Community method of law-making.[17] However, as policy objectives shifted from the focus on protecting workers *from* the market (via labour rights) to protecting workers *within* the market, for instance, through employment policy measures such as active labour market policies, to strengthen

[15] Arts 136–45 EC Treaty – now Arts 151–61 TFEU.

[16] C Kilpatrick, 'New EU Employment Governance and Constitutionalism' in G De Búrca and J Scott (eds), *Law and New Governance in the EU and US* (Hart Publishing, 2006) 127.

[17] This method can be summed up as the style of decision-making established in the Treaty of Rome, within which the Commission has the sole right of initiative with regard to legislative and policy proposals, with the European Parliament having an increasingly important voice; the Council of Ministers takes the final decision – often now by qualified majority voting – and the resulting Community law is enforced by the Court: D Ashiagbor, 'Soft Harmonisation: The "Open Method of Coordination" in the European Employment Strategy' (2004) 10(2) *European Public Law* 305.

their employability, then regulatory methods and techniques have also changed, via the adoption of 'new forms of governance'.[18]

Policy making in the realm of labour law, social policy and employment policy has long been marked by conflicts between, on the one hand, state action (intergovernmentalism) and Union competence (supranationalism); and between regulation and deregulation. The new form of governance – the 'open method of coordination', which emerged in the context of employment policy coordination – can be seen as a compromise between these two areas of contestation: an example of the EU forsaking the Community method or direct regulatory intervention, and instead seeking to achieve common goals not by imposing them, but through establishing a framework within which Member States are free to be 'self-regulating'. The overall objectives (of employment policy) are set by the European Council, but it is left to the Member States to set national and regional level targets to reach these objectives.[19] Member States are responsible for 'translating' these guidelines into national and regional policies, 'taking into account national and regional differences'.[20] The Open Method of Coordination (OMC) for employment policy is an annual, iterative procedure to improve the efficiency of labour markets through the setting of guidelines, benchmarks and indicators at the European level, along with their translation into national policies and the periodic monitoring of such implementation, mostly by means of peer review. However, the 'soft' coordination of the open method does in fact have quite a 'hard' impact – placing powerful political pressure on Member States to comply with centrally designed policies – and an explicitly 'hard' economic policy coordination backed by sanctions. That is because OMC of *employment policy* takes place in the shadow of EU *economic policy* in general, and the Stability and Growth Pact and Economic and Monetary Union in particular,[21] which constrain national employment and economic policy and necessitate strict fiscal discipline, restrictions on public expenditure, modernisation of social protection systems, and structural reforms to make labour markets economically responsive and enhance their competitiveness. As van Apeldoorn observes, such asymmetric multilevel governance ensures that socio-economic policy-making is structurally biased towards policies of neoliberal restructuring.[22]

[18] KA Armstrong, 'The Open Method of Coordination: Obstinate or Obsolete?' in R Schütze and T Tridimas, *Oxford Principles of European Union Law: The European Union Legal Order*, Vol I (Oxford University Press, 2018); D Ashiagbor, *The European Employment Strategy: Labour Market Regulation and New Governance* (Oxford University Press, 2005).

[19] Arts 145–50 TFEU (formerly, Arts 125–30 EC Treaty).

[20] Presidency Conclusions, Lisbon European Council, 23 and 24 March 2000, Bull EU-3/2000, 7–1, para 37, www.europarl.europa.eu/summits/lis1_en.htm.

[21] Enforced through multilateral surveillance and the excessive deficit procedure: the '3 per cent budget deficit rule'.

[22] B van Apeldoorn, 'The Contradictions of "Embedded Neoliberalism" and Europe's Multilevel Legitimacy Crisis: The European Project and Its Limits' in B van Apeldoorn, J Drahokoupil and L Horn (eds), *Contradictions and Limits of Neoliberal European Governance: From Lisbon to Lisbon* (Palgrave Macmillan, 2009).

This annual cycle of coordination and surveillance of the EU's economic policies, involving detailed scrutiny of Member States' plans for macroeconomic, budgetary and structural reforms, has 'hardened' in the form of the European Semester, at the core of which remains a strengthened version of the Stability and Growth Pact – fiscal policies to ensure sustainability of public finances. The 'semester' institutes a timetable, according to which the Member States receive EU-level guidance, submit their national reform programmes for evaluation at EU level, and then receive 'Country-specific recommendations' for national budgetary and reform policies.[23] Structural reforms, focusing on growth and employment in line with EU 2020 strategy mirror closely the earlier response of EU institutions to the sovereign debt crisis and eurozone crisis, which included extreme deregulatory 'reforms' imposed on those EU Member States receiving financial support from the 'Troika' of the European Commission, the European Central Bank and the International Monetary Fund (IMF). Catherine Barnard identifies the direct and indirect impact on labour law of the various responses to the crisis – the Euro Plus Pact of March 2011; the 'bail-outs' granted to Greece, Ireland and Portugal and the accompanying Memoranda of Understanding; and the European Financial Stabilisation Mechanism – as effectively amounting to EU or EU/IMF-sanctioned deregulation of employment rights at national level.[24] For example, Ireland committed itself in the Memorandum of Understanding (MoU) governing its bailout to reducing its minimum wage by one euro an hour. Portugal committed itself to cuts including reductions in bonus salary payments for civil servants and pensioners, reductions in the generosity of severance payments, and placing restrictions on dismissal rights and compensation for dismissals.[25]

Coordination of social policy has been included in the European Semester process since 2018, when the EU Pillar of Social Rights was integrated in the process with monitoring and policy coordination based on what is known as the 'social scoreboard'. Officially launched by the Commission in April 2017, the European Pillar of Social Rights, commonly known as the European Social Pillar (ESP),[26] seems to offer the potential to redress the imbalance between 'the market' and 'the social'[27] which has been so exacerbated since the Lisbon Treaty – and, before that, the Lisbon Strategy in which market fundamentalism was in the ascendancy in relation to social policy and social rights.[28]

[23] European Commission Press Release IP/21/6105, 'European Semester Autumn Package: rebounding stronger from the crisis and making Europe greener and more digital', 24 November 2021.

[24] C Barnard, 'The Financial Crisis and the Euro Plus Pact: A Labour Lawyer's Perspective' (2012) *Industrial Law Journal* 98.

[25] Ibid 110–11.

[26] European Commission, Recommendation on the European Pillar of Social Rights, C(2017) 2600 final, and Communication of 26 April 2017 establishing a European Pillar of Social Rights, COM(2017) 250 final.

[27] S Garben, 'The European Pillar of Social Rights: Effectively Addressing Displacement?' (2018) 14 *European Constitutional Law Review* 210.

[28] On the Lisbon Strategy, see European Commission, Communication from the Commission 'The Future of the European Employment Strategy (EES): A Strategy for Full Employment and Better Jobs for All', COM (2003) 6 final. See Ashiagbor, 'Soft Harmonisation' (n 17).

However, the European Semester has arguably led to a weakening of social and labour rights, and an erosion of social solidarity,[29] with the European Social Pillar having very little impact in altering this narrative. The legal basis of the Stability and Growth Pact is Articles 121 and 126 of the Treaty on the Functioning of the European Union (TFEU). Article 136 TFEU provides for specific provisions to be adopted for the euro area. It is the basis for a sanctions regulation for euro area countries, included in the so-called Six Pack and the so-called Two Pack regulations, which entail enhanced monitoring and surveillance in the euro area.[30] Thus economic policy governance and surveillance is heavily constitutionalised. In contrast, even allowing for the insertion of the European Social Pillar into the European Semester process, social policy and rights remain a second order concern. Jonathan Zeitlin and Bart Vanhercke argue that, although the Semester was conceived as a response to financial crisis, it has become 'socialised' over time.[31] However, I would contend that social rights remain subservient to making labour markets economically responsive and enhancing their competitiveness: social policy is required to be 'growth friendly' or 'jobs friendly'. Further, and more crucially, the European Social Pillar is a powerful exemplar of the pattern wherein social policy objectives are to be delivered via soft law or new governance techniques, which eschew the 'hard' law of the classic Community method, yet do not benefit from the harder edged 'surveillance and sanctions' model granted to economic policy coordination.

The European Social Pillar comprises 20 rights and principles, categorised into three chapters: on 'equal opportunities and access to the labour market', 'fair working conditions' and 'social protection and inclusion'. However, as Garben explains, the Pillar is a non-binding 'soft law' instrument,[32] which is not legally enforceable and which will, according to the Commission 'require a translation into dedicated action and/or separate pieces of legislation, at the appropriate level'.[33] One such key legislative proposal, on work life balance for parents and carers, has to date been adopted as a Directive.[34] However, on balance, the Pillar has not radically altered the long-standing dearth of legislative activity under the EU Social Policy Title.[35]

[29] C Kilpatrick, 'The Displacement of Social Europe: A Productive Lens of Inquiry' (2018) 14 *European Constitutional Law Review* 62.

[30] See the Commission's review of the 'Six Pack' and the 'Two Pack': European Commission, 'Economic governance review: Report on the application of Regulations (EU) no 1173/2011, 1174/2011, 1175/2011, 1176/2011, 1177/2011, 472/2013 and 473/20131', COM(2014) 905 final.

[31] J Zeitlin and B Vanhercke, 'Economic Governance in Europe 2020: Socialising the European Semester against the Odds?' in D Natali and B Vanhercke (eds), *Social Policy in the European Union: State of Play 2015* (ETUI and OSE, 2015).

[32] Garben, 'The European Pillar of Social Rights' (n 27) 218.

[33] European Commission, Staff Working Document accompanying the Commission Communication establishing a European Pillar of Social Rights, SWD (2017) 201 final, 2 and 3.

[34] Directive (EU) 2019/1158 of the European Parliament and of the Council of 20 June 2019 on work-life balance for parents and carers and repealing Council Directive 2010/18/EU [2019] OJ L 188/79.

[35] Garben, 'The European Pillar of Social Rights' (n 27) 223.

IV. Conclusions: The Slow Constitutionalisation of the Social

With his customary clarity of expression, Bruno explains the place of OMC within the sources of EU law.[36] I agree with his analysis that it is not quite right to describe the OMC as a form of soft law, but rather, 'an institutional process that produces policy that may or may not take a legal form'.[37] Whilst the Pillar can more clearly be said to be a soft law instrument, nevertheless, as Bruno observes, the use of rights language is 'not being matched with the enforceability that normally comes with such language'.[38]

In May 2021 the European Council adopted the Porto Declaration on social affairs,[39] accompanied by a European Commission European Pillar of Social Rights Action Plan, which 'sets out concrete initiatives to turn the European Pillar of Social Rights into reality' by 2030 in the areas of employment, skills, and social protection.[40] The language used in the Action Plan focuses on 'social targets' – in relation to employment rates, poverty and social exclusion, cooperation, dialogue – with promises to 'review', 'update' and 'adopt' policies such as the 2014 Council Recommendation on Quality Framework for Traineeships,[41] the 2020 Industrial Strategy for Europe[42] and an Action Plan on the Social Economy.[43]

In essence, therefore, whilst economic policy and 'the market' is constitutionalised and subject to a regime of sanctions (eg the excessive deficit procedure under Article 126 TFEU), 'the social' is increasingly institutionalised in a web of 'soft' techniques and instruments which mean that economic policy continues to be prioritised, with social policy structurally constrained in the role of facilitating market integration and fiscal stability.

Article 3(3) TEU, as inserted by the Lisbon Treaty 2009, commits the Union to creating 'a highly competitive social market economy'. However, Lisbon (the Treaty and the Strategy)[44] accelerated the disembedding, or weakening, of the social

[36] B De Witte, 'The Place of the OMC in the System of EU Competences and Sources of Law' (2018) 3(1) *European Papers: A Journal on Law and Integration* 207, 210.

[37] Ibid 213.

[38] Ibid 199.

[39] European Council, Press release 8 May 2021, www.consilium.europa.eu/en/press/press-releases/2021/05/08/the-porto-declaration.

[40] European Commission, The European Pillar of Social Rights Action Plan, 7 May 2021, op.europa.eu/webpub/empl/european-pillar-of-social-rights/en.

[41] Council Recommendation of 10 March 2014 on a Quality Framework for Traineeships [2014] OJ C 88/1.

[42] Commission Communication, 'Updating the 2020 New Industrial Strategy: Building a Stronger Single Market for Europe's Recovery', COM (2021) 350 final; Commission Communication, 'A New Industrial Strategy for Europe', COM (2020) 102 final.

[43] Commission Communication, 'Building an economy that works for people: An action plan for the social economy', ec.europa.eu/social/main.jsp?catId=1537&langId=en, 9 December 2021.

[44] See n 28 above.

for the sake of the market; what Christian Joerges refers to as the de-coupling of the European economic constitution from the labour and social constitutions of the nation-states.[45] I argue that a significant source of legitimacy for EU action was precisely its ability to institutionalise markets which are no longer territorially bound. The aspiration for a social market economy was sustainable, provided the market liberalisation at EU level was embedded in the social – institutions of social citizenship – originating at national level but shored up by a burgeoning supranational social dimension. Accordingly, with the above shift from labour law and social policy to economic policy governance, the EU can be said to be prioritising economic rationality over social justice at a time of increasing mistrust of the 'regional' in favour of the 'national', and in a way which undermines trust in the integration project.

[45] C Joerges, 'Europe's Economic Constitution in Crisis and the Emergence of a New Constitutional Constellation' (2014) 15(5) *German Law Journal* 985.

7

The Emergence of a European Union Law of Education

HILDEGARD SCHNEIDER

I. Introduction

Not many scholars today may know that Bruno De Witte has also been interested in and influential on, the emerging field of a European law of education.[1] In November 1987, Bruno organised a conference on European Community Law of Education at the European University Institute (EUI) in Florence. This led to the publication of an edited volume entitled *European Community Law of Education*.[2] In this chapter I will discuss the gradual evolution towards an EU law of education, and its impact on educational policies and the recognition of diplomas.

II. The Evolution of a European Union Law on Education

At that time, as Bruno also stressed in his introduction to this book, education did not belong to the policy areas that the original EEC Treaty attributed to the Community institutions. The original EEC Treaty did not even mention the word education. In a case decided in 1988 by the European Court of Justice, *Commission v Greece*,[3] in which the prohibition of EU nationals establishing a private school

[1] B De Witte, 'The Influence of European Community Law on National Systems of Higher Education' in J Pertek (ed), *General recognition of Diplomas and Free Movement of Professionals* (EIPA, 1992); B De Witte, 'The Scope of Community Powers in Education and Culture in the Light of Subsequent Practice' in R Bieber and G Ress (eds), *Die Dynamik des Europäischen Gemeinschaftsrechts* (Nomos, 1987); B De Witte, 'Equivalentie van Studieperiodes en Erkenning van Diploma's' (1992–1993) *Tijdschrift voor Onderwijsrecht en Onderwijsbeleid*, 290–96; B De Witte, 'Higher Education and the Constitution of the European Community' in C Gellert (ed), *Higher Education in Europe* (Jessica Kingsley Publishers, 1993); B De Witte, 'Recht op Onderwijs zonder Grenzen?' (1990) *Jura Falconis* 535; B De Witte, 'Educational Equality for Community Workers and their Families' in B De Witte (ed), *European Community Law of Education* (Nomos, 1989).

[2] B De Witte (ed), *European Community Law of Education* (Nomos, 1989).

[3] Case 147/86 *Commission v Greece* EU:C:1988:150.

in Greece was at issue, the Greek government had even argued that education had been deliberately excluded from the application of the Treaty as not being an economic activity but, rather, linked to the cultural life of the Member States.[4] Therefore, according to the Greek government, the rules concerning the freedom of establishment or services could not be relied upon as far as education is concerned.

This argumentation of the Greek government is reminiscent of a similar case against Italy concerning cultural goods,[5] during which the Italian government also argued that 'culture' did not fall in the ambit of the EEC Treaty and therefore 'cultural goods' were not affected by the rules concerning the free movement of goods; however, the European Court of Justice did not follow the arguments of the governments in the case against Italy or the case against Greece. The European Court of Justice held, in its 1968 judgment in the *Italian Art Treasures* case, that all products forming the object of commercial transaction come within the scope of the rules on the free movement of goods, whatever their other qualities.[6]

Following the judgment against Greece in 1988, education had to be considered as being part of an emerging branch of European law. Earlier, in 1985, the Court had given life to an until then rather dormant provision in the EEC Treaty concerning vocational training (Article 128 EEC) in its famous *Gravier* judgment.[7] According to the Court in *Gravier* the term 'vocational training' concerns 'any form of education which prepares for a qualification for a particular profession, trade or employment or which provides the necessary training and skills for such a profession, skill or employment (...), whatever the age and the level of the training of the pupils or students, and even if the training programme includes an element of general education'.[8] According to the Court the common vocational training policy constitutes 'an indispensable element in the activities of the Community, whose objectives include inter alia the free movement of persons, the mobility of labour and the improvement of the living standards of workers'. Furthermore, the Court argued that access to vocational training will promote the free movement of persons throughout the Community, by enabling them to obtain a qualification in the Member State where they intend to work. This broad view on vocational training was of vital importance for universities and their ambitions concerning a common European educational policy. Whether university studies constitute 'vocational training' was also discussed in other cases pending in that period before the Court of Justice such as *Commission v Belgium*,[9] *Blaziot and Others v*

[4] De Witte, *European Community Law of Education* (n 2) 9, referring in footnote 2 to the Conclusions of AG Slynn in Case 147/86.

[5] Case 7/68 *Commission v Italy* EU:C:1968:51.

[6] Case 7/68 *Commission v Italy* EU:C:1968:51. See also B De Witte, 'Trade in Culture: International Legal Regimes and EU Constitutional Values' in G De Búrca and J Scott (eds), *The EU and the WTO: Legal and Constitutional Aspects* (Hart Publishing, 2001) 249.

[7] Case 293/83 *Gravier v City of Liège* EU:C:1985:69.

[8] Ibid para 30.

[9] Case 293/85 *Commission v Belgium* EU:C:1988:40.

University of Liège,[10] *Lair v Universität Hannover*[11] and *Brown v Secretary of State for Scotland*.[12] With the *Gravier* judgment the Court had already laid down the legal foundation for the further development of free movement of students in the Community.[13]

During the workshop organised by Bruno in 1987 these developments and case law leading towards an emerging Community law of education as well as a Community educational policy were discussed from various and different perspectives. Some academic authors but also Member States, most prominently Germany but also Belgium, challenged the competence of the Community during that period. They feared that these developments towards a European educational policy could lead to constitutional problems in light of the division of national legislative competences between the federal and the regional level. This fear of loss of sovereignty and legislative power of the German 'Länder' was formulated rather strongly by Ingo Hochbaum in his contribution to the edited volume *European Community Law of Education*.[14] In 1974, the German government had doubted its obligation to make study grants available for children of Community migrant workers. The Court, however, had rejected this view. According to the judgment in *Casagrande*, the Community is entitled to grant educational rights in so far as this is necessary for the realisation of the free movement of workers.[15]

Another very interesting contribution to *European Community Law of Education* is the analysis of Koen Lenaerts regarding the legal basis of the original ERASMUS Decision which was adopted by the Council in June 1987.[16] The Decision established the ERASMUS programme in order to increase significantly the mobility of university students in the EEC and to promote greater cooperation between universities. As legal basis the Decision makes particular reference to Articles 128 and 235 EEC. Furthermore, reference was made to the Council Decision 63/266/EEC from April 1963 laying down general principles for implementing a common vocational training policy. In the original proposal as drafted by the Commission only Article 128 EEC and the Council Decision from 1963 were referred to. The Council, however, by unanimous vote, modified the legal

[10] Case 24/86 *Blaizot and others v University of Liège* EU:C:1988:43.

[11] Case 39/86 *Lair v Universität Hannover* EU:C:1988:322.

[12] Case 197/86 *Brown v Secretary of State for Scotland* EU:C:1988:323.

[13] AP van der Mei, *Free Movement of Persons within the European Community – Cross-Border Access to Public Benefits* (Hart Publishing, 2003) ch 5.

[14] I Hochbaum, 'The Federal Structure of Member States as a Limit to Common Educational Policy: The Case of Germany' in B De Witte (ed), *European Community Law of Education* (Nomos, 1989) See further T Oppermann, *Europäisches Gemeinschaftsrecht und deutsche Bildungsordnung, Studien zu Bildung und Wissenschaft* (Bock, 1987); I Bergreen and I Hochbaum, 'Politikfelder zwischen Länderzuständigkeit und EG-Kompetenz' in F Borkhagen, C Bruns-Klöss, G Memminger and O Stein (eds), *Die Deutschen Länder in Europa* (Nomos, 1992).

[15] Case 9/74 *Donato Casagrande v Landeshauptstadt München* EU:C:1974:74.

[16] Decision 87/327/EEC of 15 June 1987 adopting the European Community Action Scheme for the Mobility of University Students (Erasmus) [1987] OJ L 166/20. K Lenaerts, 'ERASMUS: Legal Basis and Implementation' in B De Witte (ed), *European Community Law of Education* (Nomos, 1989).

basis proposed by the Commission and included Article 235 EEC in the Decision. Consequently, with the addition of Article 235 EEC the voting had to be taken with unanimity instead of the simple majority required by Article 128 EEC.

In his chapter in *European Community Law of Education*, Koen Lenaerts referred to information in the press concerning the discussions and negotiations in the Council prior to its decision, which demonstrated that the Member States were fundamentally divided over the question on which legal basis the ERASMUS Decision should be based. According to these reports, Greece, Italy, Luxembourg, Portugal and Spain accepted that Article 128 EEC was the appropriate legal basis. In contrast, Belgium, France and the United Kingdom considered that only Article 235 EEC should be used as the legal basis, while Germany, Ireland and the Netherlands seemed to accept the Decision if both Article 128 and Article 235 EEC would be referred to as the legal basis.[17]

Finally, the compromise reached in the Council in May 1987 was indeed this dual legal basis. According to the Council, Article 128 EEC did not cover the full scale of the proposed ERASMUS programme as the term 'vocational training' of Article 128 EEC could not cover university education as a whole and the envisaged student exchange. The Commission, however, considered this issue important enough to start a procedure against the Council in August 1987.[18] In a very elaborate and detailed analysis of the ERASMUS Decision, discussing in detail the arguments of the Council and the Commission, Koen Lenaerts concluded that in his view the ERASMUS Decision necessarily entails deep involvement into the traditions of educational organisation and policy in the Member States and that the proposal went beyond the 'general principles' as referred to in Article 128 EEC. In that way, he justified the unanimous decision by the Council to include Article 235 EEC as joint legal basis next to Article 128 EEC.[19]

At the time of the conference and while Bruno was editing the book, the case *Commission v Council* was still pending at the European Court of Justice. The subject of the conference and the various contributions to the edited volume were therefore highly topical. All participants, but mainly Bruno, who had taken the initiative, can therefore be praised for the pioneering role they have played to the development of this emerging field of European law and policy making.[20]

In its judgment in the case *Commission v Council (ERASMUS)* the European Court of Justice did not follow the analysis as proposed by Koen Lenaerts. The Court, following its own *Gravier* reasoning, endorsed the Commission's view concerning the reading of Article 128 EEC. According to the Court, the task of implementing the common vocational training policy was based on the co-operation between Member States and the Community institutions and the Council

[17] See for this information Lenaerts, 'ERASMUS' (n 16) 115 and 116.

[18] Case 242/87 *Commission v Council* EU:C:1989:217.

[19] Lenaerts, 'ERASMUS' (n 16) 125.

[20] See also already B De Witte, 'The Scope of Community Powers' (n 1) 261. Concerning the further development towards a European policy of education, see also Van der Mei, *Free Movement* (n 13).

was thus entitled to adopt legal measures providing for Community action in the sphere of vocational training and imposing corresponding obligations of co-operation on the Member States.[21] After this judgment, the Commission did not hesitate to propose a wide range of measures in the field of education.[22]

The reactions following this judgment by academics and Member States differed fundamentally in tone. Some hoped for a further Europeanisation in the field of education including research, while others criticised these developments and were fearful of the increasing effect on national educational systems. In response to these declared concerns of some Member States, in 1989 the Commission stated in a Communication that it was not the objective of the Commission to harmonise the higher education sector.[23] Some Member States clearly feared that increasing student mobility would create high burdens to their national educational systems with enormous financial consequences. Student mobility and their financial support became increasingly an issue of discussion and litigation.[24]

The following introduction of two special articles[25] concerning education in the framework of the Maastricht Treaty on the European Union in 1992 has addressed some of these hopes and fears. Most importantly for the critics of these developments has without doubt been the explicit exclusion of any harmonisation of the laws and regulations of the Member States according to these articles. This prohibition of harmonisation can now be found in Articles 165(4) and 166(4) of the Treaty on the Functioning of the European Union (TFEU). A similar exclusion of harmonisation can be found in Article 167(5) TFEU with regard to the area of culture. This exclusion of harmonisation does not, however, affect other competences for the EU to act as formulated in the internal market provisions of the Treaty. The exclusion of harmonisation has, however, often created misunderstanding concerning the division of competences between the Member States and the EU. One of these misunderstandings concerns the recognition of qualifications for professional and for academic purposes. It is widely claimed that only professional recognition is covered by the internal market competences while academic recognition remains exclusively in the ambit of the Member States.[26] To support

[21] Case 242/87 *Commission v Council* EU:C:1989:217 para 11. See also H Gilliams, 'Van "Gravier" tot "Erasmus": Over de bijdrage van het Hof van Justitie tot de uitbouw van het Europees Onderwijsbeleid' (1989–1990) 53(15) *Jrg* 494; H Schneider, 'Kultur- und Bildungspolitik' in A Bleckmann, *Europarecht*, 5th edn (Carl Heymanns Verlag, 1990)

[22] See further De Witte, 'Higher Education' (n 1) 192.

[23] European Commission, Education and Training in the European Community, *Guidelines for the medium term: 1989–1992*, COM (89)236, 4.

[24] See for this aspect AP van der Mei, 'Freedom of Movement for Students: In Search of a More Satisfactory Balance between the Goal to Promote Student Mobility and the Need to Protect Education Systems' in H Schneider (ed), *Migration, Integration and Citizenship*, Vol I (Maastricht, 2005) Furthermore, and with a detailed analysis, A Hoogenboom, *Balancing Student Mobility Rights and National Higher Education Autonomy in the European Union* (Brill/Nijhoff, 2017).

[25] Originally Arts 126 (general education) and 127 (vocational training) EEC Treaty, later with the Treaty of Amsterdam re-numbered in Arts 149 and 150 EC, now Arts 165 and 166 TFEU.

[26] See further on this point, M Verbruggen, *Tussen Solidariteit en Harmonisatie: Een onderzoek naar de instrumenten voor het voeren van een Europees onderwijs* (PhD thesis, KU Leuven, 2001) 283 ff.

this view, reference is often made to Article 166(2) TFEU in which academic recognition of diplomas is mentioned and the prohibition of harmonisation in Article 166(4) TFEU. In practice it is, however, very difficult to make this distinction.

III. The Evolution of EU Law on Recognition of Diplomas

Since the 1960s, the European Community has been active in the field of diploma recognition. One of the main goals of the European Community from its very beginning was the creation of a common market for all economic activities. This includes the free movement of professionals. Therefore, national rules which have the effect of preventing persons from providing professional services or establishing themselves in another Member State have to be progressively abolished. Barriers to mobility, constituted by the requirement of a national diploma or language requirements, can constitute obstacles to completing the internal market as much as, for example, different safety standards for technical goods. The legal basis for acting in the field of diploma recognition was originally Article 57 EEC. Now, Article 53(1) TFEU provides that:

> In order to make it easier for persons to take up and pursue activities as self-employed persons, the European Parliament and the Council shall, acting in accordance with the ordinary legislative procedure, issue directives for the mutual recognition of diplomas, certificates and other evidence of formal qualifications and for the coordination of the provisions laid down by law, regulation or administrative action in Member States concerning the taking-up and pursuit of activities as self-employed persons.'

According to Article 53(2) TFEU, for the medical and pharmaceutical professions, the progressive abolition of restrictions shall be dependent upon coordination for their exercise in the various Member States.

As there has been no common educational system and the routes to professional and trade activities vary significantly between the Member States these differences can cause serious barriers to the free movement of persons.[27] This is still true, as even today, we can see mobility restrictions caused by certain, often very specific qualification requirements. The necessity for a functioning recognition system when creating an internal market for all forms of professions and trade is therefore rather obvious. As Gisella Gori has rightly stated:

> Beyond being the tool for personal development, education is also an instrument by which everyone is equipped to play an economic role in society. Accordingly, in order

[27] See further H Schneider and S Claessens, 'The Recognition of Diplomas and the Free Movement of Persons in the European Union' in H Schneider (ed), *Migration, Integration and Citizenship*, Vol I (Maastricht, 2005).

> for anyone to profit at European level from the education received, professional and academic recognition of qualifications becomes fundamental.[28]

During the years many such obstacles have been removed through the interpretation of European law by the European Court of Justice. In the 1970s and 1980s this was the case in particular where the restrictions were based on nationality or domicile restrictions. Additionally, harmonisation measures based on Article 57 EEC have been taken for certain professions in the field of trade and crafts, as well as selected professions in the health sector. Nevertheless, it has become obvious that the approach chosen by the Commission in that period was long and cumbersome.

When I met Bruno and discussed with him the possibilities of a PhD thesis in this area, the approach of the Commission towards the issue of diploma recognition had just entered into a new phase.[29] In the 1970s the harmonisation approach was very much sectoral, covering mainly health professions such as doctors, nurses, veterinary surgeons and pharmacists. For each selected profession two directives were negotiated and finally agreed upon in the Council: the Mutual Recognition Directive and the Co-ordination Directive. Experience has shown, however, that the process of drafting, agreeing upon and implementing sectoral directives was very long and laborious. In some cases, it took more than 18 years to finally pass the directives in the Council.[30] For other professions such as architects a co-ordination Directive could not be agreed upon, and for engineers the entire legislative process was stopped. The sectoral harmonisation method, was therefore abandoned by the Commission in light of the Court's *Cassis de Dijon* ruling and the Internal Market White Paper, published by the Commission in 1985.[31]

Instead of the sectoral or vertical approach, a new strategy without prior harmonisation for the mutual recognition of diplomas was introduced with Directive 89/48/EEC. Directive 89/48/EEC was thus a manifestation of the 'Europhoria' which followed the Single European Act and the prospect of the completion of an internal market by the end of 1992. The implementation of Directive 89/48/EEC in the Member States was supposed to be finalised by the beginning of 1991. This implementation was, however, no easy task as numerous professions had to be covered by the implementation measures. In some Member States this implementation had to take place not only on the national, federal level but also on the level of 'Länder' or communities, depending on the constitutional structure and legislative competences.[32] Bruno and I, together with Jacques Pertek, were asked

[28] G Gori, *Towards an EU Right to Education* (The Hague, Kluwer Law International, 2001) 235–36.
[29] See further for the developments during the past decades, I. Kortese, *The Recognition of Qualifications in the EU – Blurring the Lines of Competences between the Internal Market and Education* (PhD Thesis, Maastricht, 2020).
[30] H Schneider, *Die Anerkennung von Diplomen in der Europäischen Gemeinschaft* (Maklu, 1995) 99–160.
[31] European Commission, 'White Paper on Completion of the Internal Market', COM (85) 310.
[32] Schneider, *Die Anerkennung von Diplomen* (n 30).

by the Commission to prepare a report on the quality of implementation by the Member States. This proved to be an interesting and rewarding experience as the contact with the national co-ordinators as well as the members of the Commission gave specific insights to the research, which were otherwise very hard to get. It also provided us with various national case studies allowing us to test the quality of implementation and application in the Member States. We were able to prove that theory and practice did not align. Very often EU citizens relying on European law and their rights of free movement were the victims of incorrect or at least very restrictive interpretations by national authorities. This is still the case today, as Lavinia Kortese has recently shown in her research on the recognition of qualifications in the EU.[33]

IV. The Bologna Process and Current Developments

Today the various directives concerning the recognition of qualifications have been put together in one major legal instrument, namely Directive 2005/36/EC updated with Directive 2013/55/EU. The original intention of this operation was certainly to create more clarity as only one EU instrument would be relevant for the recognition of qualifications. In my opinion, the attempt has failed, however, as the instrument is too complicated to be understood and applied correctly by the national authorities. In addition, several other relevant developments have taken place inside and outside the EU framework since the millennium, which makes the full picture even more complicated and diffuse.[34] Sacha Garben has correctly stated that 'the area has become somewhat opaque, disorganised and at times ineffective'.[35] It can be shown that in many cases the distinction between academic and professional recognition of qualifications is not very helpful. It often adds to the confusion, misunderstanding and misapplication during the recognition process by the competent authorities in the Member States. For the mobile European citizens, it should be irrelevant for which purpose their qualifications are recognised, as long as they are recognised and transparent procedure rules are guaranteed. Very often the mobile European citizen is the victim of this lack of clarity, and consequently is faced either with a rejection of their qualification or confronted with often seemingly endless procedures.

The background of the confusion lays in the fact that too many different actors have become involved in the field during the last two decades. At the end of the 1990s, the Member States sought to take back control on the matter of education

[33] Kortese, *The Recognition of Qualifications* (n 29).
[34] Ibid ch 5, 291–369.
[35] S Garben, 'On Recognition of Qualifications for Academic and Professional Purposes' (2011) 16 *Tilburg Law Review* 127.

policies. Under the name of the 'Bologna Process' a development was initiated by the EU Member States (and beyond) in 1999. It all started with an international conference organised in connection with the celebration of the 800th anniversary of the Sorbonne University in 1998. During this meeting, the Ministers of Education of France, Germany, Italy and the United Kingdom decided to publish a 'Joint Declaration on Harmonisation of the Architecture of the European Higher Education System'. This declaration was open for the other Member States of the European Union as well as third countries to join. The Italian Minister of Education followed up this initiative with an invitation to Bologna for the following year. Following this invitation to Bologna in June 1999, originally 29 European States agreed on a Declaration that would finally and fundamentally change the structure of the national higher education systems far beyond the borders of the European Union.

This process took place, at least in the beginning, fully outside the European Union and initially without any involvement of the European Commission.[36] In this period, the negotiations concerning the Lisbon Convention on the Recognition of Qualifications concerning Higher Education in the European Region were finalised in the framework of the Council of Europe/UNESCO.[37] This additional international legal instrument dating from 1997, ratified by all Member States, has not improved the transparency and clarity in the field. Quite on the contrary, it has further contributed to the confusion. Furthermore, the procedural steps for the recognition of a certain qualification to be set on the basis of the Lisbon Recognition Convention are far from clear and often enormously time consuming.

Sacha Garben has correctly criticised this process as being very problematic in light of the existing competences of the EU to enact legislation in this field.[38] According to this reasoning, the Bologna process might have better been enacted in the legislative framework of the European Union. Today, a directive based on either the internal market competences (Articles 115 or 53 TFEU) or on Article 21(2) TFEU could have been considered. Whether such a Bologna Directive would have been politically feasible, is a different matter. It still remains to be seen whether failing to try to take back control on this matter was a missed opportunity for the Commission. Instead, the Commission has made enormous efforts to finally become involved in the Bologna process by participating as a full member

[36] For a critical analysis, see S Garben, *EU Higher Education Law: The Bologna Process and Harmonisation by Stealth* (Kluwer Law International, 2011), based on her PhD thesis defended at the EUI in 2009, with Bruno De Witte acting as one of her supervisors. See also S Garben, 'The Bologna Process: From a European Law Perspective' (2010) 16(2) *European Law Journal* 186. Furthermore, L Kortese, *The Recognition of Qualifications in the EU* (n 29) 59–82, elaborating on the follow-up developments concerning the Bologna Process.

[37] Council of Europe, Convention on the Recognition of Qualifications concerning Higher Education in the European Region, Lisbon 1997.

[38] Garben, 'On Recognition of Qualifications' (n 35); S Garben and H Schneider, 'Der Bologna Prozess: Aus der Perspektive des Europäischen Rechts betrachtet' in K Odendahl, *Europäische* (Bildungs) Union? (Berliner Wissenschafts-Verlag, 2011).

in the Bologna follow-up groups.[39] Whether this involvement has contributed to more clarity may still be questionable. In particular, the existence of numerous instruments and initiatives for recognition of qualifications originating from various actors and different organisations has created a confusing picture leading to questions concerning the application, interrelation, and hierarchy of all these instruments.[40] Unfortunately, it seems that the mobile EU citizens or students in need of recognition for professional purposes, as well as the national authorities trying to apply the various measures, are regularly lost in the regulatory jungle.

V. Concluding Remarks

I started this contribution with a discussion of the emergence of a common European education policy, the emerging European law of education, and the numerous judgments of the European Court of Justice concerning education and student mobility, most prominently the ERASMUS judgment. Bruno can certainly be called a pioneer in this field. Already during the first conference he organised at the EUI in 1987, major questions were addressed. The same can be said for the contributions at the conference concerning the common law of Europe and the future of legal education, organised in Maastricht in 1991.[41] These were events with a great vision for the future of legal and political developments in the area of education. Nobody present at these conferences, could have, however, predicted the important developments which have taken place since, including the fundamental restructuring of university education with the introduction of the bachelor–master structure due to the Bologna process. Not all legal and political developments taking place in the past decades were convincing, transparent and well-reasoned.

Yet, with his clear and analytical mind and profound knowledge, Bruno has been able to give guidance to the researchers in his team and far beyond. His contributions have given us valuable insights in European education law, as they have done in other areas of European law.

[39] On the difficult position of the European Commission, see Garben, *EU Higher Education Law* (n 36) 165 ff.

[40] See for a comprehensive analysis of the various instruments and initiatives, Kortese, *The Recognition of Qualifications in the EU* (n 29) chs 3 and 4.

[41] B De Witte and C Forder (eds), *The Common Law of Europe and the Future of Legal Education* (Kluwer 1992).

PART IV

Minorities Europe

8

Protection of Minorities in EU Law

IYIOLA SOLANKE

I. Introduction

Bruno De Witte has made a significant contribution to and exerted a strong influence on scholarship related to European Union law and European integration. A multi-lingual scholar, his works appear on reading lists around the world, meaning that his ideas have influenced generations of EU law scholars in many different places.

I had heard much about Bruno before I first met him in 2012 at a Council for European Studies (CES) conference in Barcelona. It was a superb location for a conference, very well organised and attended. Given the many good things that I had heard about him from his students, I was already pre-disposed to like him and it was therefore no surprise that we immediately got on well. I was pleasantly surprised to discover that our intellectual interests crossed in an area also close to my heart: legal protection from discrimination in the EU.

The variety of topics covered in this *Festschrift* illustrate the wide scope of Bruno's scholarship; however, like me, Bruno started his career with a doctorate on the question of minority rights. Our interests differed: while I focused on race, his particular concern was languages. His thesis was entitled *The Protection of Linguistic Diversity through Fundamental Rights*. Since defending this thesis, alongside his work on constitutional aspects of EU law, he has regularly written on the legal regulation of culture, media, education and language use, and especially the protection of minority languages. This aspect of his work is generally dedicated to engagement with law and policy to protect, promote and support minority languages in the EU.

His first publication was on linguistic diversity[1] and across the span of his long career he returned regularly to this topic, sometimes directly but then through the prism of social rights and most latterly in relation to the protection of human

[1] B De Witte, 'La pluralité ethnique et l'autonomie culturelle – étude comparative' in Y Mény (ed), *Centres et périphéries: le partage du pouvoir* (Economica, 1982).

rights.[2] It is clear that protection of minority languages remained a key concern driving all of his scholarship on EU law and the Court of Justice of the European Union (CJEU).

Bruno and I may have focused on different rights, but we share the opinion that formal equality is not enough and that positive action is a necessity. We differ in relation to the role of the EU in this area: while it is undeniable that the EEC was not created as a human rights organisation, I have more hope that it can play a positive role in the protection of minority rights.

In this short contribution, I will reflect upon this aspect of his work and how it dovetails with my own work on legal protection from racial discrimination and promotion of racial equality in the EU. I will discuss three themes: protection of minority rights in Europe; the legal basis for protection of minority rights and languages; and finally the role of the CJEU in providing that protection. In relation to the first, I will focus on Bruno's publications during the 10 years following his first publication and highlight the paradox in EU law that minority rights and racial rights are treated separately. In relation to the second, I will highlight the different fortunes of racial rights and minority rights in EU law and how Bruno brought them together. I will finally focus on Bruno's later interest in human rights, and particularly his scathing comments on Opinion 2/13 by the CJEU.

II. Equality, Minority Rights and Racial Rights

Bruno's first three publications are on linguistic equality.[3] In total, in the 10 years between 1982 and 1992, Bruno wrote seven articles on linguistic and cultural rights.[4] Two further publications[5] appeared before the first major 'break' from this topic, although it may be exaggerated to describe it as a break – it was perhaps more a practical response to the key debates in EU law which focused more on social and human rights.

[2] Co-editor of Š Imamović, M Claes and B De Witte (eds), 'The EU Fundamental Rights Landscape after Opinion 2/13' (2016) 3 *Maastricht Faculty of Law Working Paper*, 90.

[3] De Witte, 'La pluralité ethnique' (n 1); B De Witte and JU Clauss, 'Linguistic Minorities in Southern Italy: A Periphery far from the Border' in B De Marchi and AM Boileau (eds), *Boundaries and Minorities in Western Europe* (Franco Angeli Editore, 1982); B De Witte, 'Linguistic Equality: A Study in Comparative Constitutional Law' (1985) 6 *Llengua i Dret* 43, vlex.es/vid/lingustic-equality-study-comparative-216644461.

[4] B De Witte, 'Cultural Policy: The Complementarity of Negative and Positive Integration' in J Schwarze and H Schermers (eds), *Structure and Dimensions of European Community Policy* (Nomos, 1988); B De Witte, 'Cultural Policy Limits to Fundamental Rights' in A Kaufmann et al (eds), *Rechtsstaat und Menschenwürde – Festschrift für Werner Maihofer zum 70* (Klostermann, 1989); B De Witte, 'The Position of Linguistic Minorities in Italy (1973–1988)' in (1990) *Plural Societies XXI* 51; B De Witte, 'The Impact of European Community Rules on Linguistic Policies of the Member States' in F Coulmas (ed), *A Language Policy for the European Community – Prospects and Quandaries* (Mouton de Gruyter, 1991); B De Witte, 'Surviving in Babel? Language Rights and European Integration' in Y Dinstein and M Tabory (eds), *The Protection of Minorities and Human Rights* (Martinus Nijhoff, 1992).

[5] B De Witte, 'The European Community and its Minorities' in C Brölmann, R Lefeber and M Zieck (eds), *Peoples and Minorities in International Law* (Martinus Nijhoff, 1993); B De Witte, 'The Cultural

His approach to equality can be found in his article on linguistic equality (1985). In it, Bruno set out with characteristic clarity his view that the idea of equality is empty:

> Moreover, the meaning of equality is also exceedingly vague. Even when one applies the Aristotelian formula to a specific context, one merely sets the terms of the debate into sharper relief, but without beginning to give an answer. The answer is provided by a substantive value judgment, laying outside the equality formula …[6]

This is a perspective that he expresses again in later works.[7] In this article, however, he drew a distinction between 'schematic' equality – bland and general statements of equality as set out in constitutions (eg Article 3 of the German Basic Law, Article 3 of the Italian Constitution, article 5 of the Greek Constitution) – and a 'principle of equality'. The former, he argued were 'superficial' and therefore potentially useless when seeking to ensure that people do not suffer discrimination due to the language that they speak. These constitutional statements were described as a 'generic protection which treats the speakers of a minority language as abstract citizens, without acknowledging their cultural identity' and would in fact lead to domination and assimilation:

> Indeed, the absence of distinctions, the application of one-and-the-same rule to everyone is precisely the favourite instrument of linguistic domination and assimilation: everyone in the same school classes, for everyone the same radio and television programmes, for everyone the same administrative forms, irrespective of their mother tongue.[8]

In contrast to this Aristotelian concept, substantive equality was, however, worthwhile and he argued that this could 'play an extremely important role in the protection of linguistic diversity' as '"real" equality, in certain circumstances, allows for differentiations, or even requires some distinctive treatment'.

Protection of minority languages was the first topic that Bruno mentioned to me when we met. Ironically, this was a theme that I had never considered: given my focus on racial discrimination, it could be argued that this topic was equally relevant to Black[9] people in Europe belonging to minority groups linked to those

Dimension of Community Law' in Academy of European Law (ed), *Collected Courses of the Academy of European Law*, Vol I (1995).

[6] De Witte, 'Linguistic Equality' (n 3).

[7] B De Witte, 'National Equality Institutions and the Domestication of EU Non-Discrimination Law' (2011) 18(1–2) *Maastricht Journal of European Comparative Law* 157.

[8] See vlex.es/vid/lingustic-equality-study-comparative-216644461.

[9] I use Black as 'a political term with its origins in the anti-racist and civil rights movements. Whilst originally referring to people of African and Caribbean descent, the word has come to encompass both Asian and Arab people, seeing commonalities in their shared oppression.' It is used to 'a) empower these communities, less as 'ethnic minorities' but as global majorities and b) foster a sense of solidarity in the common struggles Black people face. When a person says that they are politically black, they identify themselves with these empowering sentiments rather than just a race.' Throughout this article 'the term Black is used in a political sense and will encompass those of African, Caribbean, Asian and Arab descent'. See blackfemaleprofessorsforum.org.

countries in Africa, Asia and the Caribbean colonised by European states. So why had I never thought about this?

It could be argued that this is unsurprising, coming as I do from a predominantly mono-linguistic culture where all languages beyond English are paid scant attention. However, the answer is more interesting: in EU parlance and scholarship, 'minority languages' refers only to those languages spoken in Europe by persons belonging to minority groups such as Welsh, Catalan or Basque.

Paradoxically, our concerns for equality crossed but our demographics diverged. Nonetheless, as was often the case with Bruno, we found a place of consensus. Neither of us were impressed with the EU action on this matter – albeit clearly for different reasons, I could agree with Bruno when he said that the focus in EU programmes on minority languages was too narrow:

> (…) the special priority given to the 'less widely used and less taught languages' does not refer to regional and minority languages (such as Catalan, Basque, and Welsh). This is odd, because improved knowledge of these languages seems equally able to 'lead to greater understanding among the peoples of the European Union,' which is the declared underlying aim of Lingua. There is an obvious double standard here, which contradicts the modest EU funding for minority language projects.[10]

Beyond this, the Eurocentric focus excludes those minority languages used in communities of Black Europeans across the EU, such as Patois, Urdu or Yoruba.

Bruno identified the key issue: the 'troublesome question' he wrote, is how to 'define the groups that are worthy of such special protection'.[11] Here again, we landed on consensus: for us both, there needs to be a rational social, rather than legal, basis for this. His two key arguments to justify action – in particular 'affirmative' or 'positive' action – in favour of linguistic groups include the fact that they are cultural minorities (eg a numerical minority within the country; if this is applied, it would then also include languages spoken by racialised minorities) and the fact that they are political-economic minorities (a criterion which if applied would also incorporate racialised minorities in Europe).

These ideas tally with my own, as discussed in my book on stigma and anti-discrimination law.[12] Furthermore, we agreed in our support for positive action. As he wrote:

> (…) the advantage for one group is not always symmetrical with the burden on the other (…) In other words, affirmative measures do not destroy equality, but aim precisely at establishing a more perfect equality of opportunities.[13]

[10] B De Witte, 'The Constitutional Resources for an EU Minority Protection Policy' in GN Toggenburg (ed), *Minority Protection and the Enlarged European Union: The Way Forward* (OSI, 2004) 120.

[11] De Witte, 'Linguistic Equality' (n 3).

[12] I Solanke, *Discrimination as Stigma: A Theory of Anti-discrimination Law* (Hart Publishing, 2017).

[13] B De Witte, 'From a "Common Principle of Equality" to "European Antidiscrimination Law"' (2010) 53(12) *American Behavioral Scientist* 1720.

III. Treaty Competence for Minority Rights and Racial Rights

Beyond minority languages in particular, racial rights and minority rights have fared differently in EU law. Curiously, in EU law and in scholarship on EU law, there is no overlap between minority rights and racial rights, even though the groups requiring protection under anti-racial discrimination law are *per se* minority groups. As with minority languages, minority rights in the EU are taken to refer to, for example, Russians in Germany or Portuguese in Sweden. Black Europeans – Turks in Germany, Senegalese in France, or the Surinamese in the Netherlands – are more likely to be categorised as third country nationals than minority groups.

In relation to competences in EU law, for a long time neither racial rights nor minority rights were mentioned in the Treaty – both shared the status of not being explicitly mentioned in any of the EU legal texts. As Bruno wrote:

> (…) the words 'minority' and 'minority protection' do not appear anywhere in the EU and EC Treaties. They are neither mentioned as being part of the values recognised by the European Union nor are they listed among the policy competences of the EU.

The same applied to racial rights prior to 1997 – there was no mention of protection from racial discrimination or promotion of racial equality until an amendment was made to the Treaty establishing the European Community (TEC) at Amsterdam. A new provision was inserted into the Treaty which gave the EU competence to tackle racial discrimination:

> Without prejudice to the other provisions of the Treaties and within the limits of the powers conferred by them upon the Union, the Council, acting unanimously in accordance with a special legislative procedure and after obtaining the consent of the European Parliament, may take appropriate action to combat discrimination based on sex, racial or ethnic origin, religion or belief, disability, age or sexual orientation.

As can be seen, this did not mention minority rights or minority languages, and it therefore did not provide a constitutional basis for action to protect such rights. The same applied to the Race Directive adopted in 2000 – whilst it protects the rights of racialised minorities, it does not extend to cover minorities per se.[14]

Bruno saw a chance to bridge this schism in EU scholarship. He argued that even if the authors of the Race Directive

> [m]ay have been aiming primarily at the protection of groups such as African immigrants and their descendants, the general wording used in the directive also provides protection against invidious discrimination for Roma or Basques living in France.[15]

[14] Council Directive 2000/43/EC of 29 June 2000 implementing the principle of equal treatment between persons irrespective of racial or ethnic origin [2000] OJ L 180/22.

[15] De Witte, 'The Constitutional Resources' (n 10) 107–24.

He went on to suggest that it might in fact 'become the most efficient minority protection tool in the EU for the years to come'.[16] This potential in the Race Directive remains as yet unexplored but Bruno's search for a Treaty competence did not end with this Directive.

There was in fact secondary harmonising law which pre-dated the Race Directive, such as a Directive of 1977 on the language of education of migrant children, introduced to facilitate free movement of workers, persons, goods or services.[17] It imposed a duty on Member States to ensure language education for children of EU migrants in order to facilitate these EU citizens' integration into their country of residence. However, this had not been implemented effectively:

> The implementation of this directive has been quite erratic, and the control of its implementation by the European Commission very feeble – partly due to the 'soft' language used in its substantive provisions.[18]

Bruno identified other potential sources in the EU Treaties upon which to build a minority protection policy. For example following on from the European Ministers of Culture declaration in Thessaloniki in May 2003, he promoted action in international law, under the aegis of UNESCO, to create a multilateral convention on the protection and promotion of cultural diversity, building upon work done by the Council of Europe and the International Network of Cultural Policy.[19] The EU Charter of Rights and Freedoms (CFR) was also highlighted: unlike Article 19 of the Treaty on European Union (TEU), Article 21 CFR lists membership of a national minority as a prohibited ground for discrimination, despite not promoting concrete or positive minority rights.[20]

IV. The Role of Law, Human Rights and the European Courts

In 2004, on the cusp of the largest single EU enlargement to date, Bruno wrote about 'EU language law' and the need to protect linguistic diversity in the face of a common currency and economic harmonisation.[21] The article reviewed in a critical way the manifestation of linguistic diversity in the European Treaties, the EU Charter of Rights and Freedoms, the Council, the Commission and even in the Parliament.

[16] Ibid.
[17] Ibid.
[18] Ibid.
[19] Ibid.
[20] Ibid.
[21] B De Witte, 'Language Law of the European Union: Protecting or Eroding Linguistic Diversity?' in R Craufurd Smith (ed), *Culture and European Law* (Oxford University Press, 2004).

By 2008, he was focusing more directly on the new legal regime for the protection of human rights in EU law, and the extent to which it protected linguistic diversity.[22] In one article he argued that while Article 22 CFR acknowledges the value of linguistic diversity, other Charter provisions could also be useful, in particular Article 21 CFR, which prohibits discrimination on a number of grounds, including language. By this stage, he was therefore moving from the discourse of cultural diversity to anti-discrimination and returning to the sphere of human rights first broached during his PhD.

It is possible to identify some doubt in the role of the EU as a protector of human rights. In 2004, he wrote:

> The European Community was not created as a human rights organisation, and concern for the protection of human rights only gradually appeared on the agenda of the European Union, developing in a rather piecemeal fashion.[23]

One need not look far to see that Bruno was in general sceptical of the role of courts in protecting minority languages. His assessment was very clearly that the impact of the CJEU and the European Court of Human Rights was very limited when compared with 'softer mechanisms' such as the Framework Convention on National Minorities and the Charter on Regional and Minority Languages of the Council of Europe.[24]

This scepticism spilled over in 2014, when he penned, together with Sejla Imamovic, a scathing review of the CJEU's negative opinion on the draft agreement for accession of the EU to the European Convention on Human Rights (ECHR):[25]

> In Opinion 2/13 the CJEU declared that the draft Agreement for Accession of the EU to the ECHR is not compatible with primary EU law, based on a number of objections. This article presents the Opinion and divides the Court's objections in three categories: concerns which are misconceived and should not have been raised by the CJEU at all; concerns for the CJEU's own jurisdiction which are more persuasive, but whose importance is exaggerated by the Court and concerns to preserve a different standard of fundamental rights protection in EU law derogating from the minimum standard of the Convention – a radical (and unjustified) objection, which cannot be mended by simply modifying the Accession Agreement and which makes accession next to impossible.

[22] B De Witte, 'The Protection of Linguistic Diversity through Provisions of the EU Charter other than Article 22' in X Arzoz (ed), *Respecting Linguistic Diversity in the European Union* (John Benjamins, 2008).

[23] De Witte, 'The Constitutional Resources' (n 10) 107–24.

[24] B De Witte, 'Linguistic Minorities in Western Europe: Expansion of Rights Without (Much) Litigation?' in D Anagnostou (ed), *Rights and Courts in Pursuit of Social Change. Legal Mobilisation in the Multi-Level European System* (Hart Publishing, 2014).

[25] B De Witte and Š Imamović, 'Opinion 2/13 on Accession to the ECHR: Defending the EU Legal Order against a Foreign Human Rights Court' (2015) 40 *European Law Review* 683. See also S Imamovic, M Claes and B De Witte (eds), 'The EU Fundamental Rights Landscape after Opinion 2/13' (2015) 40(5) *European Law Review* 683.

V. Conclusion

While during his academic career Bruno's intellectual journey took him into other areas, he ultimately retained a passion for the legal protection of minority languages. The question is why he felt a need to move away from this topic in the first place?

It could be argued that this is usual in an academic career, where a scholar pursues research questions as they arise. Alternatively, it could be argued that Bruno made a pragmatic choice – the lack of traction in this policy area would have led his scholarship to irrelevance and his career to an early demise. Survival required adaption. In his career we therefore see an example of the strategic academic, who builds a dual track balancing on the one hand intellectual passion with institutional pragmatism on the other. I would suggest that, while EU law and policy on areas beyond gender and disability discrimination remain marginalised in the academy, junior scholars would do well to learn from this model.

Bruno's work goes a long way to bridging the schism in the European intellectual imagination where the discourse and policy on minority rights and cultural diversity remains apart from the debate and policy evolution on racial equality. For the most part, there was no conception of equality in cultural diversity; nor a focus on culture in racial diversity. Although this linkage is now taken for granted, it did not exist during the genesis of the Race Equality Directive. In fact, the policy goals were quite distinct: cultural diversity prioritised pluralism, while racial equality promoted integration and non-discrimination. Bruno is one of the few authors who has considered the two together.

It is hard to escape the fact that his years of studying EU law and policy have left him sceptical of the role of law and the courts in protecting minority languages and promoting linguistic equality. This must be addressed: ongoing expansion, for example to the new applicant countries, will inevitably bring more minorities and more minority languages into the EU. As there is a language component to the right to good administration set out in Article 49 CFR, the EU needs to address this if it is not to fall foul of this right.

9

Minorities in the European Court of Human Rights

(Or How the 'Sleeping Beauty' Was Awakened to their Cultural and Political Assertiveness)

DIA ANAGNOSTOU

I. Introduction

The study of historical minorities and their mobilisation was the occasion that brought me into contact with Bruno De Witte some 20 years ago at the European University Institute (EUI). As a young post-doctoral fellow at the Robert Schuman Centre, I remember being nervous having to present at a seminar a paper on a small Turkish-speaking and Muslim minority in the Western Thrace (northeast of Greece) in front of an interdisciplinary audience of scholars of EU law, politics and institutions. As assigned discussant of my presentation, Bruno provided rich comments that reflected his keen interest in minorities and passionately laid out the challenges that ethnic pluralism and minority rights posed to EU Member States. By elevating a relatively little known case of regional minority assertiveness into a central matter of European integration, his remarks helped spark a lively and constructive discussion pushing my research in new directions.

My encounter with Bruno in that seminar was the beginning of a longstanding relationship involving research collaboration, cross-disciplinary mentorship and precious friendship. Our exchanges were critical in pushing me to cross over the boundaries of political science, in which I was trained, and venture into the terrain of international and European human rights law. The cross-fertilisation of my comparative politics training with human rights law, with Bruno's mentorship and collaboration, developed into a project on minority litigation in the European Court of Human Rights ('ECtHR' or 'the Strasbourg Court'), from which this chapter draws.

This chapter focuses on the period of the 1980s and early 1990s, which was a critical turning point in the ECtHR's engagement with the concerns and claims of ethnic and cultural minorities. It is well known that in the 1970s the ECtHR adopted a more activist approach, especially with respect to rights claims involving social values and mores, in which a common European consensus appeared to exist.[1] The view of the European Convention on Human Rights ('ECHR' or 'the Convention') as a 'living instrument'[2] to be interpreted in the light of societal changes, the principle of 'autonomous interpretation' from the national legal and constitutional traditions,[3] and the 'effective and practical protection' of European human rights,[4] were all enunciated in the course of that decade. This new and dynamic approach signalled the transformation of the Convention from a system founded upon intergovernmental diplomacy into a legalised rights review system.[5]

The ECtHR's assertion of its authority, however, did not initially extend to cases raising claims related to minorities and ethnic-cultural diversity. Up until the 1980s, the ECtHR and the European Commission of Human Rights (ECommHR) were reluctant to scrutinise how national governments dealt with minorities, concerned not to undermine the fledgling state support that the Court enjoyed in the first decades of its existence. Their hesitancy to review claims related to ethnic-cultural diversity began to change in the 1980s and early 1990s. It did so in response to an emerging wave of human rights litigation that originated from individuals belonging to politicised and marginalised ethnic-cultural groups. Rising litigation in this area, this chapter argues, was part and parcel of the internationalisation of mobilisation strategies for minority rights and recognition and an incipient trend of legal activism, in a context of flourishing international activities in this area. In a series of milestone decisions and judgments, the Court established its approach to claims related to the cultural identity and public participation of minorities. It paved the way for many more minority-related complaints over the next decades.

II. Minority Claims in the Early Years of the Strasbourg Court

Until the 1980s, a relatively small number of petitions were lodged by individuals from ethnic, cultural and linguistic minorities in West European countries such as Belgium, Austria, Switzerland, the United Kingdom and a few others. Only a

[1] See for instance the landmark judgment of *Sunday Times v the United Kingdom* App no 6538/74 (ECtHR, 26 April 1979).

[2] *Tyrer v UK* App no 5856/72 (ECtHR, 25 April 1978).

[3] *Engel and others v the Netherlands* App no 5100/71 (ECtHR, 8 June 1976).

[4] *Marckx v Belgium* App no 6833/74 (ECtHR, 13 June 1979).

[5] MR Madsen, 'The Protracted Institutionalization of the Strasbourg Court: From Legal Diplomacy to Integrationist Jurisprudence' in J Christoffersen and M Rask Madsen (eds), *The ECtHR between Law and Politics* (Oxford University Press, 2011).

few petitions were deemed admissible by the Commission, and less than a handful were referred to the Court for a judgment. They concerned minority culture and language, discrimination in the enjoyment of rights such as education,[6] political representation,[7] and access to justice.[8] In the early years of the Court's existence, the first petitions were linked to the language conflict between the French-speaking and the Flemish-speaking communities in Belgium.[9] They were not complaints of an individual nature but principally aimed to challenge established legal and constitutional arrangements. Aggrieved and politicised minority groups among the French-speakers petitioned the ECtHR to contest national legislation that had divided Belgium into four linguistic regions – Dutch, French and German regions and the Brussels conurbation – with each given permanent boundaries, which could not be subject to subsequent change due to demographic shifts. Legislation had also provided for the exclusive use of Dutch, French and German in the public sector in the respective regions.[10]

In the landmark *Belgian Linguistics* case – the only one that was referred to the Court for a judgment – French speakers, who were a minority in the Flemish area, claimed that education legislation discriminated against them, as they could not receive instruction in their mother tongue.[11] In a sharply divided 1968 judgment, the ECtHR opined that the right to education implied the right to be educated in the national language, but it did not require that the parents' linguistic preferences be respected. While it found that Belgium violated the right to education and the prohibition of discrimination, the judgment was 'soft' on the government: it pronounced a breach in respect to only one of the four educational acts challenged by the applicants, and only for certain French-speaking children.[12] The landmark *Belgian Linguistics* cases starkly revealed how heavily politics weighed upon the Commission and the Court, and how apprehensive states were about an international court with jurisdiction to review alleged violations over such sensitive matters as minority rights. The Belgian government had opposed the referral of the case to the Court, and it protested the judgment issued against it and threatened to withdraw its acceptance of the right to individual petition.[13]

[6] *Inhabitants of Les Fourons v Belgium* App no 2209/64 (ECommHR, 30 March 1971).

[7] *Rassemblement jurassien and Unité jurassienne v Switzerland* App no 8191/78 (ECommHR, 10 October 1979).

[8] *Isop v Austria* App no 808/60 (ECommHR, 8 March 1962).

[9] *Roger Vanden Berghe v Belgium* App no 2924/66 (ECommHR, 16 December 1968); *Un Groupe d'Habitants de Leeuw-St. Pierre v Belgium* App no 2333/64 (ECommHR, 16 December 1968).

[10] C McCrudden and B O'Leary, *Courts and Consociations: Human Rights versus Power-Sharing* (Oxford University Press, 2013) 49–50.

[11] *Case 'Relating to Certain Aspects of the Laws on the Use of Languages in Education in Belgium' v Belgium* App no 1474/62, 1677/62, 1691/62, 1769/63, 1994/63, 2126/64 (ECtHR, 23 July 1968). The applicants petitioned on behalf of their children and they were inhabitants of Alsemberg, Beersel, Antwerp, Ghent, Louvain, and Vilvorde, in the Dutch-speaking region.

[12] E Bates, *The Evolution of the ECHR* (Oxford University Press, 2010) 237–38.

[13] Ibid 185.

Minority-related complaints in the ECHR bodies mostly involved individuals from highly mobilised minorities, who were themselves involved in local, regional or national politics. They pursued ECHR litigation as an alternative and complementary to conventional national-level politics and strategies of action. Applicants were represented before the Strasbourg Court by prominent lawyers with expertise in international law. In the *Belgian Linguistics* case, for instance, counsel was Paul Guggenheim, a prominent Swiss scholar of international law and formerly a judge of an international court. Another case, the *Inhabitants of Les Fourons*, was brought by the Regional Association for the Defence of Liberties on behalf of 165 heads of families from an area to the northeast of Liege. They were represented by Léon Defosset, a lawyer with leftist leanings, who was committed to the Francophone and the federalist cause, and who would later get elected to the Belgian Senate and become a president of the Walloon party FDF. In this case too, the ECommHR declined to recognise a positive duty for the Belgian government 'to establish or subsidise a particular system of education' or education in a minority language different from the language spoken by the majority in that region and deferred to state governments.[14]

Generally, the ECommHR and the ECtHR maintained an approach which was highly deferential to national governments in the minority-related cases that they reviewed in the 1960s and until the 1980s. They rejected claims to any form of territorial autonomy and conceded a wide margin of appreciation for states in deciding what regional power-sharing structures or electoral system to establish. They also accepted the differential treatment of linguistic groups as legitimate in the context of consociational schemes aimed at achieving inter-communal balance and political stability.[15] In the late 1970s, the ECommHR rejected claims for rights violations by Jura autonomists, whose political meetings were banned for two days in 1977 in order to diffuse inter-communal conflict in the Canton of Berne. The Commission justified its decision on the grounds that the margin of appreciation that national authorities have 'is fairly broad once the authority is confronted with a foreseeable danger affecting public safety and order and must decide, often at short notice, what means to employ to prevent it'.[16] The ECHR bodies also conceded that national authorities had far-reaching discretion in justifying differences in the treatment of ethnic or religious minorities. In a case concerning the Slovene minority in the Austrian region of Carinthia, the ECommHR did not find discrimination in the refusal of state authorities to license a private radio station and to provide programmes in Slovene in public broadcasting.[17]

[14] In the *Inhabitants of Les Fourons v Belgium*, the ECommHR referred the case to the Council of Europe Committee of Ministers, which was composed of State delegates. By 1974, the Committee considered that the matter had been resolved following constitutional changes, and legislative changes that provided for subsidies to French-speaking schools in that area. See Committee of Ministers resolution in the *Inhabitants of Les Fourons v Belgium*, App no 2209/64, 30 March 1974.

[15] McCrudden and O'Leary, *Courts and Consociations* (n 10) 63–64.

[16] *Rassemblement jurassien and the Unité jurassienne v Switzerland* App no 8191/78 (ECommHR, 10 October 1979).

[17] *Informationsverein Lentia v Austria* App no 15717/89 (ECtHR, 24 November 1993).

In adopting a strongly deferential stance vis-à-vis state governments, the responses of the Court and the Commission were unreceptive to minority claims and discouraged systematic litigation.[18] In several cases, the minority-related petitions of the 1970s and 1980s were expressions of general political discontent that did not resonate with the individual frame of rights and the logic of the Convention. For instance, disgruntled Sudeten Germans, who saw their hopes for returning to and reclaiming their property in Czechoslovakia fade away with the 1973 Treaty signed between Czechoslovakia and the Federal Republic of Germany, lodged complaints in Strasbourg.[19] So did individuals and ethnic groups who were resentful about the process of Suriname's independence from the Netherlands, which allegedly passed the island not to its original Indian inhabitants but to others who had settled it under the Dutch colonial era.[20] Petitioners were not acquainted with the Convention, the nature and scope of the rights that it guaranteed, and how they were applied to provide protection. The little developed and largely unknown case law at the time prevented the Strasbourg Court from communicating with clarity how human rights are to be approached by litigants in framing their claims.

III. The Turning Point of the 1980s and Early 1990s

In the 1980s and in the first half of the 1990s, a slowly rising trend of proactive human rights litigation related to historical minorities emerged in the Strasbourg Court. Individuals from ethnic-cultural minorities and indigenous peoples in West Europe – France, Sweden, Belgium, Norway, the Netherlands and Finland – but also from politicised ethnic-religious minorities in Central East, Southeast Europe (CESE), like Greece, Spain and Turkey, brought several petitions to the ECHR bodies. Individuals from historical ethnic and linguistic minorities, minority nations and indigenous peoples, such as the Slovenes in Austria, the French-speakers in Belgium, Saami in Sweden and Finland,[21] Lapps in Norway,[22] Frisian speakers in the Netherlands,[23] Basques in Spain[24] and Bretons in France[25] brought claims to the ECHR bodies to express their

[18] B De Witte, 'Linguistic Minorities in Western Europe: Expansion of Rights Without (Much) Litigation?' in D Anagnostou (ed), *Rights and Courts in Pursuit of Social Change* (Hart Publishing, 2014).

[19] *X v Germany* App no 6742/74 (ECommHR, 10 July 1975).

[20] *X v Netherlands* App no 7230/75 (ECommHR, 4 October 1976).

[21] *Konkama and 38 Other Saami villages v Sweden* App no 27033/95(ECtHR, 25 November 1996); *Muonio Saami Village v Sweden* App no 28222/95 (ECtHR, 9 January 2001); *Johtti Sapmelaccatry and Others v Finland* App no 42969/98 (ECtHR, 18 January 2005).

[22] *G and E v Norway* App no 9278/81 and 9415/81 (ECommHR, 3 October 1983).

[23] *Fryske Nasjonale Partij v Netherlands* App no 11100/84 (ECommHR, 12 December 1985).

[24] *Castells v Spain* App no 11798/85 (ECtHR, 23 April 1992); *Herri Batasuna and Batasuna v Spain* App no 25803/04 and 25817/04 (ECtHR, 30 June 2009).

[25] *Bideault v France* App no 11261/84 (ECommHR, 1 October 1986).

grievances and advance minority-related demands vis-à-vis states. They claimed breaches related to state actions and decisions that interfered with the traditional activities and territorially based rights of indigenous people, such as rights relating to fishing and hunting, or interfered with the political participation and public expression of minorities, among other issues.

The rising trend of minority-related ECHR litigation in the 1980s to 1990s cannot be understood independently from the broader international milieu characterised by flourishing standard-setting activities and normative advancements regarding minorities. Minority protection was increasingly seen as central to the human dimension of security and a matter of international concern.[26] A milestone declaration adopted at the 1990 Copenhagen Meeting of the Organization for Security and Co-operation in Europe (OSCE) (it was CSEC – Conference on Security and Cooperation at that time) dedicated a whole chapter on the protection of minorities, including a specific reference to the 'particular problems of Roma/Gypsies' (para 40).[27] The end of the Cold War in 1989, and the disintegration of state socialist regimes in Central-East Europe, the Soviet Union and the Balkans, gave a strong impetus to these international developments around minority rights. The break-up of the former Soviet republics and of Yugoslavia in 1989–90 alerted the international community to the dangers of assimilationist and exclusionist policies against national minorities distinguished by language, religion, culture or ethnic origin.[28] European and international organisations, including the Council of Europe (CoE) were searching for ways to respond to claims raised by minorities but without endorsing any notion of collective rights that was strongly resisted by state governments.

In this international milieu, standard-setting and normative advances forged a close interconnection between human rights and the protection of minorities. As early as the 1960s, the question had been raised whether the ECHR should embrace minority rights and extend the application of its provisions to the protection of minorities.[29] The Parliamentary Assembly (PACE) and the Committee of Ministers (CoM) of the CoE had rejected proposals for an additional protocol

[26] P Thornberry and MA Martin Estebanez, *Minority Rights in Europe – A Review of the Work and Standards of the Council of Europe* (Council of Europe Publishing, 2004) 17.

[27] It established a general obligation of states to create conditions for the promotion of the identity of national minorities, and outlined a series of rights of minorities, such as to use their mother tongue, to profess and practise their religion freely, and to participate effectively in public affairs, among others. It also highlighted the importance of a democratic framework for the protection of minorities and its impact on peace and stability. See C Neukirch, K Simhandl and W Zellner, 'Implementing Minority Rights in the Framework of the CSCE/OSCE' in *Mechanisms for the Implementation of Minority Rights Standards* (Council of Europe Publishing, 2005) 160.

[28] Thornberry and Martin Estebanez, *Minority Rights in Europe* (n 26) 9–10.

[29] For the history of proposals, see P Thornberry, *International Law and the Rights of Minorities* (Clarendon Press, 1993) 304–06; C Hillgruber and M Jestaedt, *The ECHR and the Protection of National Minorities* (Verlag Wissenschaft und Politik, 1994) 13–21; A Spiliopoulou-Akermark, *Justifications of Minority Protection in International Law* (Iustus Forlag, 1997) ch 8.

to the ECHR, arguing that positive obligations for states to protect minorities must be ruled out.[30] The new proposal in the 1993 Vienna Summit to adopt an additional protocol to the ECHR on minority protection was again withdrawn due to lack of consensus among states. Instead, the CoE adopted in 1994 the Framework Convention for the Protection of National Minorities ('the Framework Convention'). The Framework Convention was the first multilateral instrument in this area and reflected the normative developments that had taken place in the preceding years.[31] The Framework Convention maintained the individual human rights frame but also acknowledged the need to safeguard the associative dimension of cultural-religious rights of minorities.[32] Despite its legally non-binding nature, it placed the protection of minorities firmly in the regime of international human rights law.

The international attention and normative advancements related to minority protection expanded opportunities and prompted minorities to invoke human rights and to mobilise before international and legal institutions, including in the ECHR system. The Court's increasing engagement with and developing approach to minority-related claims critically contributed to forging a close interlinking between human rights and minority protection. In the 1980s and early 1990s, in countries like Sweden and Norway, prominent jurists, such as Thomas Cramer, former Swedish Ombudsman, supported aboriginal rights litigation (before Norwegian and Swedish courts, and the ECHR) that became a central component of the political strategy of Sweden's Saami organisations.[33] In other cases, Norwegian Lapps voiced before the ECHR bodies a generalised grievance against the failure of Norway to recognise their language and culture, which involved historical rights to land use, reindeer breeding, hunting and fishing. In another string of petitions, French-speakers in Belgium, and Frisians aspiring for some form of local or regional autonomy in the province of Friesland (north of the Netherlands) claimed the right to use minority language in the electoral process.

The ECHR bodies consistently rejected claims to recognise the collective and cultural rights of minorities. They interpreted the Convention as not guaranteeing rights such as the use of minority language in the election process, forms of

[30] Thornberry and Martin Estebanez, *Minority rights in Europe* (n 26) 40–41; Thornberry, *International Law* (n 29) 306.

[31] Other soft-law instruments adopted within the CoE are the European Charter for Regional or Minority Languages, a Treaty specifically dealing with the historical, regional and minority languages of Europe.

[32] The FCPNM affirmed that the 'protection of a national minority can be achieved through protection of the rights of *individuals belonging to* such a minority' who 'may exercise their rights individually and in community with others' (emphasis added). See *Framework Convention for the Protection of National Minorities*, paras 31 and 37. See also F Benoît-Rohmer, *The Minority Question in Europe – texts and commentary* (Council of Europe publishing, 1996).

[33] See F Cassidy (ed), *Aboriginal Title in British Columbia: Delgamuukw v The Queen – Proceedings of a conference held September 1991* (Lantzville, BC, Oolichan Books, 1992) 273–74. Cramer represented the applicants in the case of *Östergren and Others v Sweden* App no 13572/88 (ECommHR, 1 March 1991).

territorial autonomy, or special electoral arrangements. In other cases, claims to lead a distinct way of life[34] and claims to use minority language in court as an expression of one's cultural identity,[35] were rejected at the admissibility stage. Minority claims to preserve a culturally distinct way of life when it conflicted with other public priorities or government decisions, also did not find sympathy with the ECHR bodies. In its decision in *G and E v Norway* in 1983, the Commission argued that restrictions imposed upon hunting and reindeering in areas populated by Saami, did not infringe their customary rights, which they could still enjoy in other areas. It affirmed that the Convention guarantees certain rights to everyone, but it does not recognise specific rights for minorities. While the construction of a hydroelectric dam admittedly interfered with the right to private and family life (Article 8 ECHR), the ECommHR saw it as necessary in a democratic society in the interests of the economic well-being of the country.[36]

At the same time though, the Court and the Commission, amidst significant internal dissent, began to acknowledge that certain Convention provisions were applicable and relevant to the concerns voiced by minorities. Even as it declined to extend protection to Saami customary rights when these conflicted with economic development, the ECommHR conceded that 'a minority's lifestyle may, in principle, fall under the protection of private life, family life, or home'.[37] By framing the protection of a distinct culture and way of life as a right to private and family life (Article 8 ECHR), the Commission's response to *G and E v Norway* presaged a new and potentially more receptive approach. It opened possibilities for framing claims to protect minority views and cultures as human rights and provided a basis for substantial litigation in the coming years.

Individuals belonging to minorities started to invoke Articles 8–11 ECHR – right to private and family life, religious freedom, freedom of expression and association – at times in conjunction with the non-discrimination principle (Article 14 ECHR), to claim protection of their political views, religious beliefs or cultural identity. The Commission and the Court reviewed the respective claims by applying the well-known balancing and proportionality review. They examined whether state-imposed limits on the exercise of these rights were justified in a democratic society by the need to preserve national security and territorial integrity, to prevent disorder or crime, and to protect the rights of others. Over the next decade, the Court established this approach and highlighted pluralism as a fundamental aspect of a democratic society that the Convention seeks to safeguard.[38] While pluralism was originally understood to protect the diversity of ideas and

[34] *P v UK* App no 14751/89 (ECommHR, 12 December 1990).

[35] *Bideault v France* App no 11261/84 (ECommHR, 1 October 1986).

[36] T Koivurova, 'Jurisprudence of the European Court of Human Rights Regarding Indigenous Peoples: Retrospect and Prospects' (2001) 18 *International Journal on Minority and Group Rights* 10.

[37] *G and E v Norway* App nos 9278/81 and 9415/81 (ECommHR, 3 October 1983).

[38] L Peroni, 'Minorities before the European Court of Human Rights' in J Boulden and W Kymlicka (eds), *International Approaches to Governing Ethnic Diversity* (Oxford University Press, 2015).

opinions, it was also extended to the diversity of religious beliefs, as well as of ethnic and cultural identities.[39]

The ECtHR milestone ruling of *Castells v Spain* in 1992 extended this new approach to claims related to the political expression and public participation of minorities and historical nations. In the 1980s, Spanish courts had convicted the applicant, Miguel Castells, a Member of Parliament (MP) and supporter of Basque nationalism, for publishing an article that accused the government of sheltering right-wing extremists allegedly responsible for killings.[40] The applicant was represented before the ECtHR by Douwe Korff, an academic and international human rights lawyer based in London, who was also involved in other high-profile cases before the Strasbourg Court. The ECtHR found the applicant's conviction to contravene his freedom of expression (Article 10 ECHR) and to be unnecessary in a democratic society. It stressed that it was especially important for political representatives to be able to express their views on matters of public interest, including opinions that were critical of the government. While the judgment did not in any way affirm minority rights or separatism, it showed that Articles 8–11 ECHR could provide significant protection to individuals expressing views or opinions favourable to minorities. In response to this judgment, the Spanish Constitutional Court changed its jurisprudence on issues of defamation and freedom of expression in order to conform to the ECtHR case law and to implement the judgment in *Castells*.[41]

The ECtHR further consolidated its approach vis-à-vis minority related claims invoking Articles 8–11 and 14 of the Convention, in response to complaints from ethnic-religious minorities in Southeast European countries that had accepted the right to individual petition in the 1980s and early 1990s. In Greece, Bulgaria, Turkey and elsewhere, national laws and policies imposed restrictions on the expression and associational life of minorities and came into conflict with minority aspirations and civil liberties. For example, they denied the existence of minority groups that defined themselves as Turkish (in Greece) and Macedonian (both Greece and Bulgaria). Constrained in pursuing their demands through domestic legal and political institutions, individuals belonging to religious and ethnic minorities and their organisations sought to mobilise international law and institutions – pre-eminently the ECHR.[42]

[39] J Ringelheim, *Diversite culturelle et droits de l'homme: La protection des minorities par la Convention Europeenne* (ruylant, 2006).

[40] *Castells v Spain* App no 11798/85 (ECtHR, 23 April 1992). Miguel Castells was MP in the Herri Batasuna (leftist Basque nationalist party), and leader of a political organisation linked to the separatist ETA (*Euskadi Ta Askatasuna*). He was one of the lawyers who had defended the ETA in the famous 'Burgos trial' staged by Franco in the late 1960s in order to judge and execute 16 ETA members who had been arrested. The trial marked the beginning of the end of the Francoist regime, provoking large demonstrations and international criticisms that forced Franco to commute the death penalties. See JL Sullivan, *ETA and Basque Nationalism – The Fight for Euskadi 1890–1986* (Routledge, 2015) 95.

[41] Committee of Ministers, *Resolution in* Castells v Spain DH (95) 93, 7 July 1995.

[42] These minority groups were Alevis (non-Sunni Muslims), Kurds and Armenians in Turkey, Turkish, Muslim, or Slavic-speaking and Macedonian minorities in Greece and Bulgaria, Jehovah's Witnesses in all three countries.

An early example in this string of cases was that of *Sadik Ahmet v Greece* that was lodged in 1991. The applicant, a leader of the minority in the region of Western Thrace, claimed that his sentencing by Greek courts for referring to the minority as 'Turkish' in the context of an election campaign (the Greek state recognises a Muslim minority but not a Turkish minority), violated his freedom of expression (Article 10 ECHR).[43] While the ECommHR unanimously declared the application admissible, the Court subsequently rejected it for non-exhaustion of domestic remedies – clearly concerned to distance itself from a politically sharply divisive issue. The Strasbourg Court essentially refused to adjudicate and decide on the issue, as acknowledged in the forceful dissent of two judges, reflecting a clear division in the Court's final decision (with three out of nine judges dissenting altogether). Yet, over the next decade, the ECtHR reviewed many similar petitions and found state restrictions imposed on minorities on grounds of national security and territorial integrity, to be unjustifiable in a democratic society.[44]

A rising trend of minority-related human rights litigation also focused on the Gypsy, Roma and Traveller communities.[45] Their status as a thoroughly marginalised and disadvantaged minority group in Europe was brought into the spotlight by international organisations like the OSCE, the Council of Europe, the United Nations, and the High Commissioner for the Protection of National Minorities.[46] In 1993, the High Commissioner on National Minorities published a special report on the social and economic problems of the Roma, and called for special government policies to deal with their problems in education, employment, health care and general welfare.[47]

The first complaints of Gypsies and Travellers to the ECtHR originated from the United Kingdom, a country with a public law tradition and well-developed anti-discrimination law. In the UK, legal provisions regulating where Gypsies could station their caravans, and how local administrative and planning authorities applied those provisions, gave rise to several problems and claims about breaches of the right of Gypsies and Travellers to a culturally distinct way of life. The critical factor in this litigation strand was not minority politics, but rather legal activism. A handful of UK lawyers saw the attention of international organisations to the plight of the Roma as an opportunity to pursue test case litigation. They anticipated Roma issues to become increasingly important with the accession of CESE

[43] *Sadik Ahmet v Greece* App no 18877/91 (ECtHR, 15 November 1996).

[44] D Anagnostou and Y Grozev, 'Human Rights Litigation and Restrictive State Implementation of Strasbourg Court Judgments: The Case of Ethnic Minorities from Southeast Europe' (2010) 19 *European Public Law* 401.

[45] While the word 'Gypsy' may now be considered offensive, it is used here as it was the term used in the ECHR litigation at the time.

[46] On the European and international organisations engagement with Roma rights in the 1990s, see P Vermeersch, *The Romani Movement* (Berghahn Books, 2006) ch 5.

[47] L Clements, PA Thomas and R Thomas, 'The Rights of Minorities – A Romany Perspective' (1996) 4 *OSCE Office for Democratic Institutions and Human Rights Bulletin* 6–7.

states in the ECHR, and foresaw an increase in minority-related complaints in the ECtHR from the region.[48] Some of them were university professors, and others worked in private law firms; some were specialists in social care, disability law and environmental planning, and others were acclaimed human rights and anti-discrimination lawyers. They all had in common an interest in human rights and/or in the rights of vulnerable groups and minorities. Some of them saw litigation as the only alternative to a political strategy, which was considered fruitless in view of the fact that the Roma do not 'constitute an effective pressure group or a popular cause for political vote seekers'.[49]

In the UK Travellers' cases, lawyers drew from the developing case law of the ECtHR on indigenous people, in cases like *G v Norway*, that recognised cultural identity to be part of the right to family life (Article 8 ECHR).[50] They were also aware of the limitations of the ECHR system – the individual nature of its provisions and the lack of a self-standing anti-discrimination provision – in addressing discrimination against vulnerable groups like Roma and Travellers that was often structurally entrenched in state laws and administrative practices. The restrictions placed on the ability of families to station their caravans on land that they owned, or their eviction from designated sites, arguably prevented them from leading a culturally distinct way of life and breached their right to family life.[51] The petitions also advanced the claim that such restrictions as imposed by local UK authorities, were a form of ethnic discrimination, and invoked related norms and principles contained in texts such as the Framework Convention.[52]

In the mid-1990s, in the case of *Buckley* the Court for the first time recognised that the UK environmental planning and local authority policies interfered with the right to a traditional family life under Article 8 ECHR, but found the interference to be necessary in a democratic society.[53] In a strong dissent, three (out of nine) judges countered that the multiplicity and superimposition of administrative rules excluded Gypsy Travellers from living in particular areas, leading to unjustifiable and discriminatory treatment in breach of Article 14 ECHR.[54] It was a powerful dissent that called upon the Court to recognise 'the legal difference that social, cultural or ethnic difference can make; the indirect discrimination that can ensue from a failure to recognise such difference; and the direct discrimination built into relevant national laws'.[55]

[48] Ibid 16.
[49] Ibid 5.
[50] Ibid 6–8.
[51] *P v UK* App no 14751/89 (ECommHR, 12 December 1990); *Ruby Smith v UK* App no 14455/88 (ECommHR, 4 September 1991).
[52] See eg *Chapman v United Kingdom* App no 27238/95 (ECtHR, 18 January 2001), paras 83, 93.
[53] *Buckley v United Kingdom* App no 20348/92 (ECtHR, 29 September 1996).
[54] R Sandland, 'Developing a Jurisprudence of Difference: The Protection of the Human Rights of Travelling Peoples by the ECtHR' (2008) 8 *Human Rights Law Review* 486.
[55] Ibid 487.

Over the next decade though, the Court would slowly redefine its approach to ethnic discrimination in response to many more cases from Roma and Travellers including from Central and East Europe where a transnational Roma rights movement emerged in the post-communist period. In numerous cases from countries like Bulgaria, Hungary, the Czech Republic and elsewhere, the focus of the claims that were framed and advanced shifted from asserting a distinct cultural identity to invoking the prohibition of discrimination on ethnic grounds. The Court found several human rights violations related to access by the Roma to public accommodations, residential exclusion, treatment by law enforcement bodies, minority access to public services, and segregation in education, including on grounds of structural discrimination.[56]

IV. Concluding Remarks

In the favourable normative European milieu of the 1980s and early 1990s, amidst divisions surfacing among its judges, the ECtHR developed a solid approach of applying human rights to address conflicts related to ethnic diversity in democratic societies.[57] The ECtHR relied on 'an emerging international consensus recognising the special needs of minorities and an obligation to protect their security, identity and lifestyle' in order to concede protection of a minority group's way of life under Article 8 ECHR.[58] It also referred to the CSCE Copenhagen Document on the Human Dimension and the Charter of Paris for a New Europe to uphold the right to freedom of association of minority members in Article 11 ECHR.[59] In other cases, the ECtHR explicitly referred to the Framework Convention and to findings from the Framework Convention's monitoring process to formulate its interpretation of the freedom of association (Article 11 ECHR) in relation to a minority association;[60] and to EU anti-discrimination law and case law to uphold the claim of indirect discrimination against the Roma.[61]

The preceding account of the ECtHR's encounter with an increasing number of minority-related claims in the 1980s and early 1990s shows that after many years as a 'sleeping beauty', it awakened for minorities too – more than a decade later from the time it put in place the fundamental principles of its legalisation. Minority mobilisation in the international plane, incipient legal activism and professional

[56] J Goldston, 'Public Interest Litigation in Central and Eastern Europe: Roots, Prospects, and Challenges' (2006) 28 *Human Rights Quarterly* 507.

[57] G Pentassuglia, 'The Strasbourg Court and Minority Groups: Shooting in the Dark or a New Interpretive Ethos?' (2013) 19 *International Journal of Minority and Group Rights* 2.

[58] *Chapman v United Kingdom* App no 27238/95 (ECtHR, 18 January 2001).

[59] *Sidiropoulos v Greece* App no 26695/95 (ECtHR, 10 July 1998).

[60] *Gorzelik v Poland* App no 44158/98 (ECtHR, 17 February 2004).

[61] *DH and Others v Czech Republic* App no 57325/2000 (ECtHR, 13 November 2007).

lawyers' interest in international public law, were all instrumental in framing minority issues into human rights claims. These pushed the Court to address claims related to cultural identity, public participation and discrimination against minorities, even if this was in a circumscribed and extremely cautious manner. The approach that the Court developed in its case law of the late 1980s and 1990s paved the way for many more related claims from the 1990s onwards. They rendered the ECtHR a central international legal forum for contesting various aspects of ethnic pluralism, and for addressing the marginalisation of vulnerable minorities.

10

On Democracy, Courts and Minority Rights: Mobilising Supranational Courts against Authoritarian Regimes

DILEK KURBAN

I. Introduction

What is the role of law, and specifically courts, in the protection of human rights? This question has long been fiercely debated, often framed around the democratic legitimacy, or lack thereof, of judicial review.[1] With the increasing role of Treaty-based courts in the enforcement of human rights, the focus has expanded from the national to the international level.[2] Yet, much of the debate is based on certain assumptions about the democratic credentials of political systems in which law operates and, specifically, does not take into account the particular vulnerabilities of minorities. In reality, the existence of electorally representative political bodies does not *ipso facto* attribute democratic quality to the substance of laws drafted by these institutions. Neither does their 'counter-majoritarian' nature insulate courts from the dominant political ideological frameworks in which they operate.

Where majorities decide on core issues concerning the identity of the nation, democracy does not necessarily mean equal protection under the law for all. Laws adopted by democratically accountable legislatures do not necessarily respect linguistic, ethnic and religious diversities within the nation. After all, as young Bruno De Witte had reminded in the concluding lines of his PhD dissertation, 'democracy, in the cultural as in other domains, means the recognition of the right

[1] R Dworkin, *Law's Empire* (Harvard University Press, 1986); Jeremy Waldron, *Law and Disagreement* (Oxford University Press, 1999).

[2] See eg A Stone Sweet 'Constitutional Courts and Parliamentary Democracy' (2002) 25 *West European Politics* 77.

to be different'.[3] And, as he has shown in his pioneering scholarship on minority protection in Europe, courts in established democracies are not, as such, trustable allies for minorities: 'where courts have intervened, they have not necessarily protected the weaker party, namely the speakers of the minority language, but occasionally (particularly in France) they have sought to safeguard the dominance of the majority language'.[4] Moreover, as Bruno De Witte's work on the European Court of Justice shows,[5] the notion that courts are immune to politics is a myth for supranational courts just as much as domestic ones.

Where minorities are at the behest of political majorities in the recognition and exercise of fundamental rights, and thus the promise of electoral representation is inherently limited, can law fill the justice gap? More precisely, what is the function of courts in protecting minorities against government encroachment? This brief chapter addresses these questions based on the role of supranational human rights courts in protecting minorities in authoritarian settings where minorities are 'in a very real sense political captives of the majority'.[6] It asks 'how, why, and how effectively'[7] social movements mobilise international human rights law to contest state violence by authoritarian regimes in the context of an armed conflict. I seek answers to these questions by re-visiting the findings of my PhD dissertation, supervised by Bruno De Witte and Monica Claes,[8] in light of an emerging scholarship on legal mobilisation in authoritarian and violent contexts.[9]

II. Mobilising Supranational Courts against Authoritarian Regimes

Law and society scholarship has long debated how to study the use of courts for social change. In contrast to the realist/instrumentalist view perceiving law

[3] B De Witte, *The Protection of Linguistic Diversity through Fundamental Rights* (PhD Thesis, 1985, European University Institute) 677.

[4] B De Witte, 'Linguistic Minorities in Western Europe: Expansion of Rights Without (Much) Litigation?' in D Anagnostou (ed), *Rights and Courts in Pursuit of Social Change: Legal Mobilisation in the Multi-Level European System* (Hart Publishing, 2014) 51.

[5] E Muir, M Dawson and B De Witte, 'Introduction: The European Court of Justice as a Political Actor' in M Dawson, B De Witte and E Muir, *Judicial Activism at the European Court of Justice* (Edward Elgar, 2013) 1.

[6] E Benvenisti, 'Margin of Appreciation, Consensus, and Universal Standards' (1999) 31 *International Law and Politics* 843, 848.

[7] GI Lovell, M McCann and K Taylor, 'Covering Legal Mobilisation: A Bottom-Up Analysis of *Wards Cove v. Atonio*' (2016) 41 *Law and Social Inquiry* 61, 64.

[8] Subsequently published as a monograph: D Kurban, *Limits of Supranational Justice: The European Court of Human Rights and Turkey's Kurdish Conflict* (Cambridge University Press, 2020).

[9] LJ Chua, *Mobilising Gay Singapore: Rights and Resistance in an Authoritarian State* (Temple University Press, 2014); LJ Chua and D Gilbert, 'Sexual Orientation and Gender Identity Minorities in Transition: LGBT Rights and Activism in Myanmar' (2015) 37 *Human Rights Quarterly* 1; E Gobe and L Salaymeh, 'Tunisia's "Revolutionary" Lawyers: From Professional Autonomy to Political Mobilisation' (2016) 41 *Law and Social Inquiry* 311; F van der Vet, '"When They Come for You": Legal Mobilisation

to be effective only if it leads to direct and measurable policy changes,[10] proponents of a broader notion of judicial impact have argued that law generates social transformation in complex and varied ways which cannot be reduced to the (non)enforcement of court rulings.[11] To understand circumstances in which legal mobilisation emerges and progresses, the latter advocated a bottom-up approach 'beginning with nonofficial rather than officials of law',[12] focusing on how individuals marginalised on account of race, ethnicity, class or gender may perceive, mobilise and contest the law as a form of resistance.[13]

While cautioning against 'the myth of rights', socio-legal scholars argue that litigation is most effective when part of broader political mobilisation.[14] Emphasising the law's 'double-edged'[15] function, they have produced empirical research showing 'the promise and the limits of legal mobilisation' in achieving social justice.[16] As much as this scholarship has recently been characterised as concerning social movement resistance to 'authoritarian conditions' or 'authoritarian practices',[17] its actual focus is liberal democracies. Certainly, mobilising against democratic regimes can be costly. Oppressed groups may be 'politically and personally ostracised' for mobilising the law.[18] Marginalised groups mobilising against 'authoritarian enclaves' within democracies[19] may face legal repression and even violence. Yet, even in the latter case, coercion is not universal across the state apparatus and the regime eventually resorts to corrective measures.[20] At the end of the day, activists in liberal democracies enjoy a relatively high degree of legal certainty and physical security in mobilising the law.

in New Authoritarian Russia' (2018) 52 *Law & Society Review* 301; LJ Chua, 'Legal Mobilisation and Authoritarianism' (2019) 15 *Annual Review of Law and Social Science* 355.

[10] GN Rosenberg, *The Hollow Hope: Can Courts Bring about Social Change?* (University of Chicago Press, 1991).

[11] MW McCann, *Rights at Work: Pay Equality Reform and the Politics of Legal Mobilisation* (University of Chicago Press, 1994).

[12] M McCann, 'Litigation and Legal Mobilisation' in KE Whittington, RD Kelemen and GA Caldeira (eds), *The Oxford Handbook of Law and Politics* (Oxford University Press, 2008) 524.

[13] FK Zemans, 'Legal Mobilisation: The Neglected Role of the Law in the Political System' (1983) 77 *The American Political Science Review* 690; McCann, *Rights at Work* (n 11); PA Cain, 'Litigating for Lesbian and Gay Rights: A Legal History' (1993) 79 *Virginia Law Review* 1551, SE Merry, 'Rights Talk and the Experience of Law: Implementing Women's Human Rights to Protection from Violence' (2003) 25 *Human Rights Quarterly* 343.

[14] SA Scheingold, *The Politics of Rights: Lawyers, Public Policy, and Political Change* (Yale University Press, 1974).

[15] M McCann, 'Law and Social Movements: Contemporary Perspectives' (2006) 2 *Annual Review of Law and Social Science* 17.

[16] EA Andersen, *Out of the Closets and into the Courts: Legal Opportunity Structure and Gay Rights Litigation* (University of Michigan Press, 2005) 216.

[17] Chua, 'Legal Mobilisation' (n 9) 360.

[18] L Vanhala, 'Anti-Discrimination Policy Actors and their Use of Litigation Strategies: The Influence of Identity Politics' (2009) 16 *Journal of European Public Policy* 738, 748.

[19] Chua, 'Legal Mobilisation' (n 9) 358.

[20] SE Barkan, 'Legal Control of the Southern Civil Rights Movement' (1984) 49 *American Sociological Review* 552.

In authoritarian regimes, activists not only lack the legal opportunities that liberal democracies offer, but they mobilise at great risk to their liberty and security.[21] Where mobilisation takes place in the context of violent conflicts, government backlash can be fatal. In Northern Ireland, legal advocates who exposed atrocities[22] and represented Republicans in criminal trials[23] were murdered. In Russia, activists and journalists who spoke up against atrocities in the Northern Caucasus were assassinated or disappeared.[24] In Colombia, displaced activists and human rights defenders were killed or disappeared.[25] In Turkey, Kurdish civil society leaders who spoke up against state violence were murdered, disappeared and tortured.[26] In all these cases, there were credible allegations regarding the collusion of security forces.

In recent years, a small but growing number of scholars have turned their lenses on authoritarianism, exploring social movement mobilisation against legal repression[27] and during transitions,[28] and the mobilisation of supranational courts against state coercion.[29] In exploring the impact of violence on the collective action of displaced women in Colombia, Lemaitre and Sandvik have argued that violent contexts make it much more difficult to mobilise the law due to shifting frames, vanishing resources and dangerous political opportunities.[30]

Despite these recent strides, there remains a gap in scholarship concerning legal mobilisation in contexts of authoritarianism *and* violence. In his work, van der Vet has argued that 'new authoritarian regimes', which resort to illiberal laws – rather than overt repression – in suppressing dissent, pose unique obstacles to mobilisation due to scarce opportunities and uncertainties owing to constantly changing and unpredictably enforced penal laws.[31] Leaving aside the validity of distinctions between authoritarianism and new authoritarianism,[32] van der

[21] Van der Vet, '"When They Come for You"' (n 9); Chua, 'Legal Mobilisation' (n 9).

[22] M Flaherty, 'Human Rights Violations against Defense Lawyers: The Case of Northern Ireland' (1994) 7 *Harvard Human Rights Journal* 87.

[23] K McEvoy, 'Law, Struggle, and Political Transformation in Northern Ireland' (2000) 27 *Journal of Law and Society* 542.

[24] J Lapitskaya, 'ECHR, Russia, and Chechnya: Two is not Company and Three is Definitely a Crowd' (2011) 43 *International Law and Politics* 479.

[25] J Lemaitre and KB Sandvik, 'Shifting Frames, Vanishing Resources, and Dangerous Political Opportunities: Legal Mobilisation among Displaced Women in Colombia' (2015) 49 *Law and Society Review* 5.

[26] Kurban, *Limits of Supranational Justice* (n 8).

[27] Chua, *Mobilising Gay Singapore* (n 9); Van der Vet, '"When They Come for You"' (n 9).

[28] Chua and Gilbert, 'Sexual Orientation' (n 9); Gobe and Salaymeh, 'Tunisia's "Revolutionary" Lawyers' (n 9).

[29] Van der Vet, '"When They Come for You"' (n 9); Kurban, *Limits of Supranational Justice* (n 8).

[30] Lemaitre and Sandvik, 'Shifting Frames' (n 25).

[31] Van der Vet, '"When They Come for You"' (n 9).

[32] KL Scheppele, 'Autocratic Legalism' (2018) 85 *The University of Chicago Law Review* 545; 'The Opportunism of Populists and the Defense of Constitutional Liberalism' (2019) 20 *German Law Journal* 314.

Vet's work does not concern legal mobilisation against state violence. While Lemaitre and Sandvik's work does fill that void, their findings are based on Colombia, a democratic, albeit violent, country with a strong and progressively activist constitutional court.[33] Much of the activism for and by displaced women emerged from the Constitutional Court's ruling calling for structural reforms for the displaced. Thus, Lemaitre and Sandvik's theoretical insights do not speak to authoritarian contexts where activists not only risk further violence in mobilising but also lack domestic judicial allies to turn to for protection. In the latter, supranational courts emerge as the only potential source of relief – if and where they are accessible.

Over the past decade, a bourgeoning literature has focused on supranational courts, including the European Court of Human Rights ('ECtHR' or 'the Court'). Adopting an 'optimistic faith in courts', which is prevalent in much of socio-legal scholarship,[34] scholars have characterised the ECtHR as a social movement ally due to its incremental expansion of anti-discrimination protection and exposure of legal repression and gross violations against minorities.[35] While exploring internal (inadequate resources) and external (government backlash) constraints to legal mobilisation, these studies have not looked into the barriers that the ECtHR itself might have built. This blind spot is largely due to their exclusive focus on judgments and neglect of inadmissibility decisions and strike-out rulings where the Court was *not* receptive to justiciable claims. Even in their attention on substantive rulings, however, these studies have not engaged in in-depth case law analyses to explore the relationship between victims' claims and the ECtHR's response. For instance, in enforced disappearance cases, while victims' families claim a substantive violation of the right to life, the ECtHR has often limited its rulings to procedural violations arising from governments' failure to conduct effective investigations. In both scenarios, the Court found a violation of Article 2 of the European Convention on Human Rights (ECHR), but only in the former did it hold the government responsible for the disappearance and presumed murder of the victim.

In sum, we still lack a theory that takes into account both authoritarianism and violence in exploring the prospects for effective social movement mobilisation of supranational courts.

[33] Lemaitre and Sandvik, 'Shifting Frames' (n 25).

[34] Lovell, McCann and Taylor, 'Covering Legal Mobilisation' (n 7) 63.

[35] L Hodson, *NGOs and the Struggle for Human Rights in Europe* (Hart Publishing, 2011); RA Cichowski, 'Civil Society and the European Court of Human Rights' in J Christoffersen and MR Madsen (eds), *The European Court of Human Rights between Law and Politics* (Oxford University Press, 2011) 77; D Anagnostou, 'Law and Rights' Claiming on behalf of Minorities in the Multi-level European System' in D Anagnostou (ed), *Rights and Courts in Pursuit of Social Change: Legal Mobilisation in the Multi-Level European System* (Hart Publishing, 2014) 1.

III. When Supranational Courts Hinder Legal Mobilisation

Socio-legal scholars have long stressed that whether legal mobilisation disempowers or empowers individuals 'depends on the complex, often changing dynamics of the context in which struggles occur'.[36] When the first Kurdish cases were filed with the ECtHR, the context was relatively straightforward: activists contesting an authoritarian regime engaged in state violence against a minority. While there was a significant 'disparity' in power between the applicants and the government,[37] Kurdish lawyers were able to overcome some of it with the support of British lawyers. But much of the disparity stemmed from contesting a government which denied the allegations in their totality and took advantage of the leeway that the ECHR allows for counter-terrorism. It was the combination of Turkey's authoritarianism and resort to emergency paradigm that made it difficult for Kurdish lawyers to make effective use of the right of individual petition.

Nonetheless, at the initial phase, the ECtHR was relatively assertive in its adjudication. Due to Turkey's denial of the allegations and the domestic courts' failure to establish facts, the ECHR institutions engaged in fact-finding.[38] Incrementally, although belatedly, the Court admitted circumstantial evidence in enforced disappearance cases (but not in extrajudicial killings cases), leading to the establishment of state responsibility.[39] In terms of substantive doctrine, it issued ground-breaking rulings, holding, *inter alia*, that unacknowledged detention violates the right to liberty;[40] close relatives of the disappeared may themselves be subject to inhuman treatment;[41] enforced disappearance is a substantive violation of the right to life;[42] the rape of a detainee by a state official constitutes torture;[43] and the deliberate destruction of homes by the security forces may constitute ill treatment.[44]

At the same time, while some *individual* Kurds were vindicated, the Kurds *as a people* were not. As Judge Bonello reminded in his dissenting opinion, it *was* possible to deliver justice without transgressing the boundaries of judicial review.[45] While it took the Inter-American Court of Human Rights (IACtHR)

[36] McCann, 'Law and Social Movements' (n 15) 19.

[37] M Galanter, 'Why the "Haves" Come out Ahead: Speculations on the Limits of Legal Change' (1974) 9 *Law and Society Review*, 95.

[38] P Mahoney, 'Speculating on the Future of the Reformed European Court of Human Rights' (1999) 20 *Human Rights Law Journal* 1.

[39] See eg *Kurt v Turkey* App no 15/1997/799/1002 (ECtHR, 25 May 1998); *Koku v Turkey* App no 27305/95 (ECtHR, 31 May 2005); *Osmanoğlu v Turkey* App no 48804/99 (ECtHR, 24 January 2008).

[40] *Çiçek v Turkey* App no 25704/94 (ECtHR, 27 February 2001).

[41] *Timurtaş v Turkey* App no 23531/94 (ECtHR, 13 June 2000); *İpek v. Turkey* App no 25760/94 (ECtHR, 17 February 2004).

[42] *Çakıcı v Turkey* App no 23657/94 (ECtHR, 8 July 2004).

[43] *Aydın v Turkey* GC App no 57/1996/676/866 (ECtHR, 25 September 1997).

[44] *Selçuk and Asker v Turkey* App no 12/1997/796/998-999 (ECtHR, 24 April 1998).

[45] *Tahsin Acar v Turkey* GC App no 26307/95 (ECtHR, 6 May 2003).

one judgment – and its first ever judgment – to name the Honduran policy for what it was,[46] despite having issued scathing judgments in dozens of nearly identical cases, the ECtHR has never passed judgment on the core issue: organised violence against a minority carried out and covered up by the entire state apparatus. A finding of administrative practice would have alleviated applicants from having to exhaust domestic remedies and prove the elements of crimes they attributed to the state. Instead, the ECtHR opted for a case-by-case approach. While relaxing its admissibility rules to alleviate victims from the duty to exhaust domestic remedies, it did so due to 'special circumstances' in the Kurdish region (the absence of domestic investigations, the presence of emergency rule, the risk of reprisals), not to an administrative practice.[47] The Court's reluctance did not stem from lack of information about the situation on the ground. For example, it had at its disposal fact-findings of UN and Council of Europe Treaty bodies showing that torture in Turkey was systematic. And yet, in a landmark case concerning the rape and torture under detention of a seventeen-year old Kurdish woman, the Grand Chamber found this evidence 'insufficient' to find administrative practice.[48]

In Strasbourg, Kurdish lawyers encountered a supranational court whose evidentiary standards did not match their expectations of justice. The Court was demanding that they prove not only that gross violations occurred, but also that the state was responsible for those violations. For the lawyers, Turkey's non-cooperation, for example its refusal to ensure the appearance of witnesses summoned by the ECtHR, was sufficient to shift the burden of proof to the government. For the Court, the applicants nonetheless had to prove their allegations 'beyond reasonable doubt' – an impossible feat due to the government's refusal to disclose the material evidence in its exclusive possession. Again, the ECtHR's restraint was not inevitable. The IACtHR had held that a state-sanctioned enforced disappearance policy is 'impossible to prove (…) [without] circumstantial or indirect evidence or by logical inference'[49] and admitted as evidence, for example, news reports in support of the applicants' claims. By contrast, the ECtHR refused to consider even a Turkish Parliament report which had found that security forces and proxies acting under their order or knowledge murdered prominent Kurdish dissidents.[50]

The ECtHR was also dismissive of discrimination claims. Absent a few dissenting voices who drew attention to numerous ECtHR judgments finding similar violations in strikingly similar cases lodged, without exception, by the Kurds,[51]

[46] *Velásquez Rodríguez v Honduras* Series C no 4 (IACtHR, 29 July 1988).
[47] *Akdıvar and Others v Turkey* GC App no 21893/93 (ECtHR, 16 September 1996).
[48] *Aydın v Turkey* GC App no 57/1996/676/866 (ECtHR, 25 September 1997) para 124.
[49] *Velásquez Rodríguez v Honduras* Series C no 4 (IACtHR, 29 July 1988) para 124.
[50] *Mahmut Kaya v Turkey* App no 22535/93 (ECtHR, 28 March 2000).
[51] Eg *Hasan İlhan v Turkey* App no 22494/93 (ECtHR, 9 November 2004) (dissenting opinion of Judge Loucaides); *Kişmir v Turkey*, App no 27306/95 (ECtHR, 31 May 2005) (dissenting opinion of Judge Mularoni).

the Court stood its ground. It either held that the applicants failed to substantiate their claims[52] or, without explanation, deemed it 'not necessary' to address these claims.[53] While such reluctance was characteristic of the ECtHR's Article 14 jurisprudence,[54] it was even more striking in Kurdish cases where discrimination had risen to the level of systematic and gross violations.

The Kurdish case demonstrates the difficulties of mobilising against authoritarian regimes where supranational courts are unwilling to bend their evidentiary rules even when governments refuse to discharge their contractual obligations for the establishment of facts. Where violations occur in the context of an armed conflict, the supranational authority may exhibit undue deference to the government's counter-terrorism defence even where violations are gross and systematic. At the same time, a comparative reading of jurisprudence of the world's two leading human rights courts shows that such restraint is not inherent to supranational judicial review, but a matter of choice.

IV. The Authoritarian Playbook: Transition Paradigm, Counter-opportunities and Subsidiarity

The 'constitutive capacity of the law' is not limited to social movements; it also inspires governments.[55] In liberal democracies, where judicial scrutiny is inescapable, the best that governments can do is to try to impact litigation outcomes through efforts to 'circumvent, defy, and even initiate counter-reform[s]'.[56] For authoritarian regimes facing supranational courts, the options are wider. Short of opting out, which has high reputational costs, the most effective strategy is to minimise oversight by demonstrating to the supranational authority the reliability of the domestic legal system in human rights enforcement. The transition argument is based on producing new remedies which, if found effective, enable the supranational court to issue inadmissibility rulings and boost the democratic credentials of the government. And when the supranational authority in question is prone to collaboration, it works.

By the early 2000s, it had become much more difficult for Kurdish lawyers to mobilise the ECtHR against Turkey. While the Kurds had become 'repeat players' before the ECtHR,[57] so had their adversary. The government had understood

[52] Eg *Akdıvar and Others v Turkey* GC App no 21893/93 (ECtHR, 16 September 1996).
[53] Eg *Yaşa v Turkey* App no 63/1997/847/1054 (ECtHR, 2 September 1998).
[54] P Sardaro, '*Jus Non Dicere* for Allegations of Serious Violations of Human Rights: Questionable Trends in the Recent Case Law of the Strasbourg Court' (2003) 6 *European Human Rights Law Review* 601.
[55] M McCann, 'Reform Litigation on Trial' (1992) 17 *Law and Social Inquiry* 715, 733.
[56] Ibid.
[57] Galanter, 'Why the "Haves" Come out Ahead' (n 37).

the reputational, financial and political costs of denial and non-cooperation. The authoritarian outlook had become all the more costly when the EU finally granted Turkey candidacy for membership in 1999, but made accession status contingent on, inter alia, the execution of ECtHR rulings. The democratisation paradigm would enable the ECtHR to send, with good conscience, the bulk of pending cases back to the Turkish legal system. The timing was also ripe; post-Cold War enlargement had left the ECtHR paralysed with an unmanageable docket and desperate for help. On the other side of the equation, Kurdish lawyers were fast running out of resources. British lawyers were turning their attention from Kurdish cases to the Chechen conflict after Russia's accession to the ECHR and the start of the second Chechen war.[58]

The change happened incrementally. Turkey's initial strategy was to minimise the number of adverse judgments. Starting from 2001, rather than denying the allegations, the government started to offer friendly settlements to applicants whose cases had been admitted to Strasbourg. When the latter refused, the government turned to the ECtHR and submitted unilateral declarations partially acknowledging the allegations. These documents would, for example, admit that the victim had died due to the use of excessive force. They would not, however, acknowledge state responsibility for the loss of life or promise to undertake investigations – flying in the face of established ECtHR case law on effective remedies. Yet, the strategy worked – at least initially. Invoking Article 37 of the ECHR, the Court struck out of its list several right-to-life cases, effectively penalising applicants for refusing to settle with the government.[59] This brief phase ended in 2003 when the Grand Chamber, in response to internal and external protests, found Turkey's declarations to be insufficient to merit the invocation of Article 37 and sent some, but not all, of the struck-out cases back to the list.[60]

For the Justice and Development Party (*Adalet ve Kalkınma Partisi* – AKP), which came to power on a pro-EU agenda in late 2002, the need for a more effective strategy was evident. Instead of targeting the applicants who had passed the admissibility hurdle in a piecemeal fashion, the new government adopted a proactive stance to achieve the ECtHR's wholesale rejection of repetitive cases. The most effective way out was to create *domestic* legal opportunities. The context could not be more ideal; subsidiarity was the buzz word in Strasbourg[61] and the AKP would make the best of it. Priority was given to thousands of pending Kurdish cases, particularly after the ECtHR, making use of its new powers, had issued a pilot

[58] O Solvang, 'Chechnya and the European Court of Human Rights: The Merits of Strategic Litigation' (2008) 19 *Security and Human Rights* 208.

[59] *Akman v Turkey* App no 37453/97 (ECtHR, 26 June 2001); *Haran v Turkey* App no 25754/94 (ECtHR, 26 March 2002); *T A v Turkey*, App no 26307/95 (ECtHR, 9 April 2002).

[60] *Tahsin Acar v Turkey* GC App no 26307/95 (ECtHR, 6 May 2003).

[61] R Spano, 'Universality or Diversity of Human Rights? Strasbourg in the Age of Subsidiarity' (2014) 14 *Human Rights Law Review* 487.

judgment calling for a new domestic remedy for the displaced Kurds.[62] In July 2004, only 18 days after that ECtHR ruling, in an unprecedented display of cooperation and efficiency, Turkey adopted a compensation law. In January 2006, responding in kind, the ECtHR rejected around 1,500 pending Kurdish cases on the ground that the applicants had to first exhaust this new domestic remedy which it hastily found to be effective.[63] Preoccupied with its docket crisis, the ECtHR approved a law lacking a justice component, glossing over its repeated earlier assertions that there can be no effective remedy for gross violations without the identification and punishment of perpetrators.[64]

As it familiarised itself over time with the ECtHR's growing propensity to invoke subsidiarity to handle its docket crisis, the AKP government perfected its counter-reform strategy. The goal now was to prevent cases from being admitted to begin with. The most effective way of doing that was putting in place a constitutional complaint mechanism to prolong the path to Strasbourg. Once again, the ECtHR responded expeditiously and favourably to the government. In April 2013, only seven months after the right of individual constitutional complaint entered into force in Turkey, the ECtHR rejected an applicant due to her failure to have applied to the Turkish Constitutional Court (TCC) – without first assessing whether the new remedy was effective.[65] In no time, the TCC proved its loyalty to the regime by, among others, dismissing the petitions of victims of renewed state violence in the Kurdish region,[66] and of Kurdish deputies held in prolonged pre-trial detention.[67] The TCC's complicity became all the more evident when it declined to review the applications of over 60,000 civil servants, including two of its own members, who had been summarily and collectively dismissed from their jobs on unsubstantiated allegations of being involved in the failed attempt to overthrow the government in July 2016.[68] And, when it finally addressed the issue in 2018, the ECtHR found Turkey's constitutional complaint mechanism to be an effective domestic remedy.[69]

In conclusion, after over three decades, Kurdish legal mobilisation at the ECtHR has all but failed. In the 1990s, while showing undue deference to Turkey's counter-terrorism defence, the ECtHR was at least forthcoming about the dysfunctionality of the domestic legal system. By the mid-2000s, not only was Turkey continuing

[62] *Doğan and Others v Turkey* App no 8803–8811/02, 8813/02 and 8815–8819/02 (ECtHR, 29 June 2004).

[63] *İçyer v Turkey* App no 18888/02 (ECtHR, Decision 12 January 2006).

[64] D Kurban, 'Forsaking Individual Justice: The Implications of the European Court of Human Rights' Pilot Judgment Procedure for Victims of Gross and Systematic Violations' (2016) 16 *Human Rights Law Review* 731.

[65] *Uzun v Turkey* App no 10755/13 (ECtHR, Decision 30 April 2013).

[66] Eg *Mehmet Girasun and Ömer Elçi* App no 2015/15266 (TCC, Decision – Interim Remedy – 11 September 2015).

[67] Eg *Selahattin Demirtaş* App no 2016/25189 (TCC, 21 December 2017).

[68] T Ruys and E Turkut, 'Turkey's Post-Coup 'Purification Process': Collective Dismissals of Public Servants under the European Convention on Human Rights' (2018) 18 *Human Rights Law Review* 539.

[69] *Mehmet Hasan Altan v Turkey* App no 13237/17 (ECtHR, 20 March 2018).

to make effective use of the ECHR's emergency paradigm, but it was now successfully presenting itself to Strasbourg as a reliable partner in the enforcement of the Convention. The more the ECtHR was preoccupied with its docket crisis, the more susceptible it became to Turkey's tactical maneuvers and, consequently, the less of a human rights court. Certainly, Kurdish lawyers still 'go to Strasbourg'. Yet, they do so out of habit rather than conviction; for them, petitioning the ECtHR has become 'somewhat like appealing to the High Court of Appeals'.[70] Moreover, in light of the Turkish courts' continued complicity with state violence and authoritarianism, the ECtHR remains the only judicial authority to grant some relief to the handful victims who make it to Strasbourg.

V. Mobilising Supranational Courts against Authoritarianism and Violence

In his PhD dissertation, Bruno De Witte had shown a pragmatic way out for minority rights advocates; rather than insisting on the recognition of minority rights, which is ideal but not attainable, lawyers should see how they can make use of existing human rights norms to advance language rights.[71] Speaking to that invitation nearly four decades later, this chapter told the story of one such effort in an authoritarian setting.

While presenting a significant opportunity, the availability of supranational judicial oversight does not *ipso facto* guarantee victims' access to it. In addition to evidentiary, admissibility and standing hurdles that may emanate from supranational courts, lawyers contesting authoritarian regimes face additional obstacles compared to those in liberal democracies. First, they are extremely dependent on external financial, human and information resources to engage in sustained legal mobilisation. More often than not, these resources vanish not only because the attention of international donors and legal experts shift to other violent contexts, but also because mobilising supranational courts brings even more government repression, leading to the loss of hard-gained domestic resources due to the death, imprisonment, (self-) exile or withdrawal of the handful of lawyers with hard-earned expertise and experience in supranational litigation. Those few activists who survive government retaliation and manage to have the ear of a supranational court face a further challenge: having to prove claims 'beyond reasonable doubt' in the face of government denial and in the absence of fact-finding by domestic courts. Given that authoritarian regimes, by definition, owe their power to the lack of the rule of law, supranational courts' insistence on hard evidence in such situations impedes victims' access to justice.

[70] Interview with Meral Danış Beştaş, Diyarbakır, 1 October 2013.
[71] De Witte, *The Protection of Linguistic Diversity* (n 3).

The Kurdish case shows that, as much as they provide a platform to social movements to contest state violence and provide some relief to some victims, supranational courts may also constrain mobilisation against authoritarian regimes, particularly where the contested violations occur under the guise of counter-terrorism and in the context of an armed conflict. There is an evident need for new theories to explain why and how this may or may not occur. What explains the IACtHR's and the ECtHR's fundamentally different jurisprudential approaches to standards of evidence, burden of proof and state responsibility, given the similarities of their mandates? In contexts where local activists face diminishing opportunities and resources, shifting supranational and domestic legal frames, and enduring authoritarianism and state violence, what are the ways in which supranational human rights courts enable or impede effective mobilisation against state violence? It is only when we have the analytical and theoretical tools to answer these questions that we can meaningfully assess the effectiveness of legal mobilisation against and supranational oversight of authoritarian regimes.

PART V

Scholarly Europe

11

How to Introduce the EU Legal Order? Some Thoughts on Framework and Method

ELISE MUIR

1. Introduction

Legal scholars, and an EU legal scholar such as Bruno De Witte is no exception, propose analytical frameworks and tools into which rules may be fitted. These frameworks and tools may be used as starting points to understand, discuss and assess existing as well as forthcoming developments.[1] In that sense, the legal grammar proposed by the scholar introducing an area of law may deeply influence the reader or audience, in particular in an area of law that is as dynamic and diffuse as EU law.[2] Precisely because of the importance of the conceptual choices on which introductions to a specific area of law rely, as well as due to changes in the academic landscape in which European legal scholars operate,[3] EU law scholars are increasingly often invited to make the normative underpinnings of their approach and methodological choices more explicit.

The wealth of Bruno's writings, as well as the guidance and support that he gives to colleagues and more junior academics, has done its 'narrative work beneath the surface'[4] to diffuse his vision of the EU among many of his collaborators, readers and students. Yet, and although he himself observed that 'legal scholars display a

[1] See S Vogenauer, 'An Empire of Light? II: Learning and Lawmaking in Germany Today' (2006) 26 *Oxford Journal of Legal Studies* 627–63, 636 and 647.

[2] See W Twining, W Farnsworth, S Vogenauer and F Tesón, 'The Role of Academics in the Legal System' in P Cane and M Tushnet (eds), *The Oxford Handbook of Legal Studies* (Oxford University Press, 2003) 920, 927–29 and 937. On the specificity of EU law see N Walker, 'Legal Theory and the European Union: A 25th Anniversary Essay' (2005) 25 *Oxford Journal of Legal Studies* 581, 582–83.

[3] As most helpfully explained by R van Gestel and H Micklitz, 'Why Methods Matter in European Legal Scholarship' (2014) 20(3) *European Law Journal* 292.

[4] LH Edwards, 'Once Upon a Time in Law: Myth, Metaphor, and Authority' (2010) 77 *Tennessee Law Review* 884.

surprising lack of interest in legal scholarship, or at least they tend not to make it an object of their writing',[5] his own work is not often explicitly theoretical or detailed on his methodological choices.

Despite Bruno's overall fairly discreet tone on these matters, this chapter seeks to identify some of the main characteristics of his approach to the EU legal order as inferred from reading and collaborating with him. The focus is on two fundamental and intricate questions related to the choice of framework and methods: what is the EU? (section II) and what does the study of the EU legal order entail? (section III). In addressing each of these two questions in turn, this contribution elaborates on how I draw on Bruno's work to shape my approach to introducing the EU legal order[6] with a view to enabling an educated beginner to gain a more immediate sense of the ways in which EU law is made and operates.[7]

II. What is the European Union?

There is much didactic appeal for EU legal scholars in introducing the EU by drawing an analogy between the latter and a state-like structure, in particular by adopting a 'constitutional' approach. Undeniably, the EU Treaties, and legal sources of equal legal rank such as the Charter of Fundamental Rights of the EU, play a central and forceful role in the EU legal system.

The EU Treaties in particular perform three main functions. They define fundamental values, objectives, principles and certain rules of substantive law, such as those ensuring the functioning of the internal market and the monetary union, contributing to creating 'an ever closer union between the peoples of Europe'.[8] The EU Treaties also set out the rules for the functioning of the legal system, such as the institutional design and procedures for decision-making at EU level. Finally, they define the existence of, and the way to exercise, EU competences which allow the principles and rules set out therein to be complemented by, implemented and enforced across the EU legal order. The EU Treaties further rank at the top of the hierarchy of EU norms and deploy a vast array of legal effects in national legal orders. These results from their primacy over national law, the direct effect of some of its provisions in national legal orders as well as a far-reaching duty of sincere cooperation that is binding on EU organs and on the Member States. These shape the interplay between the EU legal system and others in powerful ways.

[5] B De Witte, 'European Union Law: A Unified Academic Discipline?' in A Vauchez and B De Witte (eds), *Lawyering Europe: European Law as a Transnational Social Field* (Hart Publishing, 2013) 101–02.

[6] This chapter thereby also explains some of the choices made in E Muir, *An Introduction to the EU Legal Order* (Cambridge University Press, 2022, forthcoming).

[7] Paraphrasing E Korkea-aho, 'Mainstreaming the "Uninvited Backstairs Influences": Lobbyists as Regulated Actors in EU Law Research' (forthcoming).

[8] Art 1, para 2 of the Treaty on European Union (TEU).

The said Treaties therefore perform the functions of a 'basic constitutional charter' of the EU and have a decisive impact on its 'constitutional structure', to borrow the choice of words of the Court of Justice of the European Union.[9] The Charter of Fundamental Rights of the European Union, which has the same legal authority as the EU Treaties since 2009, adds to the constitutional overtone of EU primary law.[10] In this context, the choice for a 'constitutional' approach could assist an educated beginner in the field in readily grasping the hierarchy of EU norms, as well as some of the key dynamics of the EU legal order and functions of the main EU institutions.

Yet, the draft Treaty establishing a *Constitution* for Europe from 2004 was never fully ratified, and thus did not enter into force. As is well known, the Treaty of Lisbon that was adopted in its stead was stripped of what the drafters considered to be its constitutional attributes with a view to ensuring ratification, '[t]he constitutional concept [… was] abandoned'.[11] For this very simple reason, adopting a constitutional lens for the purpose of providing an introduction to the EU legal order is not straightforward.[12] The constitutional implications of the process of European integration may be better discussed as an advanced subject matter. This indeed requires opening up a critical reflection on the deep changes that EU law has itself undergone and triggered in domestic legal systems, as well as on how this relates to the contemporary dynamics of both constitutional law and international law.[13]

In the aftermath of the entry into force of the Treaty of Lisbon and thus after the failure of the draft Treaty establishing a Constitution for Europe, Bruno recalled and explained in his writings how he understands the EU 'as an international legal experiment'.[14] His argument is that sharply separating the EU from the field of international law might be misguided both because this would overestimate the novelty of EU law, and because it would underestimate the capacity

[9] Respectively: Case 294/83 *Les Verts* EU:C:1986:166 and Case C-621/18 *Wightman* EU:C:2018:999, para 45.5.

[10] See also on fundamental rights and the 'constitutional framework' of the EU, Opinion 2/13 on *Accession of the European Union to the European Convention for the Protection of Human Rights and Fundamental Freedoms* EU:C:2014:2454, paras 167–77.

[11] Council of the European Union, Presidency Conclusions, Brussels, 21 and 22 June 2007, 11177/1/07 REV 1, Annex 1, point I.1.

[12] I am grateful to Edouard Dirrig for sharing his views on the matter.

[13] Engaging with such exercises see for instance K Lenaerts, P Van Nuffel and T Corthaut, *EU Constitutional Law* (Oxford University Press, 2021); E Dubout, *Droit constitutionnel de l'Union européenne* (Bruylant, 2021); R Schütze, *The Changing Structure of European Law*, vol I (Oxford University Press, 2009) and vol II (Oxford University Press, 2017); A Bailleux, and H Dumont, *Le pacte constitutionnel européen – Tome 1. Fondements du droit institutionnel de l'Union* (Bruylant, 2015).

[14] B De Witte, 'The European Union as an international legal experiment' in G De Búrca and J Weiler (eds), *The Worlds of European Constitutionalism* (Cambridge University Press, 2011) 19–56. The subsequent overview of Bruno's argument paraphrases from his book chapter. Geert de Baere rightfully drew my attention to the fact that Bruno's approach to the matter may be traced back to some of his early writings: B De Witte, 'Retour à *Costa*: La primauté du droit communautaire à la lumière du droit international' (1983) *EUI Working Paper* 49.

of international law to develop innovative features in contexts other than that of European integration. Whilst he acknowledges that it would be somewhat 'odd or artificial' to discuss the EU as an international organisation, he calls for addressing the oddity of the EU without denying its international law foundations and dynamics. As he stresses, after all even the 2004 'Constitution for Europe' would have been enshrined in an international Treaty.

Bruno himself does not elaborate much on specific labels that could be used to describe the EU legal order, to avoid using a constitutional narrative. In the context of seeking to provide an introduction to the EU legal order, it may actually be impossible to put a label on the specific type of regional integration that the EU represents as it warrants further reflecting on, and in fact re-defining, the labels themselves. The focus thus shifts on seeking to characterise the nature of the EU legal order through a set of chosen expressions and features rather than a single label.

Seeking to take Bruno's legitimate concerns into account when designing an introduction to the EU legal order, I do not engage with a discussion on labels and instead indeed attempt to describe the specifics of the EU legal order. I opt for stressing that the EU differs from other models of regional integration because it encompasses a particularly ambitious range of policy areas, and deploys powerful legal effects. While stressing that the international Treaties on which the EU is founded have primarily been adopted through intergovernmental techniques, it is noted that the legal effects that derive from these Treaties largely depart from these techniques. This is not only due to the primacy and direct effect of EU law, but to the full legal machinery on which the operation of these principles rely and to which they apply.[15]

Emphasis is then placed on the governance model on which the EU relies, which is often said to be 'supranational'. Such a system of governance acknowledges the importance of the interests of each individual State party to the organisation. Meanwhile, it *also* makes space for the representation of other interests such as those of the citizens of the State parties, as well as for the idea of a 'common good' – or 'a measure of 'aboveness'[16] – going beyond the mere addition of the interests of each individual State party.[17] The 'Community method' that characterises the

[15] As illustrated again recently in B De Witte, 'Direct Effect, Primacy, and the Nature of the Legal Order' in P Craig and G De Búrca, *The Evolution of EU Law* (Oxford University Press, 2021) ch 7. Bruno has repeatedly stressed that primacy and direct effect do not in themselves set EU law aside from international law. Yet, as Bruno also notes, 'what is probably the most convincing argument for the view that the EU has ceased to be an international organization (…) is not based on particular characteristics of the EU (…) but rather on the combination of a number of peculiarities': B De Witte 'The European Union as an International Legal Experiment' in G De Búrca and J Weiler (eds), *The Worlds of European Constitutionalism* (Cambridge University Press, 2011) 50.

[16] For a more in-depth discussion of how the concept may be usefully articulated see J Weiler, 'The Community System: The Dual Character of Supranationalism' (1981) 1(1) *Yearbook of European Law* 268.

[17] See further K Lenaerts and P Van Nuffel, *European Union Law*, 3rd edn (Sweet & Maxwell, 2011) 16–19 and 25.

particular dynamics of decision-making within the EU since its early days is thus introduced, before elaborating on the extraordinary legal setting enabling a vast array of legal norms to be integrated in domestic legal systems within the EU legal order.

The supranational nature of the process of European integration hereby characterised is understood as not negating the existence and importance of dialogue between representatives of the Member States at European level on interests that they deem to be of particular importance to them. Such examples abound. In recent years, for instance, we have seen solutions to crises – such as the Covid-19 pandemic – being addressed by emergency gatherings of the representatives of the governments of the Member States within the EU institutional framework.[18] One may also note the existence of occasional difficulties with distinguishing between Member States acting collectively as part of an EU institution, or collectively in their sovereign capacity, as illustrated in relation to the 'EU–Turkey statement'.[19] The EU legal order simply does not exist in a vacuum. For another example, the Member States of the EU may conclude agreements between themselves in areas of non-exclusive EU competences, such as the Treaty establishing the European Stability Mechanism.[20]

In an attempt to address Bruno's concerns regarding how to define what the EU legal order is (as introduced above), my proposal therefore consists in stressing that the EU has grown to be overall increasingly supranational, with greater emphasis of the main features of today's version of the Community method over time; while simultaneously noting that the EU has unquestionably asserted itself as a forum where responsibility is organised and decisions are taken by the Member States to act jointly.[21] This approach may be more nuanced than merely introducing the EU as being 'a variant of constitutionalist approaches in all but name', as Bruno's work has been characterised.[22]

The distinction between the logic of a supranational approach relying on a powerful common institutional framework complemented with a set of integrated legal tools, and that by which Member States create a 'sphere in which to do things together' through intergovernmental dialogue, is not black-and-white – both exist side by side.[23] While there may be tensions between the two logics, they can be

[18] Eg European Council, Conclusions on the recovery plan and multiannual financial framework for 2021–2027, 17 to 21 July 2021, EUCO 10/20, and Conclusions on the MFF and Next Generation EU, COVID-19, climate change, security and external relations, 10 to 11 December 2021, EUCO 22/20.

[19] As illustrated in Case T-192/16 *NF v European Council* EU:T:2017:128, paras 69–71 on the 'EU–Turkey statement' of 18 March 2016.

[20] Treaty establishing the European Stability Mechanism, signed on 2 February 2012 T/ESM 2012-LT; Case C-370/12 *Pringle* EU:C:2012:756, paras 93–107.

[21] Paraphrasing L Van Middelaar, *Alarums and Excursions: Improvising Politics on the European Stage* (Agenda Publishing, 2019) 167. Bruno himself relies on the work of this author in his recent writings. B De Witte, 'Legal Methods for the Study of EU Institutional Practice' (forthcoming).

[22] As reported by J Komárek, 'Whose Ideas Matter? Studying the Origins of European Constitutional Imaginaries' (forthcoming).

[23] Ibid 165–66.

understood as primarily complementing each other in the EU legal order. This is well illustrated by the development of the Schengen area and the Dublin system. These were developed between certain Member States of the EU, yet outside the Treaty framework, to support or deepen EU policies[24] and are now subject to the 'Community method'.[25]

III. What Does a Legal Introduction to the EU Legal Order Entail?

For the purpose of providing a legal introduction to the EU legal order, and alongside Bruno's own approach, scholars often opt for the scholarly tradition concerned with understanding the internal coherence of a legal system.[26] This relies on the doctrinal method requiring 'rational reconstruction' of law.[27] This is not to suggest that other prongs of legal research, such as socio-legal research, or the insights from other disciplines, such as political science, are not relevant and important to inform legal scholars and the way they introduce their field. Quite to the contrary, these are crucial to oxygenate EU legal scholarship; they helpfully complement doctrinal legal work. For instance, they shed light on a large number of institutional practices that have developed 'in the shadow of the law'.[28] For that purpose, while being truthful to the doctrinal approach, Bruno has called for open and new ways of studying EU law,[29] and has himself implemented this approach in several of his writings.

[24] As the preamble of the Schengen agreement states, the five State parties (also Member States of the European Economic Community): 'ANIMÉS de la volonté de parvenir à la suppression des contrôles aux frontières communes dans la circulation des ressortissants des États membres des Communautés européennes et d'y faciliter la circulation des marchandises et des services' (Agreement of 14 June 1985 on the gradual abolition of checks at their common borders). See also Convention of 15 June 1990 determining the State responsible for examining applications for asylum lodged in one of the Member States of the European Communities (Dublin Convention), Preamble (3) and (4) and Treaty of 2 February 2012 Establishing the European Stability Mechanism, Preamble.

[25] B De Witte, 'An Undivided Union? Differentiated Integration in Post-Brexit Times' (2018) 55 *Common Market Law Review* 227, 234, 236 and 241–44.

[26] This is not to deny the normative dimension of legal doctrinal research. As MacCormick notes, in legal doctrine 'the organising principles are normative in character'; and further on the distinction between normative and legal doctrinal approaches see N MacCormick, 'Four Quadrants of Jurisprudence' in W Krawietz et al (eds), *Prescriptive Formality and Normative Rationality in Modern Legal Systems* (Duncker & Humblot, 1994) 53, 69.

[27] Ibid 54 and 57. See also, on 'doctrinal constructivism', A von Bogdandy, 'The Past and Promise of Doctrinal Constructivism: A Strategy for Responding to the Challenges Facing Constitutional Scholarship in Europe' (2009) 7(3) *International Journal of Constitutional Law* 364.

[28] De Witte, 'Legal Methods' (n 21).

[29] B De Witte, 'European Union Law: A Unified Academic Discipline?' in A Vauchez and B De Witte (eds), *Lawyering Europe: European Law as a Transnational Social Field* (Hart Publishing, 2013) 116. Also reflecting on what European legal methodology entails and in defence of a revitalised form of doctrinal legal research: R Gestel and H Micklitz, 'Why Methods Matter in European Legal Scholarship' (2014) 20(3) *European Law Journal* 292.

EU lawyers – and I include myself in that category – tend to spend much time exploring the intricacies of the case law of the Court of Justice of the European Union.[30] This approach is perfectly understandable, as the latter's key function is to 'ensure that in the interpretation and application of the [EU] Treaties the law is observed'[31] and the Court's case law has played a very important role in the development and maturing of the EU legal order. Yet, working alongside Bruno, one is often reminded of the importance of keeping in mind the broader picture. Be it in times of constitutional change,[32] in times of crisis,[33] or – and perhaps in particular – in the daily life of the EU,[34] such a picture is gained primarily by looking at the work of a broad range of key political actors.[35] Bruno's work, together with Antoine Vauchez in particular, invites us to look beyond the usual suspects in the institutional landscape of the EU and to adopt an open posture in the definition of relevant actors, exploring for instance the function of the legal services of a given institution or professional (judicial) networks.[36]

Bruno's approach on these points may weigh on my decision to start introductions to the EU legal order by devoting attention to 'actors' *before* discussing 'competences'. This choice allows a dynamic approach to the EU legal order to be taken: it acknowledges the role of actors other than the traditional EU institutions involved in the exercise of EU competences and a focus on the interpretation of the powers of these institutions. For instance, the Member States are important actors owing to the decisive role that they play, such as in reform of the EU Treaties,[37] in the decision on the EU's own resources,[38] or in the process of accession by the EU to the European Convention on Human Rights.[39] EU citizens have also been

[30] Inviting broadening the angle and providing an overview of the related academic debate: J Shaw, 'The European Union: Discipline Building Meets Polity Building' in P Cane and M Tushnet (eds), *The Oxford Handbook of Legal Studies* (Oxford University Press, 2003).

[31] Art 19(1) TEU.

[32] See for instance on the process leading to the drafting of the defunct Treaty establishing a Constitution for Europe: B De Witte, 'Simplification and reorganization of the European Treaties' (2002) 39 *Common Market Law Review* 1255.

[33] See for instance B De Witte, 'Euro Crisis Responses and the EU Legal Order: Increased Institutional Variation or Constitutional Mutation?' (2015) 11(3) *European Constitutional Law Review* 434 and 'The European Union's COVID-19 Recovery Plan: The Legal Engineering of an Economic Policy Shift' (2021) 58(3) *Common Market Law Review* 635.

[34] Among others: B De Witte, 'New Institutions for Promoting Equality in Europe: Legal Transfers, National Bricolage and European Governance' (2012) 60(1) *American Journal of Comparative Law* 49; B De Witte, 'An Undivided Union? Differentiated Integration in Post-Brexit Times' (2018) 55(2) *Common Market Law Review* 227.

[35] See also J Shaw, 'The European Union: Discipline Building Meets Polity Building' in P Cane and M Tushnet (eds), *The Oxford Handbook of Legal Studies* (Oxford University Press, 2003) 330.

[36] A Vauchez and B De Witte (eds), *Lawyering Europe: European Law as a Transnational Social Field* (Hart Publishing, 2013); see respectively the chapters by J-P Jacqué, on the one hand, and M De Visser and M Claes, on the other. For another example see also C Kilpatrick and B De Witte, 'Introducing the Role of Collective Actors and Preliminary References in the Enforcement of EU Fundamental Rights Law' (2017) *EU Working Paper* 17, 1–6.

[37] Art 48 TEU.

[38] Art 311 of the Treaty on the Functioning of the European Union (TFEU).

[39] Art 218(8) TFEU.

carved a special place in the design of the EU legal order: they give purpose to the process of EU integration, serve as a source of institutional legitimacy, and contribute to the system of checks and balances on which the EU institutional design rests.[40]

Furthermore, by opting for 'actors'[41] rather than 'institutions' as the entry point into the relevant chapter of an introductory course or textbook, the chosen lens makes it possible to look at EU institutions *and* their aids, as well as beyond, for instance at EU agencies and atypical bodies such as the Euro Group. Although these are hardly mentioned in the main provisions of the EU Treaties,[42] an introduction to the EU legal order ought to accommodate the need to fit them in. That is necessary to provide an overview of the broad range of those involved in shaping the EU legal order.

On a related note, Bruno has often called for attention being paid in EU law scholarship to legal practice.[43] This is indeed inescapable for the purpose of introducing as well as researching the dynamics of the EU legal order because legal practice is so often 'raw law'.[44] How indeed could one explain the logic of the ordinary legislative procedure without mentioning trilogues?[45] How could one shed light on the role of the European Parliament in the process leading to the appointment of the President of the Commission and its members without mention of the 'Spitzenkandidaten process'[46] (as fallible as it may be) or the practice of individual hearings of Commissioners designates?[47] How could one explain the logic of the infringement action without looking at its administrative practice?[48] While not losing sight of the hierarchy of norms, as well as of the role of law in framing practices,[49] one cannot omit the role of practice in oiling the system of norms and feeding into it.

[40] Eg Art 3(1–2) TEU; Art 10 TEU.

[41] See further R Gabled, *Au-delà de la prise de décision: décrire la répartition des rôles en droit de l'Union européenne* (PhD Thesis, 2019, European University Institute).

[42] Today the existence of the Euro Group is anchored in Art 137 TFEU and Protocol 14 on the Euro Group [2016] OJ C 202; yet, in the view of the Court of Justice, these provisions do 'not alter its intergovernmental nature in the slightest' (Joined Cases C-597/18 P, C-598/18 P, C-603/18 P and C-604/18 P, *Council v K Chrysostomides & Co and others* EU:C:2020:1028, para 87).

[43] See for instance B De Witte, 'EMU as Constitutional Law' in F Amtenbrink, C Herrmann and R Repasi (eds), *The EU Law of Economic and Monetary Union* (Oxford University Press, 2020) ch 11; De Witte, 'Legal Methods' (n 21).

[44] On the notion of 'raw law' and on the 'feed-back effect' between practice and doctrinal legal scholarship, see N MacCormick, 'Four Quadrants of Jurisprudence' in W Krawietz, et al (eds), *Prescriptive Formality and Normative Rationality in Modern Legal Systems* (Duncker & Humblot 1994) 57.

[45] The importance of these trilateral negotiations is now acknowledged by institutional players: Parliament, Council and Commission, Interinstitutional Agreement on Better Law-Making [2016] OJ L 123/1, points 32–40; see also for instance Case T-540/15 *De Capitani* EU:T:2018:167, paras 70–71.

[46] It is based on a creative reading of Art 17(7), subpara 1, TEU.

[47] Recognised in Parliament, Rules of Procedure, Rule 125.

[48] See Commission, Communication on EU law: Better results through better application [2017] OJ C18/10; and Commission, 'Commission staff working document – general statistical overview – part 1', 2019 Report on monitoring the application of EU law, 31 July 2020.

[49] On the relationship between law and practice in the choice of legal basis see P Leino, 'The Institutional Politics of Objective Choice: Competence as a Framework for Argumentation' in S Garben

IV. Concluding Remarks: The Personal Dimension of EU Law Scholarship

Being part of an academic community open to discussion is crucial for the purpose of first shaping, and in turn outlining, one's understanding of the fundamentals of EU law. Sound academic exchanges are the only way of progressing on the path towards a better understanding of the complex legal system we seek to capture. I have often turned to Bruno for feedback and discussion. His responses were always swift, warm, sharp, engaging, and critical yet attentive.

In my reading, his work is primarily driven by the pursuit of an ever better understanding of the legal system on which the EU legal order rests and develops. The lens of analysis is viscerally pro-European, as well as cautiously optimistic. For that purpose, Bruno has always shown a particular sensitivity to the challenges and constraints which key actors are faced with in shaping that legal order with a form of 'legal pragmatism'.[50] Bruno engages in this task through the lens of doctrinal legal analysis. He examines major challenges with a rock-solid legal tool box, without losing track of the overall quest for joint solutions by Member States and EU institutions. I always find comfort in the way he values experimentalism over dogmatism because the EU is such a difficult object to fit into ready-made boxes, yet proceeds with great legal rigor.

Now theoretical choices and methodological approaches are not enough to grasp the identity of an EU law scholar and the related contribution to the field. There is also a strong personal dimension. It is just as important for a great EU scholar to pay attention to inter-cultural exchange, openness and mutual respect, as it is to abide to the canons of the legal discipline and seek to address theoretical and methodological challenges in the field. The intention is not to be emotional here – the point being made is of an academic nature. How does one set the parameters in which a healthy and lively scholarly community grows and flourishes? I shall ask Bruno …

and I Govaere (eds.), *The Division of Competences between the EU and the Member States: Reflections on the Past, the Present and the Future* (Hart Publishing, 2017).

[50] On Bruno De Witte and 'Pragmatism and EU Law' see N Nic Shuibhne, chapter twelve in the present volume.

12

Pragmatism and EU Law

NIAMH NIC SHUIBHNE

I. Introduction

I would venture that Bruno De Witte is the archetypal pragmatist, and for the purposes of this edited volume, I aim to explore a concept of *legal pragmatism* that emerges from my reading of his extensive scholarship across three key areas of EU law.

The idea of tracing the implications of legal pragmatism was triggered by returning, first, to how I came to know Bruno's work in the first place when I was a PhD researcher – through his field-defining work that interrogates whether EU law provides appropriate space for national (and/or more local) cultural and linguistic diversity. The variety of legal pragmatism that emerges in that context is outlined in this chapter through reflecting on the justification system that applies in EU free movement law as a system based on *functional pragmatism* (section II). Another strand of Bruno's work – on differentiated integration – offers the sense of more *structured pragmatism* (section III): of a framework for diversity more closely fixed to specified Treaty boundaries that also explicitly articulate a protected legal core. However, a connective link to section II manifests through the fact that a concern to overcome protectionism and to progress the achievement of a borderless internal market constrains the scope of functional pragmatism in EU free movement law. Pragmatism is therefore affordable, in other words, because there is also a protected (if more implicit) legal core at the heart of the free movement justification system, which can offer precisely the balance 'between flexibility and disintegration' that Bruno has advocated more generally.[1] Conversely, it will be shown that the structured pragmatism discussed in section III does not equate to rigidity; that there is space for creativity and difference even where there are more explicit structural constraints.

Bruno has also reflected deeply on the recurring episodes of crisis that have been encountered by EU law and governance (section IV). But it will be argued

[1] Eg B De Witte, A Ott and E Vos (eds), *Between Flexibility and Disintegration: The Trajectory of Differentiation in EU Law* (Edward Elgar Publishing, 2017).

that, here, the protected core of EU law is possibly more vulnerable. In his scholarship, Bruno challenges us to see but not exaggerate the systemic implications that the necessarily pragmatic management of acute events produces. In that light, the chapter asks: what does a pragmatic approach to EU law mean when it reaches limits that a pragmatist might not themselves transcend yet might still be transcended by others?

II. Protecting Space for National Diversity: Functional Pragmatism

In several areas of EU law, scholars work out pragmatic ways to explain the simultaneous firmness and looseness that EU legal principles can spark. Explaining the primacy of EU law and the respective (and sometimes in tension) national and supranational perspectives on the source of primacy's authority through the language of constitutional and/or legal pluralism provides a strong example.[2] The justification space in EU free movement law provides another, conveying the idea of *functional pragmatism* in two key respects. First, we should acknowledge the significance of the judicial step taken in *Van Binsbergen*[3] and *Cassis de Dijon*,[4] which expanded the range of public interest defences for national restrictions of free movement rights in ways that carved a novel framework that is still applied today. The idea of functional pragmatism is suggested by how the Court of Justice left the finite public interest list constituted by the Treaty derogation framework in place[5] and attached it to the most protectionist (eg directly discriminatory) restrictions of free movement rights, on the one hand; while quietly enabling a way to hear and evaluate pretty much any public interest argument a Member State might conceive – normally, only when the restrictions in question are either indirectly discriminatory or not discriminatory at all but still preventing or impeding market access,[6] though sometimes (and again very pragmatically) for directly

[2] See eg the essays in G Davies and M Avbelj (eds), *Research Handbook on Legal Pluralism and EU Law* (Edward Elgar Publishing, 2018).

[3] Case 33/74 *Van Binsbergen* EU:C:1974:131, para 14: 'the requirement that persons whose functions are to assist the administration of justice must be permanently established for professional purposes within the jurisdiction of certain courts or tribunals cannot be considered incompatible with the provisions of Articles 59 and 60 [EEC], where such requirement *is objectively justified* by the need to ensure observance of professional rules of conduct connected, in particular, with the administration of justice and with respect for professional ethics' (emphasis added).

[4] Case 120/87 *Cassis de Dijon* EU:C:1979:42, para 8: 'Obstacles to movement within the Community resulting from disparities between the national laws relating to the marketing of the products in question must be accepted in so far as those provisions may be recognized as being *necessary in order to satisfy mandatory requirements* relating in particular to the effectiveness of fiscal supervision, the protection of public health, the fairness of commercial transactions and the defence of the consumer' (emphasis added).

[5] See esp Arts 36, 45(3), 52(1), 62 and 65 TFEU.

[6] For the contemporary expression of public interest justification in free movement law, see eg Case C-384/08 *Attanasio Group Srl* EU:C:2010:133, para 50 ('overriding reasons in the public interest capable of justifying restrictions on the fundamental freedoms guaranteed by the Treaty').

discriminatory restrictions too, in order to reflect the changing importance of specific public interest arguments over time.[7]

Second, the determination of *legitimate* justification is just an inherently pragmatic reasoning exercise more generally, and especially when the proportionality (ie the appropriateness and necessity) of a contested restriction is being decided. In a striking reflection on precisely that point, former Judge Rosas (writing extra-judicially) suggested that

> [h]ere is an example where the result of reconciling, or as the case may be, balancing of different interests will not depend so much on the actual formulation used in the judgment but rather on perceptions among the sitting judges of what is fair and reasonable, based on an overall assessment of all relevant factors and whether the problem for the proper functioning of the internal market is deemed to be minor or more serious

adding too that

> [i]t almost goes without saying that the final outcome could be different had the case been decided by another chamber of the Court than the one to which the case has been referred.[8]

The Court's efforts to find a compromise when potentially applicable perspectives are not easy to reconcile also reflects pragmatism: for example, through asserting that even though justifications 'of a purely economic nature cannot constitute overriding reasons in the public interest justifying a restriction of a fundamental freedom guaranteed by the Treaties (…) national legislation may constitute a justified restriction on a fundamental freedom when it is dictated *by reasons of an economic nature* in the pursuit of an objective in the public interest'.[9]

Similarly, consider the classic statement in *Van Duyn*, where the Court ruled that 'the concept of public policy must be interpreted strictly, so that its scope cannot be determined unilaterally by each Member State without being subject to control by the institutions of the [Union]', while confirming, at the same time, that the particular circumstances justifying recourse to the concept of public policy *may vary from one country to another* and from one period to another, and it is therefore necessary in this matter to allow the competent national authorities an area of discretion within the limits imposed by the Treaty'.[10] The fact that public interest grounds can be locally – distinctively – expressed bridges back to Bruno's longstanding interest in the legal protection of cultural and linguistic diversity.[11]

[7] Eg Case C-531/07 *Fachverband der Buch – und Medienwirtschaft* EU:C:2009:276, paras 32–34; Case C-591/17 *Austria v Germany* EU:C:2019:504, para 75.

[8] A Rosas, 'Foreword' in P Koutrakos, N Nic Shuibhne and P Syrpis (eds), *Exceptions from EU Free Movement Law: Derogation, Justification and Proportionality* (Hart Publishing, 2016) vi.

[9] Joined Cases C-105/12 to C-107/12 *Essent and Others* EU:C:2013:677, paras 51–52 (emphasis added).

[10] Case 41/74 *Van Duyn* EU:C:1974:133, para. 18 (emphasis added).

[11] Eg B De Witte, 'Surviving in Babel? Language Rights and European Integration' in Y Dinstein and M Tabory (eds), *The Protection of Minorities and Human Rights* (Martinus Nijhoff, 1992) 277; B De Witte, 'A Competence to Protect: The Pursuit of Non-Market Aims Through Internal Market

In *Runevič-Vardyn and Wardyn*, the Court affirmed that 'the provisions of European Union law do not preclude the adoption of a policy for the protection and promotion of a language of a Member State which is both the national language and the first official language'.[12] That recognition was more explicitly extended to cover 'the adoption of a policy for the protection and promotion *of one or more* official languages of a Member State' in *Las*.[13]

Importantly for present purposes, two points in particular can be highlighted. First, Article 3(3) of the Treaty on European Union (TEU) and Article 22 of the Charter of Fundamental Rights underline in EU primary law that the Union is obliged to respect its rich cultural and linguistic diversity; and Article 4(2) TEU, which establishes that the Union must also respect the national identity of its Member States, also embraces protection of a State's official national language.[14] This introduces the significance of norms captured by the EU Treaties. Second, threading through both Bruno's scholarship in this field and the relevant case law of the Court, there is clear recognition that locality will be tolerated – or more than that, that it will be respected – only within *limits*. In *Van Duyn*, for example, the Court emphasised the role of Union supervision to ensure that free movement rights would still be sufficiently *effective*. The significance of proportionality review is expressed in *Runevič-Vardyn and Wardyn* and *Las*. Similarly, Bruno has shown how the standardisation impulse of economic integration and the local impulse of linguistic diversity can be balanced: indeed, that they must be balanced.[15] His distinction between the making of both 'strategic choice[s]' and 'substantive choice[s]'[16] in this analysis recalls the idea of pragmatism; but he does recognise the valid claims of both standardisation and difference in the context of the EU's internal market, as well as the vital importance of not enabling discriminatory restrictions and thus of confronting protectionism. Bruno is also very critical of the uncertainty and unpredictability that ensue when things become *too* detached from recognisable and consistently applied limits. In such circumstances, he makes repeated appeals for greater coherence.[17]

A pragmatic approach to justification and proportionality can facilitate the smooth navigation of apparently competing currents, shifting the balance this way

Legislation' in P Syrpis (ed), *The Judiciary, the Legislator and the Internal Market* (Cambridge University Press, 2012) 25; B De Witte, 'Language Rights in the Work of the European Union' in I Ulasiuk, L Hadirca and W Romans (eds), *Language Policy and Conflict Prevention* (Brill, 2018) 221.

[12] Case C-391/09 *Runevič-Vardyn and Wardyn* EU:C:2011:291, para 85.

[13] Case C-202/11 *Las* EU:C:2013:239, para 25 (emphasis added).

[14] Case C-391/09 *Runevič-Vardyn and Wardyn* EU:C:2011:291, para 86.

[15] Eg B De Witte, 'The Impact of European Community Rules on Linguistic Policies of the Member States' in F Coulmas (ed), *A Language Policy for the European Community: Prospects and Quandaries* (Mouton de Gruyter, 1991) 163.

[16] Ibid 165.

[17] Eg B De Witte, 'Cultural policy justifications' in P Koutrakos, N Nic Shuibhne and P Syrpis (eds), *Exceptions from EU Free Movement Law. Derogation, Justification and Proportionality* (Hart Publishing, 2016) 127; B De Witte 'Internal Market Law and National Language Policies' in K Purnhagen and P Rott (eds), *Varieties of European Economic Law and Regulation. Liber amicorum for Hans Micklitz* (Springer, 2014) 419.

or that way on a case-by-case basis. However, at the same time, that navigation should happen within defined parameters so that we do not end up with *dysfunctional* pragmatism; within a protected legal core rooted in the Treaties and also, I would argue, in the 'specific characteristics'[18] of the EU legal order and the principles of Union law that the EU's institutions articulate – and to which, no less importantly, they must adhere.

III. Conceiving a System of Differentiated Integration: Structured Pragmatism

The idea of pragmatism within limits finds particularly prescriptive reflection in another of Bruno's areas of interest: in the *structured pragmatism* suggested by the Treaty framework that governs enhanced cooperation.[19] Title IV TEU and Articles 326–334 of the Treaty on the Functioning of the European Union (TFEU) establish that framework – and here, a protected legal core is made plain: exclusive Union competences are excluded (Article 20(1) TEU) and common foreign and security policy entails a distinct procedure (Article 329(2) TFEU); initiatives must still 'further the objectives of the Union, protect its interests and reinforce its integration process' (Article 20(1) TEU); they must 'comply with the Treaties and Union law' (Article 326 TFEU); 'not undermine the internal market or economic, social and territorial cohesion [or] constitute a barrier to or discrimination in trade between Member States, nor (…) distort competition between them' (Article 326 TFEU); and they must 'respect the competences, rights and obligations of those Member States which do not participate in it' (Article 327 TFEU). In other words, yes, there is an organised way for States to do different things in different configurations, but not in certain areas or without respecting agreed rules of the game; flexibility can be enabled, but not in all respects.

For Bruno, the conditionality attached to enhanced cooperation is rationalised by the fact that 'the participating states receive the benefit of using the EU institutional system to adopt policies only among themselves instead of for the whole EU' – and he is characteristically pragmatic about this, suggesting that the 'numerous substantive and procedural conditions' that apply is a 'very reasonable price to pay' on balance.[20] Exhibiting another Bruno trait, there is also some optimism: it is not that the Treaty framework on enhanced cooperation is too burdensome for greater deployment but rather that the 'continuing reluctance' of

[18] Opinion 2/13 of the Court EU:C:2014:2454, paras 165–77.

[19] Resonating with Bruno's characterisation of differentiated integration as a 'structural element of the EU legal order': B De Witte, 'The Law as Tool and Constraint of Differentiated Integration', EUI Working Paper RSCAS 2019/47, cadmus.eui.eu/bitstream/handle/1814/63604/RSCAS_2019_47.pdf?sequence=1&isAllowed=y.

[20] Ibid 6.

Member States to engage it 'is, arguably, testimony to the enduring strength of the consensus culture inside the Council'.[21] But what resonates most for present purposes when re-reading Bruno's work in this field is how it highlights the ways in which differentiation has progresses *around* as distinct from *within* the enhanced cooperation Treaty framework per se.[22] Thus, whereas conceiving of justification as functional pragmatism could accommodate the articulating and enforcing of a protected legal core in a field that innately bends toward diversity, the paradox found in conceiving of differentiated integration as structured pragmatism is that it shifts our attention to what might potentially represent forms of escape from articulated legal limits.

In some respects, differentiated integration beyond the specific mechanism of enhanced cooperation is just a phenomenon of EU law and its Treaty system already. In that sense, Bruno highlights the longstanding approach to derogation from Treaty obligations effected through the equal status in primary law of opt-out by Protocol; inbuilt Treaty mechanisms such as Article 136(1) TFEU, which enables the adoption of 'measures specific to those Member States whose currency is the euro'; and international agreements that the Member States may still conclude in their own capacity. Bruno has therefore rightly observed that '[t]he various forms of differentiation that have spread so profusely during the past 20 years have not formally challenged the existence of one EU legal order; and there are rather firm criteria to determine whether a legal norm belongs to the EU legal order or not'.[23] Crucially, though, he intimates that 'the formal criteria for deciding what belongs to the EU legal order' must 'still function *well*'.[24]

For example, Bruno has demonstrated that there is a long history to the practice of treaties that Member States conclude under international rather than under EU law.[25] Assessing more specifically international treaties that the Member States conclude 'even when the subject matter of their agreement is close to European Union policies', he describes 'the Schengen experience' as a positive model' since 'it offers an example of both the potential of such agreements to overcome a blockage within the Union's decision-making system, and the possibility for their later re-integration within the EU legal system'.[26] However, in his work on differentiated integration, Bruno has also acknowledged that, across different examples, 'the contours of the EU legal order have become rather fuzzy'; in particular, he has cautioned that 'the easy and almost insouciant recourse to variable geometry also

[21] Ibid 6–7.

[22] For an early example, see eg B De Witte, D Hanf and E Vos (eds), *The Many Faces of Differentiation in the EU* (Intersentia Publishing, 2001).

[23] De Witte, 'The Law as Tool and Constraint' (n 19) 4.

[24] Ibid (emphasis added).

[25] B De Witte and T Martinelli, 'Treaties between EU Member States as Quasi-instruments of EU Law' in M Cremona and C Kilpatrick (eds), *EU Legal Acts: Challenges and Transformations* (Oxford University Press, 2018) 157.

[26] De Witte, 'The Law as Tool and Constraint' (n 19) 8.

comes with a lack of transparency, complicated accountability mechanisms, and a neglect of intra-state solidarity', which presents 'serious challenges for the constitutional integrity of the EU'.[27] Bridging to a third key area of Bruno's academic contributions, are these challenges amplified in the EU's management of crisis and emergency? Does legal pragmatism steer us through such events all the more effectively, or do we reach, in that context, the limits of pragmatism?

IV. Managing Crisis and Emergency: At the Limits of Pragmatism?

Bruno's contributions to the debate on how the Union does deal, and should deal, with crisis and emergency, exhibit traits identified with respect to both functional and structured pragmatism in the previous sections of this chapter. In essence, his work underlines both the importance of working within articulated legal parameters and, at the same time, the importance of approaching those parameters with pragmatism where necessary. In the zone of flexibility, we might look for structure; in the zone of structure, we might look for flexibility. This is, surely, the essence of legal pragmatism.

As introduced in section II, in Bruno's work I see above all a profound respect for, deep understanding of, and forensic engagement with, the legal parameters set by the Treaties. It is there, for example, in his assessment that '[b]ecause of the hierarchy between primary law (the Treaties) and secondary law (the enhanced cooperation instruments), it is clear that enhanced cooperation can only validly come into being if it respects the constraints imposed by the Treaties'.[28] Extensive Treaty surgery is a characteristic of all of his writing. In this way, his analytical skill reminds all of us to root our thinking in the Treaties – to take them seriously as the politically negotiated repository of EU primary law, and to start with the Treaties when we need to work through any EU legal puzzle. At the same time, though, he embraces the role that interpretation plays in determining the meaning of relevant Treaty provisions as well as the principles of EU constitutional law that are not present in the Treaties at all: on the latter point, for example, that '[i]n its case law, the Court of Justice has consistently held that the primacy of EU law extends not only to measures of national law but also to agreements between two or more member states, which must be disapplied by national courts if they are inconsistent with EU law'.[29] He also agrees that not all constitutional constraints are

[27] B De Witte, 'Variable Geometry and Differentiation as Structural Features of the EU Legal Order' in B De Witte, A Ott and E Vos (eds), *Between Flexibility and Disintegration: The Trajectory of Differentiation in EU Law* (Edward Elgar Publishing, 2019) 9 at 25.
[28] De Witte, 'The Law as Tool and Constraint' (n 19) 11.
[29] Ibid 12.

located in the Treaty framework, noting, for example, that '[t]he constraints that limit recourse to separate international agreements cannot be found in the Treaty text; they rather result from the inherent primacy of EU law over the national law of the Member States'.[30]

All of these dimensions are evident in a recent contribution on Article 4(2) TEU, where Bruno states in the very first line of the abstract that '[t]he main argument of this article is that the meaning of the national identity clause of Article 4 (2) TEU *should be limited to what its text actually states*, namely to a guarantee for the constitutional structures of the European Union (EU) Member States'.[31] This perspective is not, as Bruno makes clear, about personal preference, but, instead, because '[s]uch a broader meaning is not needed, since *primary EU law* contains many other provisions that protect national diversity, all of which have a specific meaning and role in the EU legal order'.[32] Equally, though, the wider concern is not ignored: that '[g]iving Article 4(2) the broader meaning is harmful, as it opens the door to abusive and superficial uses of identity as a justification for non-compliance with EU law obligations from the side of the Member State'.[33]

Traces of legal pragmatism are even more strongly evident in Bruno's analyses of crisis-adjunct situations. He has argued, for example, that '[t]he Court's rather lenient approach to the compatibility of inter se treaties with EU law may be explained by the fact that the stakes were very high in *Pringle*, so that arriving at a negative verdict on the ESM treaty was, despite the arguments of many legal scholars, never a realistic option'.[34] More recently, in his novel conception of 'EU emergency law',[35] a pragmatic approach is again vividly evident. Here, for example, commenting on collective Member State action taken under international rather than EU law, he agrees that this represents 'an escape from some of the constraints of EU law, in particular from the judicial review exercised by the Court of Justice, *but not an escape from law as such*, since the conclusion, ratification and application of those agreements are subject to the rules of international law'.[36] Bruno's crafting

[30] B De Witte, 'Overcoming the Single Country Veto in EU Reform' (2020) 5 *European Papers: A Journal on Law and Integration* 983–85.

[31] B De Witte, 'Article 4(2) TEU as a Protection of the *Institutional* Diversity of the Member States' (2021) 27 *European Public Law* 559 (emphasis added).

[32] Ibid (emphasis added).

[33] Ibid.

[34] De Witte and Martinelli, 'Treaties between EU Member States' (n 25) 180; Case C-370/12 *Pringle* EU:C:2012:756. See further, B De Witte and T Beukers, 'The Court of Justice Approves the Creation of the European Stability Mechanism Outside the EU Legal Order: *Pringle*' (2013) 50 *Common Market Law Review* 80, which even concludes on the statement that '[a]ll in all, the Court has given, in *Pringle*, a well-reasoned judgment expressing a good mixture of legal principle and political pragmatism' 848.

[35] B De Witte, Guest Editorial, 'EU Emergency Law and its Impact on the EU Legal Order: European Crises and EU Emergency Law' (2022) 59 *Common Market Law Review* 3. He defines 'EU emergency law' as 'the rules of primary and secondary EU law that serve to address *sudden* threats to the core values and structures of the Union and its Member States', thus distinguishing it as a 'narrower concept' compared to 'EU crisis law' (4, emphasis added).

[36] Ibid 13 (emphasis added).

of a 'formal definition of the constitutional law of the EMU (namely, the norms of primary law relating directly or indirectly to Economic and Monetary Union)' offers the further insight that, by contrast, 'the many legal or policy changes that happened during the financial crisis period should not all be qualified as *constitutional* changes'.[37] His reasoning again exhibits a pragmatic quality:

> As an illustration of this distinction between constitutional and infra-constitutional change, take the evolution of the European Central Bank's (ECB) monetary policy. The content of that policy has undeniably changed since 2008, in particular by means of the use of the so-called unconventional measures of intervention on the secondary bond markets. The ECB did not articulate this as a constitutional change, but rather as a change of policy within the broad confines of its monetary policy mandate as defined by the Treaties. The applicants in the *Gauweiler* and *Weiss* cases thought otherwise and argued that this was not a mere policy change, but one which had constitutional effects, making the ECB step outside the limits of its Treaty-defined mandate as laid down in Article 127 TFEU and breaching the prohibition of monetary financing of Article 123 TFEU. The Court of Justice, instead, approved the interpretation proposed by the ECB. In doing so, it showed a considerable amount of judicial deference, but that attitude itself may be a reflection of the constitutional choice made at the time of the Maastricht Treaty to assert the independence of the ECB, and therefore also grant it broad discretion in fulfilling its Treaty mandate.[38]

It is another marker of pragmatism that Bruno acknowledges – and accepts – the *dynamic* nature of EU constitutionalism. For example, he suggests, again in the context of EMU, that perspectives of continuity and of transformation 'can be reconciled if one accepts that constitutional change does not only happen, in the European Union, by means of formal changes in the text of primary law, but also by means of changing *judicial interpretation* of the norms of primary law, or by *institutional practice* that transforms the significance or effect of written norms of primary EU law'.[39]

However, it would be a mistake to presume that Bruno avoids criticism of legal overstretch. All of the work reflected upon for the purposes of this chapter is replete with careful attention to cautions and to constraints, expressed with Bruno's characteristic directness and reflecting his underlying commitment to constitutionalism. To provide just one concrete example, Bruno has stated that he is open to engaging enhanced cooperation in order to 'allow for the circumvention of the unanimity requirement where it is still in place (especially for taxation), and more generally (…) allow like-minded States to take forward their cooperation, using the instruments of EU law and side lining the acrimonious resistance of

[37] B De Witte, 'EMU as Constitutional Law' in F Amtenbrink, C Herrmann, and R Repasi (eds), *The EU Law of Economic and Monetary Union* (Oxford University Press, 2020) 278–79 (emphasis in original).

[38] Ibid. Case C-62/14 *Gauweiler and others* EU:C:2015:400; Case C-493/17 *Weiss and others* EU:C:2018:1000.

[39] De Witte, 'EMU as Constitutional Law' (n 37) 291 (emphasis in original).

other States', while counselling, at the same time, that 'institutional transformation of the Union requires, now more than ever, a willingness to reform EU treaty-making, including a painful re-consideration of the "taboo" rule that European treaty revision requires the unanimous agreement of all the Member States'.[40]

But perhaps the point is that it is the legal pragmatist's *first* instinct to find a given EU (or national) act *within* rather than *outwith* the scope of the Treaties, eg unless there are serious and demonstrable *legal* reasons to find otherwise. There are significant advantages to that approach: not only but especially in phases of crisis and/or emergency since it reinforces the value of calm and measured steadiness, tempering otherwise understandable inclinations to panic, turmoil or volatility. A well-known example is Bruno's balanced assessment of the Court as being a '*little* selfish' (emphasis added) vis-à-vis its case law on mechanisms for international dispute settlement in the light of the principle of autonomy of EU law.[41] Similarly, he contrasts the 'radical' claim 'that either single euro crisis reforms, or their cumulative effect, have led to a mutation of the constitutional law of the European Union' with the 'more moderate' perspective that the 'euro crisis response is marked by a further increase in this institutional variation within EU law, between EMU law and other areas, but the overall constitutional system, as last re-arranged by the Lisbon Treaty, is not affected in a major way'[42] – both preferring and defending, in the end, the latter characterisation. Showing again the optimistic dimension of his pragmatism, he has also suggested that 'the conclusion of side agreements under international law is not to be seen as a flight from the rule of law, but as recourse to a different system of legal regulation *which was justified by the nature of the measures that the states decided to enact*' and even more strikingly, while 'it is true that some of the complex "rule-work" emerging from the eurozone crisis failed to meet the rule-of-law requirements of clarity and predictability, (…) this could be a temporary lapse rather than a structural decline of constitutional integrity'.[43]

[40] De Witte, 'Overcoming the Single Country Veto' (n 30) 987–88.

[41] B De Witte, 'A Selfish Court? The Court of Justice and the Design of International Dispute Settlement beyond the European Union' in M Cremona and A Thies (eds), *The European Court of Justice and External Relations Law: Constitutional Challenges* (Hart Publishing, 2014) 33–46: '[n]evertheless, the jurisprudence of the Court of Justice on the permissibility of creating new international courts certainly casts a shadow on the international initiatives of the EU and of its Member States. Nobody can criticise the Court of Justice for wanting to preserve the unique nature of the adjudication system established by the European Treaties, and fine-tuned by the Court itself in the course of time. But we would nevertheless conclude by arguing that the Court, in preserving the autonomy of the EU legal order in the face of rival international adjudication systems, has occasionally been a little selfish, showing more concern for its own role than for the advancement of the broader agenda of promoting the international rule of law'. The points of criticism of the Court for its reasoning in Opinion 2/13, more specifically, are arguably sharper in B De Witte and S Imamović, 'Opinion 2/13 on Accession to the ECHR. Defending the EU Legal Order against a Foreign Human Rights Court' (2015) 50 *European Law Review* 683.

[42] B De Witte, 'Euro Crisis Responses and the EU Legal Order: Increased Institutional Variation or Constitutional Mutation?' (2015) 11 *European Constitutional Law Review* 434, 444–45. As an aside, note the delightfully pragmatic observation at the end of 446 and into 447.

[43] Ibid 452.

The perspectives that Bruno has applied not only to responses to the eurozone crisis but also to scholarship assessing them[44] also find expression in his take on the measures adopted at Union level to address regulatory challenges produced by the Covid-19 pandemic. His assessment of these measures is framed explicitly as the 'legal engineering of an economic policy shift' and with reference to the idea that 'the craftsmanship by the legal services of the EU institutions provided the tools for common action within the constraints imposed by the EU legal order as it stands'.[45] Once again, his detailed exploration of the legal bases and procedural conditions specified in the Treaties established the requisite constitutional propriety, but the importance of space for interpretation is also underlined. Note also the pragmatic observation that '[t]his conclusion does not imply that the current vertical and horizontal division of powers is optimal, but, in the absence of a realistic possibility to revise the Treaties, the authors of the recovery plan had to work with the available legal tools'.[46]

However, Bruno's assessment of the part played by the European Council, in particular, stands in contrast with the view presented in the Editorial Comment in, somewhat ironically, the previous issue of the same journal in which his article is published: for example, in the editors' argument that 'the conditionality incident epitomizes the disproportionally powerful role the European Council is left to play in the EU, (…) which casts a long shadow over the EU institutional framework' and that while '[a]dmitting that the various crises the EU has gone through may justify a more prominent role for an institution that operates as the EU crisis-manager in chief, this evolution does not sit easily with the notion that, since the Treaty of Lisbon, the European Council has become a formal part of that institutional framework'.[47] More generally, the Editorial's criticism of the adoption of the recovery plan from a rule of law perspective – thus also, a Treaty-rooted perspective in light of Article 2 TEU – with respect to the concessions extended to Hungary and Poland does not pull punches.[48]

For Bruno, applying a pragmatic perspective facilitates the argument that 'in almost every instance of EU crisis response in the past decade, the legal constraints imposed by EU primary law were respected by the EU institutions, even when the measures adopted may often have been politically sub-optimal'.[49] I am less sure that we have always stayed in the sphere of *politically* sub-optimal. I am also less sure that the formal criteria that we need to apply to ensure appropriate scrutiny in these circumstances are 'still function[ing] *well*'.[50] At one level, Bruno's warning

[44] See again ibid and esp 445–53.

[45] B De Witte, 'The European Union's Covid-19 Recovery Plan: The Legal Engineering of an Economic Policy Shift' (2021) 58 *Common Market Law Review* 635, 638.

[46] Ibid 681.

[47] Editorial Comments, 'Compromising (on) the General Conditionality Mechanism and the Rule of Law' (2021) 58 *Common Market Law Review* 267, 280.

[48] Ibid esp 277 *et seq.*

[49] De Witte, 'EU Emergency Law' (n 35) 17.

[50] De Witte, 'The Law as Tool and Constraint' (n 19) 4 (emphasis added).

not to extrapolate systemic collapse from admittedly 'questionable and legally dubious'[51] legal developments undoubtedly and quite directly tempered my own evaluation of the impact of Brexit not on the EU itself but on EU law.[52] More specifically, it forced me to refine concrete and evidence-based points of concern, which coalesced in the end around three themes: 'fixed outcomes determined by ostensibly non-binding measures; the closing down of pathways for judicial review through emphasising form over substance; and a still incoherent articulation of the legal coordinates of Union membership'.[53] Not as a generalisation but on these specific examples, I am less sure that there is 'not an escape from law as such'.[54] Some months later, reading through and seeing links across Bruno's extraordinary contribution to EU legal scholarship, the questions posed here therefore concern whether legal pragmatism has limits and, if so, where these limits might be located. Going back to the idea extracted from Bruno's work on cultural and linguistic diversity as well as differentiated integration: what is the legal core that we must protect, the traversing of which *does* 'escape law as such'?

It is striking that Bruno often adopts a word that (like 'normally') is dear to the hearts and pens of all pragmatic lawyers: *quasi* – such as, for example, his depiction of the Treaty's 'quasi-accession procedure' for euro area membership.[55] And it is very Bruno (including linguistically) that he coined the term '*à la carte ma non troppo*'.[56] These ostensibly unremarkable turns of phrase are in fact what triggered my suggested portrait of Bruno as a legal pragmatist. I have been fortunate to have remained in academic conversation with him for more than two decades already and so, to continue that conversation, the fundamental question I would now ask him is this: can pragmatism sustain as a virtuous concept of EU law when there seem to be few(er) Bruno-types responsible for negotiating its implications in practice?

It is possible that the pragmatic perspective long evident in Bruno's work connects increasingly to a far from trivial concern: that the Union itself endures notwithstanding the existential risks that cycle after cycle of crisis have exacerbated. For example, along with Diane Fromage, Bruno writes in a *European Public Law* guest editorial that

> [t]here is indeed little doubt that the European Union (EU) is currently at a decisive juncture that will influence its future role and operating mode as is evidenced by several phenomena including the fact that one of its Member States has left for the first time

[51] De Witte, 'Euro Crisis Responses' (n 42) 453 ('whereas some legal solutions and crisis mechanisms may appear questionable and legally dubious, I do not see evidence of a brutal setting aside of the rule of law in the name of political expediency, but rather a major effort to deal with urgent matters in a constitution-compatible way').

[52] N Nic Shuibhne, 'Did Brexit Change EU Law?' (2021) 74 *Current Legal Problems* 105.

[53] Ibid 107.

[54] De Witte, 'EU Emergency Law' (n 35) 13.

[55] De Witte, 'The Law as Tool and Constraint' (n 19) 5. See similarly De Witte and Martinelli, 'Treaties between EU Member States' (n 25).

[56] De Witte, 'The Law as Tool and Constraint' (n 19) 7 ('*a la carte* but not too much').

> ever, that its core values are increasingly and recurrently under threat, while it is, at the same time, called to play a major role to counter the negative effects of the current pandemic.[57]

How should we, as legal scholars, negotiate the obligation to interrogate the constitutional propriety of the Union's activities without fuelling the tiresome but entirely real shadow of the Union's existential fragility? More than ever, we need committed constitutionalists and Treaty scientists of pragmatic demeanour to navigate these challenges, and so we hope for them. My own pragmatic postscript is that we must also plan for the fact that we do not always get them.

[57] D Fromage and B De Witte, 'National Constitutional Identity Ten Years On: State of Play and Future Perspectives' (2021) 27 *European Public Law* 411.

PART VI

Rethinking Academia: Bruno De Witte

13

Rethinking Academia: Bruno De Witte

RUTH RUBIO MARÍN

If you ask yourself how is it possible that somebody who, like Bruno, has cultivated such an extensive academic network would retire from academia with a *Liber Amicarum* which almost exclusively includes the voices of female colleagues the answer is simple: this is, probably, what would make most sense to him.[1]

Having been increasingly involved in projects of similar nature to honour retiring colleagues, Bruno did not spare his views: of course he would say yes every time he was asked to contribute but every time, he was left with the burning doubt as to whether these expressions of affection and gratitude really accomplished their goal. This is why, when approached by Ellen Vos and Monica Claes to be part of his own *Liber Amicarum*, I was immediately relieved to learn that those invited to contribute had mostly been selected from the close circle of female academic friends Bruno has actively cultivated throughout his academic career.

If one asks oneself how a project conceived in this way could make sense in a world which has become inevitably suspicious of the image of one honoured male surrounded by many female voices the answer is also simple: only for Bruno. Only for Bruno because, male as he is (as far as I know he has never changed views on this), Bruno is, academically speaking, one of us. Nothing but complete 'horizontality' in his approach and no secrets. Bruno has always been open about the fact that he is most at ease and has most fun when working with female colleagues (sorry, guys, though you know he likes some of you very much too and that he also likes soccer!) As Ellen and Monica wrote to me, Bruno has always celebrated the fact that Maastricht Centre for European Law has a majority of women, in part because Bruno believes that, in general 'women tend to be somewhat less full of themselves'.

The fact is, I am not sure Bruno has ever asked himself the question as to why exactly this is the case but maybe a *Liber Amicarum* which celebrates his academic legacy is the place to ponder not only the impact of his ideas but also the impact of

[1] When preparing this chapter, I invited contributors to this volume to share with me their impressions about Bruno's way of understanding and living academic life to create this collective portrait of him.

his way of conceiving and performing academic life and, in that sense, an invitation for us all to 'rethink academia'. When I asked Veerle, his wife, who, I believe was also partly responsible for this design choice, why she thinks Bruno prefers to work with women, she shrugged her shoulders, as if I was asking her why we humans breathe air (this is just the way it is), but also immediately recalled the fact that Bruno was raised in a household with four sisters and suggested that this very simple fact is probably connected to his preference and ease around women – something he will clearly recognise. When I look back at the many years of acquaintance with Bruno – at many academic enterprises ranging from joint teaching, supervising and conference attendance – I suspect the answer also has to do with the type of academic persona Bruno embodies. Who knows how much of this was influenced by his early childhood experience. Be it as it may, my guess is that, when we look back and ponder the impact Bruno has had on our own academic lives, many of us will feel that, beyond his academic ideas, it was the kind of academic persona that he embodied that inspired us.

Bruno, unlike many other male academics of similar great prestige, is, in essence, a team player. He is a 'we', rather than an academic 'I'. He draws genuine joy from discussing ideas with others, caring very little about the distinctions and academic credentials of his interlocutor, and this turns him into a naturally caring and generous academic. He is someone who would be approached not only by his supervisees but by his colleagues, as well as by younger scholars in search of a good and active listener, as somebody always willing to offer another angle and eager to point to the recent relevant work of others, not only himself, when this is called for. This attitude has permeated his supervisorial style. In the words of Ellen,

> I met Bruno and started to work in Maastricht as an assistant professor, he never made me feel that he was my boss. The relationship was always based on a sense of equality and true interest in what I was doing, encouraging me to carry out the research that I was genuinely interested in.

No surprise then that so many wanted to be supervised by Bruno and that indeed Bruno has supervised so many. Moreover, the fact remains that Bruno has ended up with many more 'mentees' than official 'supervisees' (of which he has had many too!), and, why so many of his mentees and supervisees have sought to establish life-long ties with him. After all, as Dilek Kurban rightly points out, Bruno

> has never seen supervising and mentoring limited to 'work', be it academic or not, but has had a holistic approach to it, mindful of the mentees/supervisee's emotional, psychological needs, wishes, issues, expectations. His advice is never just about work, but extends to entire life, with all its dimensions and complexities.

Bruno has never been drawn into running an academic institution, though he will openly recognise the merit and need for this and thanked those of his colleagues who have taken that burden. This is not to say that he does not contribute greatly to the ethos of the academic institutions he inhabits. For one, his sense of humour and soft manners are known to have the power to tone down the airs of self-importance so common in academic circles, which are all too often testosterone laden. Also, as Elise Muir puts it:

> Bruno's contribution to academia also flows from his belief in transparency. Bruno speaks his mind, modestly yet confidently, and not only on matters of legal analysis and interpretation but also on managerial aspects of academia. He keeps away from obscure decision-making procedures, is open on what matters to him and places trust in fair and open competition. His ability to say things as he sees them, unhindered and well-intentioned, is always a powerful reminder of the basics of sound academic relationships.

In other ways, he is more of a kind rebel preaching by example. Bruno has little respect for the things we are all increasingly encouraged to do in order to magnify our academic power and impact, such as fundraising, living up to standard measurement mechanisms, or basically anything that could guide him away from the fundamental choice he made in life: to devote his profession to reading, thinking, writing, discussing with others and guiding others who made a similar choice. Because he is not about self-grandeur or ego-boosting, Bruno will always listen to what others have to say rather than be the first to raise his hand, and when speaking will systematically do so with a form of kindness and respect that ensures that the speaker will never feel personally threatened or offended no matter how strongly challenged; however, Bruno will not shy away from expressing disagreement when disagreement is called for. His chosen wording will always be a form that conveys a 'we are all in this together, trying to figure it out … here is my take' approach rather than 'I know better'. 'What always strikes me', Monica Claes writes to me,

> is that he does not try to convince his interlocutors that they are wrong and he is right. He simply has his own view, and adduces arguments, carefully explaining and substantiating them, but he does not seek to change people's mind. If they are not convinced, so be it. There is then also an end to the discussion, and an agreement to disagree. This works the other way around. He will often say 'I follow your reasoning, I understand the point that you are making, but I simply do not agree'. And always respectfully (without the need to say that, because it is self-evident).

And often indeed, he will not agree, because in fact Bruno can be quite stubborn. Monica recalls, in laughter, how Walter van Gerven once told her privately 'it is such a pity that he won't let himself be directed'.

Rather than staying within a comfort zone and becoming ever more specialised in a certain topic or subdiscipline, he has been guided by curiosity, rather than pride or comfort. Bruno features as a fox in the 'fox versus groundhog' typology of academics he likes to refer to, since instead of digging deeper and deeper into one single issue, he has preferred to diversify his academic curiosity by wandering from one topic to the next, always looking for new challenges, for the big picture, for the missing links, even if this has inevitably translated into articles rather than monographs as his preferred form of publication. Moreover, because Bruno will often say yes to invitations from colleagues to contribute to conferences and joint projects, much of his great work and many of his original ideas are to be found in book chapters too. Bruno simply could afford the luxury of not minding how many points in the scale that measures standard forms of academic success the different writing formats would grant him. This has never mattered to him, and it is in these subtle and silent ways that he has systematically expressed rebellion and helped shape institutional culture – leading by example.

That he could afford the luxury to do so, does not mean that Bruno did not pay a price for stepping out of the norm. As Gráinne de Búrca rightly pointed out to me in discussing Bruno and his ways,

> to some extent, this kind of intellectual contribution – generous, responsive and inclusive, driven more by a sense of academic community and by the pleasure of engagement and collaboration than by a desire for recognition, status or reputational advancement – can come at a cost. The academic world still primarily encourages and recognises a different kind of scholar and scholarship, privileging sole-authored work, eye-catching theses, and grand claims, and rewarding strategically positioned research agendas. These are the kinds of careers that tend to attract the garlands, the awards, the honorary doctorates, the public recognition. Whereas the deep value of the kind of collective, thoughtful, generous, community-spirited work, including research, mentoring, teaching and advising that has comprised so much of Bruno's academic contribution is far less often recognised and celebrated by conventional accolades and awards.

This is why we take this *Liber Amicarum* to be not only a kind of public recognition and an expression of appreciation for all Bruno has given to the contributors to this volume and the academic community more generally, but also as an invitation to challenge the way many think of academic careers and their ways to success. For instance, when the driving force behind academic success is passion more than ambition, will one be spared at least some of the evils of pathological workaholism? I have often wondered this watching Bruno. Saturdays or Sundays are not an exception, and will typically find Bruno at some point with a paper or a thesis in his hands, and a coloured pencil to mark the text he is reading with comments. Always a pencil, never a pen, maybe subconsciously choosing a form that allowed, if necessary, after revisitation, easy erasure – that is, a non-definitive, non-final form. Yet in spite of this hard work, Bruno has never come across as a socially impeded workaholic. For Bruno, life always comes first, and the conflict is rarely there, because he always conveys the joy of life that intellectuals partake in when every experience – whether it be enjoying a novel, reading the newspaper, taking a walk or going on a longer trip – becomes yet another opportunity to wonder, to learn, to question oneself, to allow oneself to be surprised by new forms of knowledge and discoveries. This and his infinite sense of humour, including about himself, have not only made the departmental meetings at both the European University Institute and Maastricht lighter, but have also made Bruno's professional drive and ambition feel light on others.

Being genuinely interested in everything, Bruno has always been approached by colleagues and students from many disciplines focusing on the thinker, rather than the discipline; the issues, rather than the language; the ideas rather than their format. In that sense too, Bruno has remained a genuine generalist at a time when overspecialisation makes it increasingly challenging to be one: a man of Renaissance well suited for the Florentine and polyglot environment he chose to spend most of his academic career in, before leaving the EUI to return to his beloved and equally vibrant, women-led department in Maastricht.

A true European at heart, it only took Bruno a few academic incursions into the American way to reaffirm his Europeanness and eschew options that he might have had in more competitive environments after ending his term at the EUI. Gráinne and I recall him attending a workshop on antidiscrimination law we both organised in the same US institution in the spring of 2014, which we believe confirmed his desire to remain academically rooted in the old continent. Maybe it was the stress he observed in all of us, or the competitive forms of articulating criticism, or the fact that there never seemed to be a break from academic discussion, not even over lunch or dinner! Or perhaps, after all, it was just the jetlag that diminished his enjoyment of those events.

The fact is that was the one time – the only time – I have seen Bruno academically stressed out. For the rest, he has simply gently carried the inner stress of being always late for a deadline as a result of never learning to say no to friends and colleagues who asked him to write a paper, take part in a conference, or read a piece of work. For all of us, Bruno has always counted as an unconditional yes. No surprise then when the last time I saw him, just a few weeks ago, and asked him what he would miss the most when retiring from his academic life in the years to come, Bruno did not have to think twice: having people, old and new, contact him to meet and share their ideas and lives with him. Meeting colleagues in various parts of the world to continue the conversation always left half open – always written in pencil, never in pen. No coincidence then, if I happen to think that this too is what we, the inner circle of Bruno's female colleagues and other friends, will probably miss the most if he really retires from academic life: something, we all suspect, is not likely to really happen very soon.

INDEX

www.ingramcontent.com/pod-product-compliance
Ingram Content Group UK Ltd.
Pitfield, Milton Keynes, MK11 3LW, UK
UKHW021907150926
475560UK00003B/221

9 781509 959693